Microsoft®

Access 2000

Illustrated Introductory

Microsoft®
Access 2000
Illustrated Introductory

Lisa Friedrichsen

COURSE
TECHNOLOGY

Thomson Learning™

MICROSOFT OFFICE
USER SPECIALIST

APPROVED COURSEWARE

ONE MAIN STREET, CAMBRIDGE, MA 02142

Australia • Canada • Denmark • Japan • Mexico • New Zealand • Philippines
Puerto Rico • Singapore • South Africa • Spain • United Kingdom • United States

Microsoft Access 2000—Illustrated Introductory is published by Course Technology

Senior Product Manager:	Kathryn Schooling
Product Manager:	Jennifer A. Duffy, Rebecca VanEsselstine
Associate Product Manager:	Emily Heberlein
Contributing Author:	Elizabeth Eisner Reding
Production Editor:	Elena Montillo
Developmental Editor:	Rachel Biheller Bunin
Marketing Manager:	Karen Bartlett
Editorial Assistant:	Stacie Parillo
Composition House:	GEX, Inc.
QA Manuscript Reviewer:	Nicole Ashton, Jeff Schwartz, Alex White
Text Designer:	Joseph Lee, Joseph Lee Designs
Cover Designer:	Doug Goodman, Doug Goodman Designs

Trademarks

Course Technology and the Open Book logo are registered trademarks of Course Technology.

Illustrated Projects and the Illustrated Series are trademarks of Course Technology.

Some of the product names and company names used in this book have been used for identification purposes only and may be trademarks or registered trademarks of their respective manufacturers and sellers.

Microsoft and the Microsoft Office User Specialist Logo are registered trademarks of Microsoft Corporation in the United States and other countries. Course Technology is an independent entity from Microsoft Corporation, and not affiliated with Microsoft Corporation in any manner. This publication may be used in assisting students to prepare for a Microsoft Office User Specialist Exam. Neither Microsoft Corporation, its designated review company, nor Course Technology warrants that use of this publication will ensure passing the relevant Exam.

Use of the Microsoft Office User Specialist Approved Courseware Logo on this product signifies that it has been independently reviewed and approved in complying with the following standards:

Acceptable coverage of all content related to the Microsoft Office Exam entitled Microsoft Access 2000 and sufficient performance-based exercises that relate closely to all required content, based on sampling of text.

For more information contact:

Course Technology
One Main Street
Cambridge, MA 02142

or find us on the World Wide Web at: www.course.com

Disclaimer

Course Technology reserves the right to revise this publication and make changes from time to time in its content without notice.

ISBN 0-7600-6070-3

Printed in the United States of America

6 7 8 9 BM 04 03 02

The Illustrated Series Offers the Entire Package for your Microsoft Office 2000 Needs

Office 2000 MOUS Certification Coverage

The Illustrated Series offers a growing number of Microsoft-approved titles that cover the objectives required to pass the Office 2000 MOUS (Microsoft Office User Specialist) exams. After studying with any of the approved Illustrated titles (see list on inside cover), you will have mastered the Core and Expert skills necessary to pass any Office 2000 MOUS exam. In addition, **Access 2000 MOUS Certification Objectives** at the end of the book map to where specific MOUS skills can be found in each lesson and where students can find additional practice.

Helpful New Features

The Illustrated Series responded to Customer Feedback by adding a **Project Files list** at the back of the book for easy reference, Changing the red font in the Steps to green for easier reading, and Adding New Conceptual lessons to units to give students the extra information they need when learning Office 2000.

New Exciting Case and Innovative On-Line Companion

There is an exciting new case study used throughout our textbooks, a fictitious company called MediaLoft, designed to be "real-world" in nature by introducing the kinds of activities that students will encounter when working with Microsoft Office 2000. The **MediaLoft Web site**, available at www.course.com/illustrated/medialoft, is an innovative Student Online Companion which enhances and augments the printed page by bringing students onto the Web for a dynamic and continually updated learning experience. The MediaLoft site mirrors the case study used throughout the book, creating a real-world intranet site for this chain of bookstore cafés. This Companion is used to complete the WebWorks exercise in each unit of this book, and to allow students to become familiar with the business application of an intranet site.

Enhance Any Illustrated Text with these Exciting Products!

Course CBT

Enhance your students' Office 2000 classroom learning experience with self-paced computer-based training on CD-ROM. Course CBT engages students with interactive multimedia and hands-on simulations that reinforce and complement the concepts and skills covered in the textbook. All the content is aligned with the MOUS program, making it a great preparation tool for the certification exams. Course CBT also includes extensive pre- and post-assessments that test students' mastery of skills.

Course Assessment

How well do your students *really* know Microsoft Office? Course Assessment is a performance-based testing program that measures students' proficiency in Microsoft Office 2000. Previously known as SAM, Course Assessment is available for Office 2000 in either a live or simulated environment. You can use Course Assessment to place students into or out of courses, monitor their performance throughout a course, and help prepare them for the MOUS certification exams.

Create Your Ideal Course Package with CourseKits™

If one book doesn't offer all the coverage you need, create a course package that does. With Course Technology's CourseKits—our mix-and-match approach to selecting texts—you have the freedom to combine products from more than one series. When you choose any two or more Course Technology products for one course, we'll discount the price and package them together so your students can pick up one convenient bundle at the bookstore.

For more information about any of these offerings or other Course Technology products, contact your sales representative or visit our web site at:

www.course.com

Preface

Welcome to *Microsoft Access 2000—Illustrated Introductory*. This highly visual book offers users a hands-on introduction to the aspects of Microsoft Access 2000 and also serves as an excellent reference for future use. If you would like additional coverage of Microsoft Access 2000, we also offer *Microsoft Access 2000—Illustrated Second Course*, a logical continuation of the Introductory edition.

► Organization and Coverage

This text contains eight units that cover basic through intermediate Access skills. In these units, students learn how to create, modify, and use relational databases, including developing simple to complex tables, queries, forms, and reports.

► About this Approach

What makes the Illustrated approach so effective at teaching software skills? It's quite simple. Each skill is presented on two facing pages, with the step-by-step instructions on the left page, and large screen illustrations on the right. Students can focus on a single skill without having to turn the page. This unique design makes information extremely accessible and easy to absorb, and provides a great reference for after the course is over. This hands-on approach also makes it ideal for both self-paced or instructor-led classes.

Each lesson, or "information display," contains the following elements:

Each 2-page spread focuses on a single skill.

Clear step-by-step directions explain how to complete the specific task, with what students are to type in green. When students follow the numbered steps, they quickly learn how each procedure is performed and what the results will be.

Concise text that introduces the basic principles discussed in the lesson. Procedures are easier to learn when concepts fit into a framework.

Creating Related Tables

Access

Once you have developed a valid relational database design on paper, you are ready to define the tables in Access. All characteristics of a table including field names, data types, field descriptions, field properties, and key fields are defined in the table's Design view. In a relational database, it is important to define the length and data type of the linking field the same way in both tables to create a successful link. ◀ Using his new database design, David creates the Attendance table.

Steps

1. Start Access and open the **Training-E** database on your Project Disk
   The Courses and Employees tables already exist in the database.

2. Click **Tables** on the Objects Bar if it is not already selected, then click the **New Table button** 🖾 in the Training-E database window
   You will enter the fields for the Attendance table directly into the table's Design view.

3. Click **Design View** in the New Table dialog box, then click **OK**
   Field names should be as short as possible, but long enough to be descriptive. The field name entered in a table's Design view is used as the default name for the field in all later queries, forms, and reports.

   QuickTip
   Press [Enter] or [Tab] to move to the next column in a table's Design view window.

4. Maximize the **Table1: Table** window, type **LogNo**, press **[Enter]**, type **a** to select the AutoNumber Data Type, then press **[Enter]** twice to bypass the Description column and move to the second row
   The LogNo is a unique number used to identify each record in the Attendance table (each occurrence of an employee taking a course). The AutoNumber data type, which automatically sequences each new record with the next available integer, works well for this field. When entering data types, you can type the first letter of the data type; for example, type "T" for Text, "D" for Date/Time, or "C" for Currency. You can also click the Data Type list arrow, then select the data type from the list.

5. Type the other fields, entering the data types as shown in Table E-2
   Field descriptions entered in a table's Design view are optional. In Datasheet view, the description of a field appears in the status bar, and therefore provides further clarification about what type of data should be entered in the field. The SSN field will serve as the linking field between the Attendance and Employee tables. The CourseID field will serve as the linking field between the Attendance and Courses tables. You are not required to use the same field name in both tables, but doing so makes it easier to understand the link between the related tables later.

6. Click **LogNo** in the Field Name column, then click the **Primary Key button** 🔑 on the Table Design toolbar
   The LogNo field serves as the primary key field in this table.

CLUES TO USE

Comparing linked tables to imported tables

A **linked table** is a table created in another database product, or another program such as Excel, that is stored in a file outside the open database. You can add, delete, and edit records in a linked table from within Access, but you can't change its structure. An **imported table** creates a copy of the information from the external file and places it in a new Access table in your database.

► ACCESS E-6 **MODIFYING A DATABASE STRUCTURE**

Hints as well as trouble-shooting advice, right where you need it — next to the step itself.

Clues to Use boxes provide concise information that either expands on one component of the major lesson skill or describes an independent task that is in some way related to the major lesson skill.

Every lesson features large-size, full-color representations of what the students' screen should look like after completing the numbered steps.

FIGURE E-3: Design view for the Attendance table

TABLE E-2: Additional fields for the Attendance Table

field name	data type	description
SSN	Text	Employee's SSN
CourseID	Text	Course ID number
Attended	Date/Time	Date the course was taken
Passed	Yes/No	Did the employee pass the final test?

Quickly accessible summaries of key terms, toolbar buttons, or keyboard alternatives connected with the lesson material. Students can refer easily to this information when working on their own projects at a later time.

The page numbers are designed like a road map. Access indicates the Access section, E indicates the fifth unit, and 7 indicates the page within the unit.

Other Features

The two-page lesson format featured in this book provides the new user with a powerful learning experience. Additionally, this book contains the following features:

► MOUS Certification Coverage

Each unit opener has a ⌐MOUS⌐ next to it to indicate where Microsoft Office User Specialist (MOUS) skills are covered. In addition, there is a MOUS appendix which contains a grid that maps to where specific Core Access MOUS skills can be found in each lesson and where students can find additional practice. This textbook thoroughly prepares students to learn the Core skills needed to pass the Access 2000 MOUS exam. *Microsoft Access-Illustrated Complete, 0-7600-6072-X*, teaches students the Expert skills needed for the Access 2000 Expert MOUS exam.

► Real-World Case

The case study used throughout the textbook, a fictitious company called MediaLoft, is designed to be "'real-world" in nature and introduces the kinds of activities that students will encounter when working with Microsoft Access 2000. With a real-world case, the process of solving problems will be more meaningful to students.

Students can also enhance their skills by completing the WebWorks exercises in each unit by going to the innovative Student Online Companion, available at **www.course.com/illustrated/medialoft**. The MediaLoft site mirrors the case study by acting as the company's intranet site, further allowing students to become familiar with applicable business scenarios.

► End of Unit Material

Each unit concludes with a Concepts Review that tests students' understanding of what they learned in the unit. The Concepts Review is followed by a Skills Review, which provides students with additional hands-on practice of the skills. The Skills Review is followed by Independent Challenges, which pose case problems for students to solve. At least one Independent Challenge in each unit asks students to use the World Wide Web to solve the problem as indicated by a Web Work icon. The Visual Workshops that follow the Independent Challenges help students develop critical thinking skills. Students are shown completed Web pages or screens and are asked to re-create them.

Access 2000

Instructor's Resource Kit

The Instructor's Resource Kit is Course Technology's way of putting the resources and information needed to teach and learn effectively into your hands. With an integrated array of teaching and learning tools that offers you and your students a broad range of technology-based instructional options, we believe this kit represents the highest quality and most cutting edge resources available to instructors today. Many of these resources are available at www.course.com. The resources available with this book are:

MediaLoft Web site   Available at **www.course.com/illustrated/medialoft**, this innovative Student Online Companion enhances and augments the printed page by bringing students onto the Web for a dynamic and continually updated learning experience. The MediaLoft site mirrors the case study used throughout the book, creating a real-world intranet site for this fictitious company, a national chain of bookstore cafés. This Companion is used to complete the WebWorks exercise in each unit of this book, and to allow students to become familiar with the business application of an intranet site.

Instructor's Manual   Available as an electronic file, the Instructor's Manual is quality-assurance tested and includes unit overviews, detailed lecture topics for each unit with teaching tips, an Upgrader's Guide, solutions to all lessons and end-of-unit material, and extra Independent Challenges. The Instructor's Manual is available on the Instructor's Resource Kit CD-ROM, or you can download it from **www.course.com**.

Course Test Manager   Designed by Course Technology, this Windows-based testing software helps instructors design, administer, and print tests and pre-tests. A full-featured program, Course Test Manager also has an online testing component that allows students to take tests at the computer and have their exams automatically graded.

Course Faculty Online Companion   You can browse this textbook's password-protected site to obtain the Instructor's Manual, Solution Files, Project Files, and any updates to the text. Contact your Customer Service Representative for the site address and password.

Project Files   Project Files contain all of the data that students will use to complete the lessons and end-of-unit material. A Readme file includes instructions for using the files. Adopters of this text are granted the right to install the Project Files on any standalone computer or network. The Project Files are available on the Instructor's Resource Kit CD-ROM, the Review Pack, and can also be downloaded from www.course.com.

Solution Files   Solution Files contain every file students are asked to create or modify in the lessons and end-of-unit material. A Help file on the Instructor's Resource Kit includes information for using the Solution Files.

Figure Files   Figure files contain all the figures from the book in bitmap format. Use the figure files to create transparency masters or in a PowerPoint presentation.

WebCT   WebCT is a tool used to create Web-based educational environments and also uses WWW browsers as the interface for the course-building environment. The site is hosted on your school campus, allowing complete control over the information. WebCT has its own internal communication system, offering internal e-mail, a Bulletin Board, and a Chat room.

Course Technology offers pre-existing supplemental information to help in your WebCT class creation, such as a suggested Syllabus, Lecture Notes, Figures in the Book / Course Presenter, Student Downloads, and Test Banks in which you can schedule an exam, create reports, and more.

Brief Contents

Contents

Access 2000

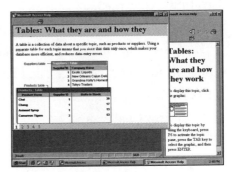

Contents

Using Tables and Queries

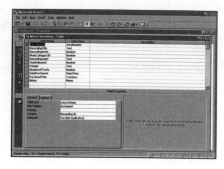

Using Forms

Contents

Creating Multiple Table Queries

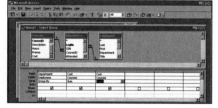

Developing Forms and Subforms

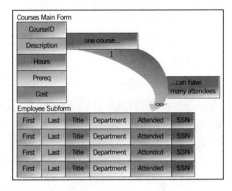

Building Complex Reports

Contents

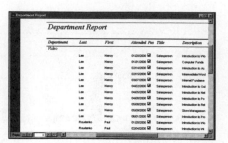

Getting
Started with Access 2000

Objectives

- MOUS ► **Define database software**
- MOUS ► **Learn database terminology**
- ► **Start Access and open a database**
- MOUS ► **View the database window**
- MOUS ► **Navigate records**
- MOUS ► **Enter records**
- MOUS ► **Edit records**
- MOUS ► **Preview and print a datasheet**
- MOUS ► **Get Help and exit Access**

In this unit, you will learn the purpose, advantages, and terminology of Microsoft Access 2000, a database software. You will also learn how to open a database and how to use the different elements of the Access window. You'll learn how to get help. You'll learn how to navigate through a database, enter and update data, and preview and print data. John Kim is the director of shipping at MediaLoft, a nationwide chain of bookstore cafés that sells books, music, and videos. Recently, MediaLoft switched to Access from an index card system for storing and maintaining customer information. John will use Access to enter and maintain this critical information for MediaLoft.

Defining Database Software

Microsoft Access 2000 is a database software program that runs on Windows. **Database software** is used to manage data that can be organized into lists of related information, such as customers, products, vendors, employees, projects, or sales. Many small companies record customer, inventory, and sales information in a spreadsheet program such as Microsoft Excel. While this electronic format is more productive than writing information on index cards, Excel still lacks many of the database advantages provided by Access. Refer to Table A-1 for a comparison of the two programs. John reviews the advantages that database software has over a manual index card system.

Data entry is faster and easier

Before inexpensive microcomputers, small businesses used manual paper systems, such as index cards, to record each customer, sale, and inventory item as illustrated in Figure A-1. Using an electronic database such as Access, you can create on-screen data entry forms, which make managing a database easier, more accurate, and more efficient than using index cards.

Information retrieval is faster and easier

Retrieving information on an index card system is tedious because the cards have to be physically handled, sorted, and stored. Also, one error in filing can cause serious retrieval problems later. With Access you can quickly search for, display, and print information on customers, sales, or inventory.

Information can be viewed and sorted in multiple ways

A card system allows you to sort the cards in only one order, unless the cards are duplicated for a second arrangement. Customer and inventory cards were generally sorted alphabetically by name. Sales index cards were usually sorted by date. In this system, complete customer and product information was recorded on each of their individual cards as well as on the corresponding sale cards. This quickly compromises data accuracy. Access allows you to view or sort the information from one or more subjects simultaneously. For example, you might want to know all the customers who purchased a particular product or all the products purchased by a particular customer. A change made to the data in one view of Access is automatically updated in every other view or report.

Information is more secure

Index cards can be torn, misplaced, and stolen. There is no password required to read them, and a disaster, such as a flood or fire, could completely destroy them. You can back up an Access database file on a regular basis and store the file at an offsite location. You can also password protect data so only those users with appropriate security clearances can view or manipulate the data.

Information can be shared among several users

An index card system is limited to those users who can physically reach it. If one user keeps a card for an extended period of time, then others cannot use or update that information. Access databases are inherently multiuser. More than one person can be entering, updating, and using the data at the same time.

Duplicate data entry is minimized

The index card system requires that the user duplicate the customer and product information on each sales card. With Access, you only need to enter each piece of information once. Figure A-2 shows a possible structure for an Access database to record sales.

FIGURE A-1: Using index cards to organize sales data

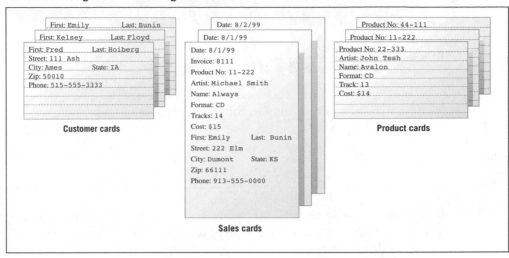

FIGURE A-2: Using Access, an electronic relational database, to organize sales data

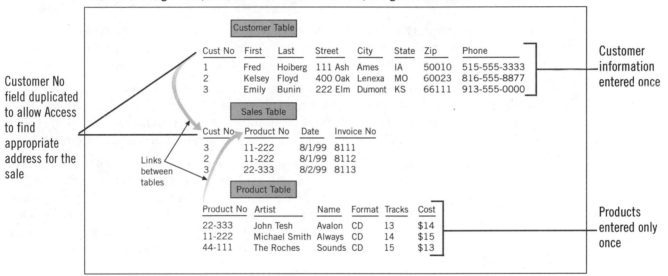

TABLE A-1: Comparing Excel to Access

feature	Excel	Access
Layout	Provides a natural tabular layout for easy data entry	Provides a spreadsheet "view" as well as forms which arrange data in a variety of ways
Storage	Limited to approximately 65,000 records per sheet	Able to store any number of records up to 2 gigabytes
Linked tables	Manages single lists of information	Allows links between lists of information to reduce data entry redundancy
Reporting	Limited to a spreadsheet printout	Provides sophisticated reporting features such as multiple headers and footers and calculations on groups of records
Security	Very limited	Each user can be given access to only the records and fields they need
Multiuser capabilities	Does not allow multiple users to simultaneously enter and update data	Allows multiple users to simultaneously enter and update data
Data entry screens	Provides limited data entry screens	Provides the ability to create extensive data entry screens called forms

Learning Database Terminology

To become familiar with Access, you need to understand basic database terminology. John reviews the terms and concepts that define a database.

Details

 A **database** is a collection of information associated with a topic (for example, sales of products to customers). The smallest piece of information in a database is called a **field**, or category of information, such as the customer's name, city, state, or phone number. A **key field** is a field that contains unique information for each record. A group of related fields, such as all demographic information for one customer, is called a **record**. In Access, a collection of records for a single subject, such as all of the customer records, is called a **table**, as shown in Figure A-3.

 An Access database is a **relational database**, in which more than one table, such as the Customer, Sales, and Product tables, can share information. The term "relational database" comes from the fact that two tables are linked, or related, by a common field.

 Tables, therefore, are the most important **object** in an Access database because they contain all of the data within the database. An Access database may also contain six other objects, which serve to enhance the usability and value of the data. The objects in an Access database are tables, queries, forms, reports, pages, macros, and modules, and they are summarized in Table A-2.

 Data can be entered and edited in four of the objects: tables, queries, forms, and pages. The relationship between tables, queries, forms, and reports is shown in Figure A-4. Regardless of how the data is entered, it is physically stored in a table object. Data can be printed from a table, query, form, page, or report object. The macro and module objects are used to provide additional database productivity and automation features. All of the objects (except for the page objects, which are used to create Web pages) are stored in one database file.

TABLE A-2: Access objects and their purpose

object	purpose
Table	Contains all of the raw data within the database in a spreadsheet-like view; tables can be linked with a common field to share information and therefore minimize data redundancy
Query	Provides a spreadsheet-like view of the data similar to tables, but a query can be designed to provide the user with a subset of fields or records from one or more tables; queries are created when a user has a "question" about the data in the database
Form	Provides an easy-to-use data entry screen, which generally shows only one record at a time
Report	Provides a professional printout of data that may contain enhancements such as headers, footers, and calculations on groups of records
Page	Creates Web pages from Access objects as well as provides Web page connectivity features to an Access database, also called Data Access Page
Macro	Stores a collection of keystrokes or commands, such as printing several reports or displaying a toolbar when a form opens
Module	Stores Visual Basic programming code that extends the functions and automated processes of Access

FIGURE A-3: Tables contain fields and records

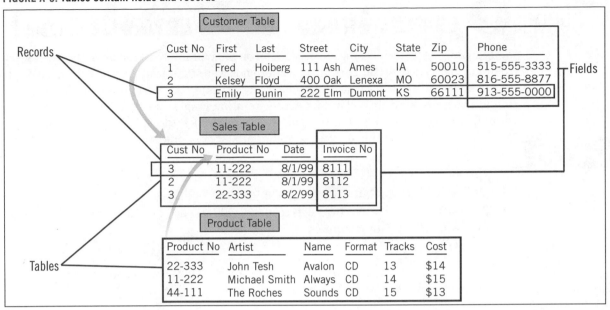

FIGURE A-4: The relationship between Access objects

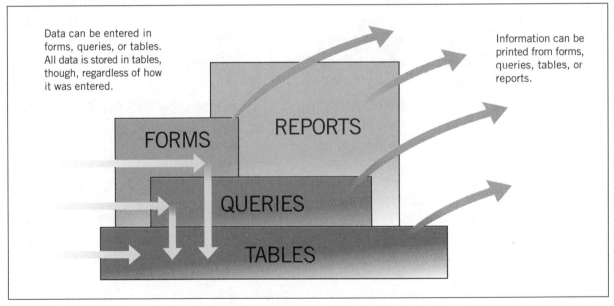

Data can be entered in forms, queries, or tables. All data is stored in tables, though, regardless of how it was entered.

Information can be printed from forms, queries, tables, or reports.

Access 2000

Starting Access and Opening a Database

You can start Access by clicking the Access icon on the Windows desktop or on the Microsoft Office Shortcut Bar. Since not all computers will provide a shortcut icon on the desktop or display the Office Shortcut Bar, you can always find Access by clicking the Start button on the taskbar, pointing to Programs, and then choosing Access from the Programs menu. You can open a database from within Access or by finding the database file on the desktop, in My Computer, or in Windows Explorer, and then opening it. John starts Access and opens the MediaLoft-A database.

Steps

1. Click the **Start button** [Start] on the taskbar
The Start button is in the lower-left corner of the taskbar. You can use the Start menu to start any program on your computer.

Trouble?

If you can't locate Microsoft Access on the Programs menu, point to the Microsoft Office group and look for Access there.

2. Point to **Programs**
Access is generally located on the Programs menu. All the programs, or applications, stored on your computer can be found here.

3. Click **Microsoft Access**
Access opens and displays the Access dialog box, from which you can start a new database or open an existing file.

QuickTip

Make a copy of your Project Disk before you use it.

4. Insert your Project Disk in the appropriate disk drive
To complete the units in this book, you need a Project Disk. See your instructor or technical support person for assistance.

5. Click **More Files**, then click **OK**
The Open dialog box appears, as shown in Figure A-5. Depending on the databases and folders stored on your computer, your dialog box may look slightly different.

Trouble?

These lessons assume your Project Disk is in drive A. If you are using a different drive, substitute that drive for drive A in the steps.

6. Click the **Look in list arrow**, then click **3½ Floppy (A:)**
A list of the files on your Project Disk appears in the Open dialog box.

7. Click the **MediaLoft-A** database file, click **Open**, then click the **Maximize button** on the title bar if the Access window does not fill the screen
The MediaLoft-A database opens as shown in Figure A-6.

CLUES TO USE

Personalized toolbars and menus in Office 2000

Office 2000 toolbars and menus modify themselves to your working style. The toolbars you see when you first start a program include the most frequently used buttons. To locate a button not visible on a toolbar, click the More Buttons button at the end of the toolbar to see the list of additional toolbar buttons. As you work, the program adds the buttons you use to the visible toolbars and moves the buttons you haven't used in a while to the More Buttons list. Similarly, menus adjust to your work habits. Short menus appear when you first click a menu command. To view additional menu commands, point to the double-arrow at the bottom of the menu, leave the pointer on the menu name after you've clicked the menu, or double-click the menu name. If you select a command that's not on the short menu, the program automatically adds it to the short menus. You can return personalized toolbars and menus to their original settings by clicking Tools on the menu bar, then clicking Customize. On the Options tab in the Customize dialog box, click Reset my usage data, click Yes to close the alert box, then close the Customize dialog box. Resetting usage data erases changes made automatically to your menus and toolbars. It does not affect the options you customize.

FIGURE A-5: Open dialog box

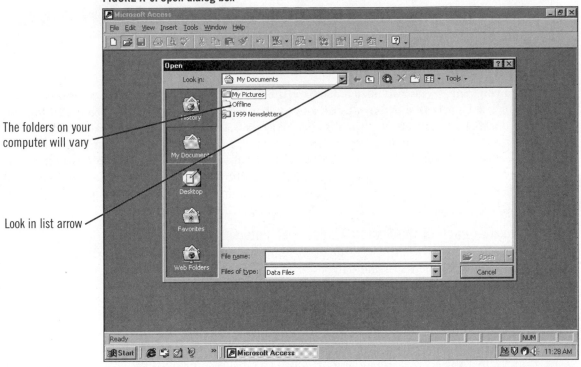

The folders on your computer will vary

Look in list arrow

FIGURE A-6: MediaLoft-A database

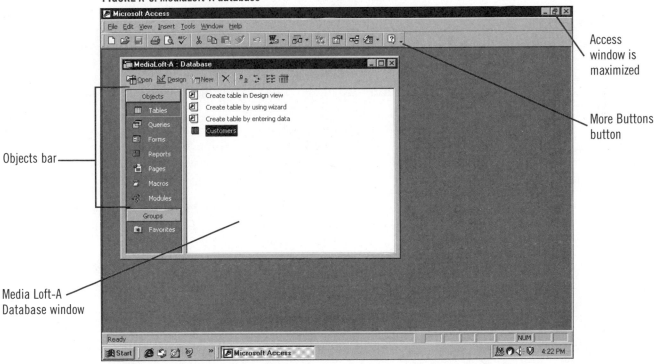

Access window is maximized

More Buttons button

Objects bar

Media Loft-A Database window

Viewing the Database Window

When you start Access and open a database, the **database window** displays common Windows elements such as a title bar, menu bar, and toolbar. Clicking the Objects or Groups buttons on the Objects bar alternatively expands and collapses that section of the database window. If all the objects don't display in the expanded section, click the small arrow at the top or bottom of the section to scroll the list. The **Objects** area displays the seven types of objects that can be accessed by clicking the object type you want. The **Groups** area displays other commonly used files and folders, such as the Favorites folder. ✒ John explores the MediaLoft-A database.

1. **Look at each of the Access window elements shown in Figure A-7**
   The Objects bar on the left side of the database window displays the seven object types. The other elements of the database window are summarized in Table A-3. Because the Tables object is selected, the buttons you need to create a new table or to work with the existing table are displayed in the MediaLoft-A Database window.

2. **Click File on the menu bar**
   The File menu contains commands for opening a new or existing database, saving a database in a variety of formats, and printing. The menu commands vary depending on which window or database object is currently in use.

3. **Point to Edit on the menu bar, point to View, point to Insert, point to Tools, point to Window, point to Help, move the pointer off the menu, then press [Esc] twice**
   All menus close when you press [Esc]. Pressing [Esc] a second time deselects the menu.

4. **Point to the New button ☐ on the Database toolbar**
   Pointing to a toolbar button causes a descriptive **ScreenTip** to automatically appear, providing a short description of the button. The buttons on the toolbars represent the most commonly used Access features. Toolbar buttons change just as menu options change depending on which window and database object are currently in use.

5. **Point to the Open button ☞ on the Database toolbar, then point to the Save button ☐ on the Database toolbar**
   Sometimes toolbar buttons or menu options are dimmed which means that they are currently unavailable. For example, the Save button is dimmed because it doesn't make sense to save the MediaLoft-A database right now because you haven't made any changes to it yet.

6. **Click Queries on the Objects bar**
   The query object window provides several ways to create a new query and displays the names of previously created queries, as shown in Figure A-8. There are three previously created query objects displayed within the MediaLoft-A Database window.

7. **Click Forms on the Objects bar, then click Reports on the Objects bar**
   The MediaLoft-A database contains the Customers table, three queries, a customer entry form, and three reports.

Viewing objects

You can change the way you view the objects in the database window by clicking the last four buttons on the toolbar. You can view the objects as Large Icons , Small Icons , in a List (this is the default view), and with Details . The Details view shows a longer description of the object, as well as the date the object was last modified and the date it was originally created.

FIGURE A-7: MediaLoft-A database screen elements

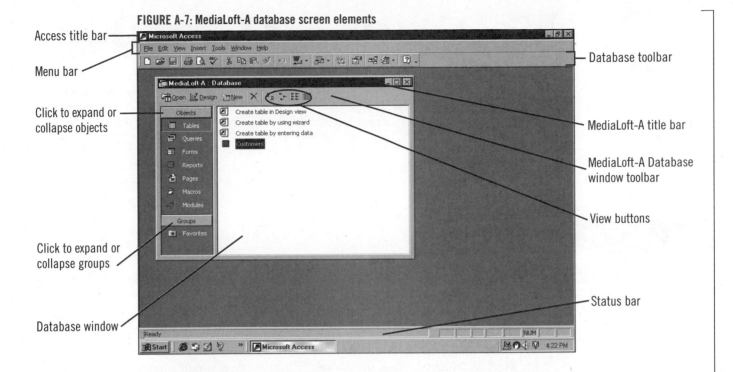

Access title bar

Menu bar

Database toolbar

Click to expand or collapse objects

MediaLoft-A title bar

MediaLoft-A Database window toolbar

View buttons

Click to expand or collapse groups

Database window

Status bar

FIGURE A-8: MediaLoft-A query objects

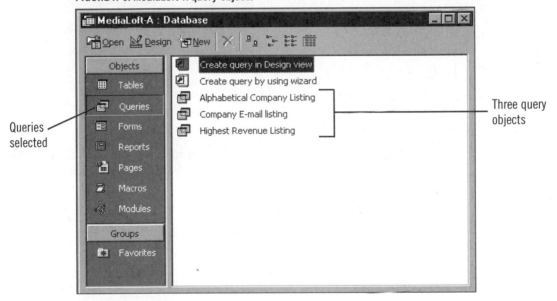

Queries selected

Three query objects

TABLE A-3: Elements of the database window

element	description
Database toolbar	Contains buttons for commonly performed tasks
Database window	Provides access to the objects within the database
Menu bar	Contains menus used in Access
Objects bar	Allows you to view a list of the object type chosen
Database window toolbar	Contains buttons you use to open, modify, create, delete, or view objects
Status bar	Displays messages regarding the current database operation
Title bar	Contains program name (Access) and filename of active database

Navigating Records

Your ability to navigate through the fields and records of a database is key to your productivity and success with the database. You navigate through the information in **Navigation mode** in the table's **datasheet**, a spreadsheet-like grid that displays fields as columns and records as rows. John opens the database and reviews the table containing information about MediaLoft's customers.

QuickTip

You can also double-click an object to open it.

1. **Click Tables on the Objects bar, click Customers, then click the Open button 📧 on the MediaLoft-A Database window toolbar**

   The datasheet for the Customers table opens, as shown in Figure A-9. The datasheet contains 27 customer records with 13 fields of information for each record. **Field names** are listed at the top of each column. The number of the selected record in the datasheet is displayed in the **Specific Record box** at the bottom of the datasheet window. Depending on the size of your monitor and the resolution of your computer system, you may see a different number of fields. If all of the fields don't display, you can scroll to the right to see the rest.

2. **Press [Tab] to move to Sprint**

   Sprint is the entry in the second field, Company, of the first record.

3. **Press [Enter]**

   The data, Aaron, is selected in the third field, First. Pressing either [Tab] or [Enter] moves the focus to the next field. **Focus** refers to which field would be edited if you started typing.

4. **Press [↓]**

   The focus moves to the Kelsey entry in the First field of the second record. The **current record symbol** in the **record selector box** also identifies which record you are navigating. The Next Record and Previous Record **navigation buttons** can also be used to navigate the datasheet.

5. **Press [Ctrl][End]**

   The focus moves to the last field of the last record. You can also use the Last Record navigation button to move to the last record.

6. **Press [Ctrl][Home]**

   The focus moves to the first field of the first record. You can also use the First Record navigation button to move to the first record. A complete listing of navigation keystrokes to move the focus between fields and records is shown in Table A-4.

Changing to Edit mode

If you click a field with the mouse pointer instead of pressing the [Tab] or [Enter] to navigate through the datasheet, you change from Navigation mode to **Edit mode**. In Edit mode, Access assumes that you are trying to edit that particular field, so keystrokes such as [Ctrl][End], [Ctrl][Home], [←], and [→] move the insertion point *within* the field. To return to Navigation mode, press [Tab] or [Enter] which moves the focus to the next field, or press [↑] or [↓] which moves the focus to a different record.

FIGURE A-9: Customers datasheet

FIGURE A-9: Customers datasheet

Labels around the figure:
- Current record symbol
- Current focus
- Records
- Record selector box
- Specific Record box
- Navigation buttons
- Field name
- Total number of records
- Fields

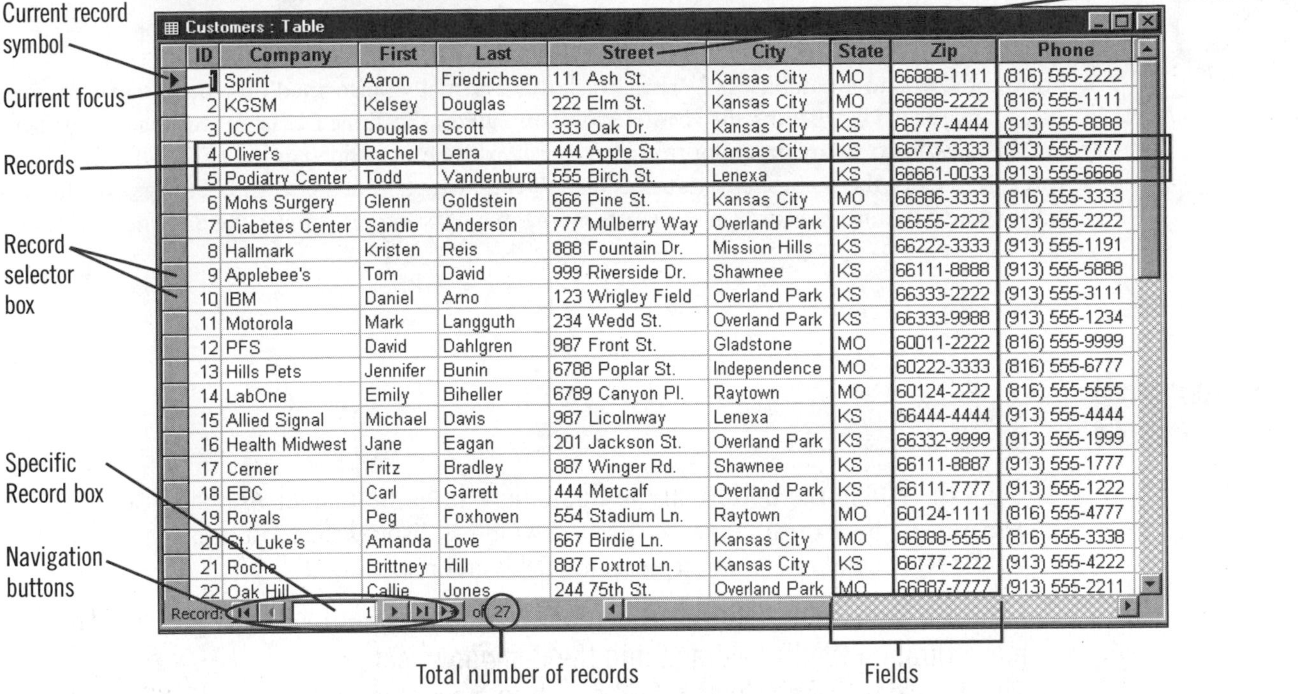

ID	Company	First	Last	Street	City	State	Zip	Phone
1	Sprint	Aaron	Friedrichsen	111 Ash St.	Kansas City	MO	66888-1111	(816) 555-2222
2	KGSM	Kelsey	Douglas	222 Elm St.	Kansas City	MO	66888-2222	(816) 555-1111
3	JCCC	Douglas	Scott	333 Oak Dr.	Kansas City	KS	66777-4444	(913) 555-8888
4	Oliver's	Rachel	Lena	444 Apple St.	Kansas City	KS	66777-3333	(913) 555-7777
5	Podiatry Center	Todd	Vandenburg	555 Birch St.	Lenexa	KS	66661-0033	(913) 555-6666
6	Mohs Surgery	Glenn	Goldstein	666 Pine St.	Kansas City	MO	66886-3333	(816) 555-3333
7	Diabetes Center	Sandie	Anderson	777 Mulberry Way	Overland Park	KS	66555-2222	(913) 555-2222
8	Hallmark	Kristen	Reis	888 Fountain Dr.	Mission Hills	KS	66222-3333	(913) 555-1191
9	Applebee's	Tom	David	999 Riverside Dr.	Shawnee	KS	66111-8888	(913) 555-5888
10	IBM	Daniel	Arno	123 Wrigley Field	Overland Park	KS	66333-2222	(913) 555-3111
11	Motorola	Mark	Langguth	234 Wedd St.	Overland Park	KS	66333-9988	(913) 555-1234
12	PFS	David	Dahlgren	987 Front St.	Gladstone	MO	60011-2222	(816) 555-9999
13	Hills Pets	Jennifer	Bunin	6788 Poplar St.	Independence	MO	60222-3333	(816) 555-6777
14	LabOne	Emily	Biheller	6789 Canyon Pl.	Raytown	MO	60124-2222	(816) 555-5555
15	Allied Signal	Michael	Davis	987 Licolnway	Lenexa	KS	66444-4444	(913) 555-4444
16	Health Midwest	Jane	Eagan	201 Jackson St.	Overland Park	KS	66332-9999	(913) 555-1999
17	Cerner	Fritz	Bradley	887 Winger Rd.	Shawnee	KS	66111-8887	(913) 555-1777
18	EBC	Carl	Garrett	444 Metcalf	Overland Park	KS	66111-7777	(913) 555-1222
19	Royals	Peg	Foxhoven	554 Stadium Ln.	Raytown	MO	60124-1111	(816) 555-4777
20	St. Luke's	Amanda	Love	667 Birdie Ln.	Kansas City	MO	66888-5555	(816) 555-3338
21	Roche	Brittney	Hill	887 Foxtrot Ln.	Kansas City	KS	66777-2222	(913) 555-4222
22	Oak Hill	Callie	Jones	244 75th St.	Overland Park	MO	66887-7777	(913) 555-2211

Record: 1 of 27

TABLE A-4: Navigation mode keyboard shortcuts

shortcut key	to move to the
[Tab], [Enter] or [→]	Next field of the current record
[Shift][Tab] or [←]	Previous field of the current record
[Home]	First field of the current record
[End]	Last field of the current record
[Ctrl][Home]	First field of the first record
[Ctrl][End]	Last field of the last record
[↑]	Current field of the previous record
[↓]	Current field of the next record
[Ctrl][↑]	Current field of the first record
[Ctrl][↓]	Current field of the last record
[F5]	Specific record

Entering Records

Adding records to a database is a critical task that is usually performed on a daily basis. You can add a new record by clicking the **New Record button** on the Table Datasheet toolbar or by clicking the New Record navigation button. A new record is always added at the end of the datasheet. You can reorder the records in a datasheet by sorting, which you will learn later. John is ready to add two new records in the Customers table. First he maximizes the datasheet window.

Steps

1. Click the **Maximize button** on the Customers Table datasheet window title bar

   Maximizing both the Access and datasheet windows displays the most information possible on the screen and allows you to see more fields and records.

2. Click the **New Record button** ▶※ on the Table Datasheet toolbar, then press **[Tab]** to move through the ID field and into the Company field

   The ID field is an **AutoNumber** field, which automatically assigns a new number each time you add a record.

3. Type **CIO**, press **[Tab]**, type **Lisa**, press **[Tab]**, type **Lang**, press **[Tab]**, type **420 Locust St.**, press **[Tab]**, type **Lenexa**, press **[Tab]**, type **KS**, press **[Tab]**, type **66111-8899**, press **[Tab]**, type **9135551189**, press **[Tab]**, type **9135551889**, press **[Tab]**, type **9/6/69**, press **[Tab]**, type **lang@cio.com**, press **[Tab]**, type **5433.22**, then press **[Enter]**

   The ID for the record for Lisa Lang is 28. AutoNumber fields should not be used as a counter for how many records you have in a table. Think of the AutoNumber field as an arbitrary but unique number for each record. The value in an AutoNumber field increments by one for each new record and cannot be edited or reused even if the entire record is deleted. The purpose of an AutoNumber field is to uniquely identify each new record. It logs how many records have been added to the datasheet since the creation of the datasheet, and not how many records are currently in the datasheet.

Trouble?

The ID number for the new records may be different in your database.

4. Enter the new record for Rachel Best shown in the table below

in field:	type:	in field:	type:
ID	29	Zip	65555-4444
Company	RBB Events	Phone	913-555-2289
First	Rachel	Fax	913-555-2889
Last	Best	Birthdate	8/20/68
Street	500 Sunset Blvd.	Email	Best@rbb.com
City	Manhattan	YTDSales	5998.33
State	KS		

Compare your updated datasheet with Figure A-10.

FIGURE A-10: Customers table with two new records

Table Datasheet toolbar

Both windows are maximized

New record button

Two new records

New record button

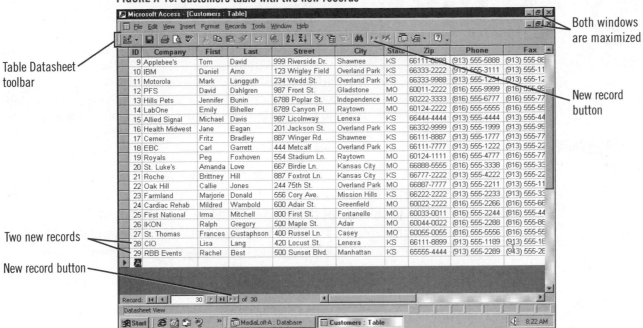

FIGURE A-11: Moving a field

Mouse pointer

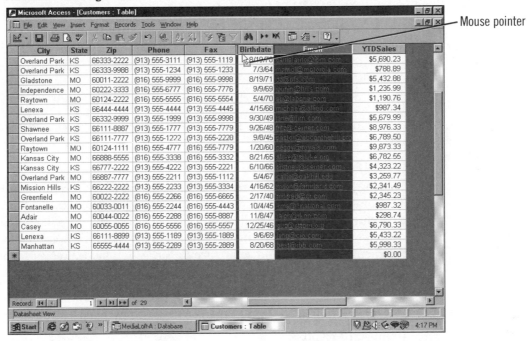

Moving datasheet columns

You can reorganize the fields in a datasheet by dragging the field name left or right. Figure A-11 shows how the mouse pointer changes to ⬚, as the Email field is moved to the left. The black vertical line represents the new location between the Fax and Birthdate fields. Release the mouse button when you have appropriately positioned the field.

Editing Records

Updating information in databases is another important daily task required to keep your database current. To change the contents of an existing record, click the field you'd like to change to switch to Edit mode, then type the new information. You can delete any unwanted data by clicking the field and using the [Backspace] and [Delete] keys to delete text to the left and right of the insertion point. Other data entry keystrokes are summarized in Table A-5. ▰▰ John needs to make some corrections to the datasheet of the Customers table. He starts by correcting an error in the Street field of the first record.

Steps 123 4

1. **Press [Ctrl][Home] to move to the first record, click to the right of 111 Ash St. in the Street field, press [Backspace] three times to delete St., then type Dr.**
   When you are editing a record, the **edit record symbol**, which looks like a small pencil, appears in the record selector box to the left of the current record, as shown in Figure A-12.

2. **Click to the right of Hallmark in the Company field in record 8, press [Spacebar], type Cards, then press [↓] to move to the next record**
   You do not need to explicitly save new records or changes to existing records because Access saves the new data as soon as you move to another record or close the data sheet.

3. **Click Shawnee in the City field for record 17, then press [Ctrl]['] (⟦ ⟧)** *button next to enter*
   The entry changes from "Shawnee" to "Overland Park." [Ctrl]['] inserts the data from the same field in the previous record.

4. **Click to the left of EBC in the Company field for record 18, press [Delete] to remove the E, press [Tab] to move to the next field, then type Doug**
   "Doug" replaces the current entry "Carl" in the First field. Notice the edit record symbol in the record selector box to the left of record 18. Since you are still editing this record, you can undo the changes.

5. **Press [Esc]**
   The Doug entry changes back to Carl. Pressing [Esc] once removes the current field's editing changes.

6. **Press [Esc] again**
   Pressing [Esc] a second time removes all changes made to the record you are currently editing. The company entry is restored to EBC. The ability to use the [Esc] key in edit mode to remove data entry changes is dependent on whether or not you are still editing the record (as evidenced by the edit record symbol to the left of the record). Once you move to another record, the changes are saved, and you return to Navigation mode. In Navigation mode you can no longer use the [Esc] key to remove editing changes, but you can click the **Undo button** 🔙 on the Table Database toolbar to undo the last change you made.

7. **Press [↓] to move to Peg in the First field of record 19, type Peggy, then press [↓] to move to record 20**
   Since you are no longer editing record 19, the [Esc] key has no effect on the last change.

QuickTip
The ScreenTip for the Undo button displays the action you can undo.

8. **Click the Undo button 🔙 on the Table Datasheet toolbar**
   You undo the last edit and Peggy is changed back to Peg. Access only allows you to undo your last action. You can also delete a record directly from the datasheet.

9. **Click the Allied Signal ID 15 Record Selector box, click the Delete Record button ⊠ on the Table Datasheet toolbar, then click Yes to confirm that you want to delete the record**
   You cannot undo a record deletion operation.

FIGURE A-12: Editing records

Edit record symbol

Insertion point

ID	Company	First	Last	Street	City	State	Zip	Phone	Fax
1	Sprint	Aaron	Friedrichsen	111 Ash Dr.	Kansas City	MO	66888-1111	(816) 555-2222	(816) 555-22
2	KGSM	Kelsey	Douglas	222 Elm St.	Kansas City	MO	66888-2222	(816) 555-1111	(816) 555-11
3	JCCC	Douglas	Scott	333 Oak Dr.	Kansas City	KS	66777-4444	(913) 555-8888	(913) 555-88
4	Oliver's	Rachel	Lena	444 Apple St.	Kansas City	KS	66777-3333	(913) 555-7777	(913) 555-77
5	Podiatry Center	Todd	Vandenburg	555 Birch St.	Lenexa	KS	66661-0033	(913) 555-6666	(913) 555-66
6	Mohs Surgery	Glenn	Goldstein	666 Pine St.	Kansas City	MO	66886-3333	(816) 555-3333	(816) 555-22
7	Diabetes Center	Sandie	Anderson	777 Mulberry Way	Overland Park	KS	66555-2222	(913) 555-2222	(913) 555-22
8	Hallmark	Kristen	Reis	888 Fountain Dr.	Mission Hills	KS	66222-3333	(913) 555-1191	(913) 555-11
9	Applebee's	Tom	David	999 Riverside Dr.	Shawnee	KS	66111-8888	(913) 555-5888	(913) 555-88
10	IBM	Daniel	Arno	123 Wrigley Field	Overland Park	KS	66333-2222	(913) 555-3111	(913) 555-11
11	Motorola	Mark	Langguth	234 Wedd St.	Overland Park	KS	66333-9988	(913) 555-1234	(913) 555-12
12	PFS	David	Dahlgren	987 Front St.	Gladstone	MO	60011-2222	(816) 555-9999	(816) 555-99
13	Hills Pets	Jennifer	Bunin	6788 Poplar St.	Independence	MO	60222-3333	(816) 555-6777	(816) 555-77
14	LabOne	Emily	Biheller	6789 Canyon Pl.	Raytown	MO	60124-2222	(816) 555-5555	(816) 555-55
15	Allied Signal	Michael	Davis	987 Licolnway	Lenexa	KS	66444-4444	(913) 555-4444	(913) 555-44
16	Health Midwest	Jane	Eagan	201 Jackson St.	Overland Park	KS	66332-9999	(913) 555-1999	(913) 555-99
17	Cerner	Fritz	Bradley	887 Winger Rd.	Shawnee	KS	66111-8887	(913) 555-1777	(913) 555-77
18	EBC	Carl	Garrett	444 Metcalf	Overland Park	KS	66111-7777	(913) 555-1222	(913) 555-22
19	Royals	Peg	Foxhoven	554 Stadium Ln.	Raytown	MO	60124-1111	(816) 555-4777	(816) 555-77
20	St. Luke's	Amanda	Love	667 Birdie Ln.	Kansas City	MO	66888-5555	(816) 555-3338	(816) 555-33
21	Roche	Brittney	Hill	887 Foxtrot Ln.	Kansas City	KS	66777-2222	(913) 555-4222	(913) 555-22
22	Oak Hill	Callie	Jones	244 75th St.	Overland Park	MO	66887-7777	(913) 555-2211	(913) 555-11
23	Farmland	Marjorie	Donald	556 Cory Ave.	Mission Hills	KS	66222-2222	(913) 555-2233	(913) 555-33
24	Cardiac Rehab	Mildred	Wambold	600 Adair St.	Greenfield	MO	60022-2222	(816) 555-2266	(816) 555-66
25	First National	Irma	Mitchell	800 First St.	Fontanelle	MO	60033-0011	(816) 555-2244	(816) 555-44

Record: 1 of 29

Datasheet View

Start | MediaLoft-A : Database | Customers : Table | 4:19 PM

TABLE A-5: Edit mode keyboard shortcuts

editing keystroke	action
[Backspace]	Deletes one character to the left of the insertion point
[Delete]	Deletes one character to the right of the insertion point
[F2]	Switches to Edit mode from Navigation mode
[Esc]	Undoes the change to the current field
[Esc][Esc]	Undoes the change to the current record
[F7]	Starts the spell check feature
[Ctrl][']	Inserts the value from the same field in the previous record into the current field
[Ctrl][;]	Inserts the current date in a date field

CLUES TO USE

Resizing datasheet columns

You can resize the width of the field in a datasheet by dragging the thin black line that separates the field names to the left or right. The mouse pointer changes to ✛ as you resize the field to make it wider or narrower. Release the mouse button when you have resized the field.

Previewing and Printing a Datasheet

After entering and editing the records in a table, you can print the datasheet to obtain a hard copy of it. Before printing the datasheet, you should preview it to see how it will look when printed. Often you will want to make adjustments to margins and page orientation. ➤ John is ready to preview and print the datasheet.

Steps

QuickTip

If you need your name on the printed solution, enter your name as a new record in the datasheet.

1. Click the Print Preview button 🔍 **on the Table Database toolbar**
The datasheet appears as a miniature page in the Print Preview window, as shown in Figure A-14. The Print Preview toolbar provides options for printing, viewing more than one page, and sending the information to Word or Excel.

2. Click 🔍 **on the top of the miniature datasheet**
By magnifying this view of the datasheet, you can see its header, which includes the object name, Customers, in the center of the top of the page and the date on the right.

3. Scroll down to view the bottom of the page
The footer displays a page number centered on the bottom.

4. Click the Two Pages button ▣ **on the Print Preview toolbar**
You decide to increase the top margin of the printout.

5. Click File on the menu bar, then click Page Setup
The Page Setup dialog box opens, as shown in Figure A-15. This dialog box provides options for changing margins, removing the headings (the header and footer), and changing page orientation from portrait (default) to landscape on the Page tab.

6. Double-click 1" in the Top text box, type 2, then click OK
The modified datasheet appears in the window. Satisfied with the layout for the printout, you'll print the datasheet and close the Print Preview window.

7. Click the Print button 🖨 **on the Print Preview toolbar, then click Close**
The datasheet appears on the screen.

Hiding fields

Sometimes you don't need all the fields of a datasheet on a printout. To temporarily hide a field from viewing and therefore from a resulting datasheet printout, click the field name, click Format on the menu bar, and then click Hide Columns. To redisplay the column, click Format, then Unhide Columns. The Unhide Columns dialog box, shown in Figure A-13, opens. The empty columns check boxes indicate the columns that are hidden. Clicking the check boxes will bring the columns back into view on the datasheet.

FIGURE A-13: Unhide Columns dialog box

These fields are currently hidden

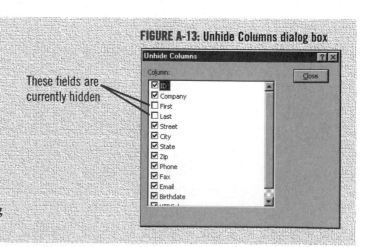

FIGURE A-14: Datasheet in print preview (portrait orientation)

Print Preview toolbar

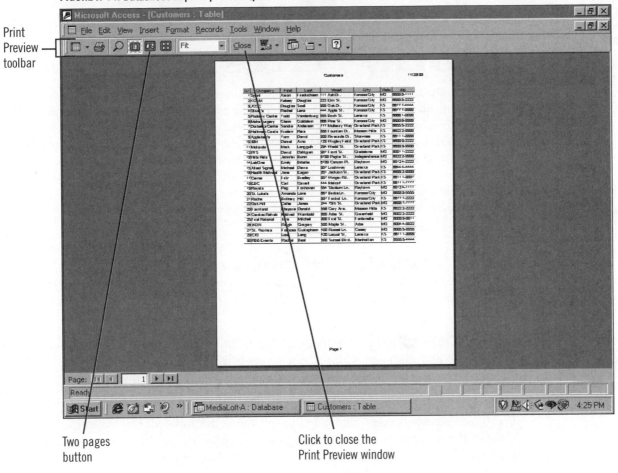

Two pages button

Click to close the Print Preview window

FIGURE A-15: Page Setup dialog box

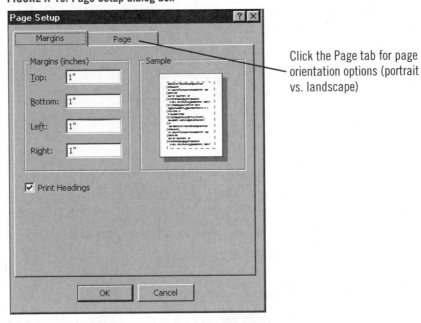

Click the Page tab for page orientation options (portrait vs. landscape)

Access 2000

Access 2000

Getting Help and Exiting Access

When you have finished working in your database, you need to close the object you were working in, such as a table datasheet, and then close the database. To close a table, click Close on the File menu or click the object's Close button located in the upper-right corner of the menu bar. Once you have closed all open objects, you can exit the program. As with most programs, if you try to exit Access and have not yet saved changes to open objects, Access will prompt you to save your changes. You can use the Help system to learn more about the program and get help. ➤ John has finished working with Access for now, so he closes the Customers table and MediaLoft-A database. Before exiting, he learns more about the Help system, and then exits Access.

Steps 1234

1. **Click the Close button for the Customers datasheet**
   The MediaLoft-A database window displays. If you make any structural changes to the datasheet such as moving, resizing, or hiding columns, you will be prompted to save those changes.

2. **Click the Close button for the MediaLoft-A Database, as shown in Figure A-16**
   The MediaLoft-A database is closed, but Access is still running so you could open another database or explore the Help system to learn more about Access at this time.

3. **Click Help on the menu bar, then click Microsoft Access Help**
   The Office Assistant opens and offers to get the help you need. You can further explore some of the concepts you have learned by finding information in the Access Help system. Table A-6 summarizes the options on the Access Help menu, which provides in-depth information on Access features.

4. **Type What is a table, click Search, click Tables: what they are and how they work, then click the graphic as shown in Figure A-17**

5. **Read the information, then click each of the five pages**

6. **Close the Access Help windows**

Trouble?
Do not remove your Project Disk from drive A until you have exited Access.

7. **Click File on the menu bar, then click Exit**
   You have exited Access.

Shutting down your computer

Never shut off a computer before the screen indicates that it is safe to do so. If you shut off a computer during the initial Windows load process (the screen displays the Windows logo and a cloud background at this time) or before the screen indicates that it is safe to do so, you can corrupt your Windows files.

FIGURE A-16: Closing a database

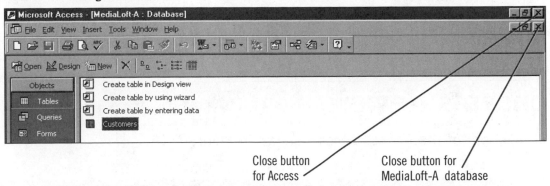

Close button
for Access

Close button for
MediaLoft-A database

FIGURE A-17: Access Help window

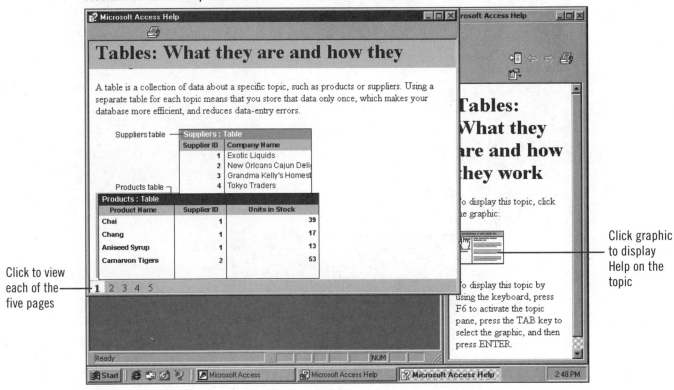

Click to view
each of the
five pages

Click graphic
to display
Help on the
topic

TABLE A-6: Help menu options

menu option	description
Microsoft Access Help	Opens the Office Assistant; type a question to open the entire Microsoft Access Help manual in a separate window in which you can search for information by the table of contents, index, or keyword
Show the Office Assistant	Presents the Office Assistant, an automated character that provides tips and interactive prompts while you are working
Hide the Office Assistant	Temporarily closes the Office Assistant for the working session
What's This	Changes the mouse pointer to ▷?; this special mouse pointer provides a short explanation of the icon or menu option that you click
Office on the Web	If you are connected to the Web, provides additional Microsoft information and support articles; this Web-based information is updated daily
Detect and Repair	Analyzes a database for possible data corruption and attempts to repair problems
About Microsoft Access	Provides the version and product ID of Access

Practice

► Concepts Review

Label each element of the Access window shown in Figure A-18.

FIGURE A-18

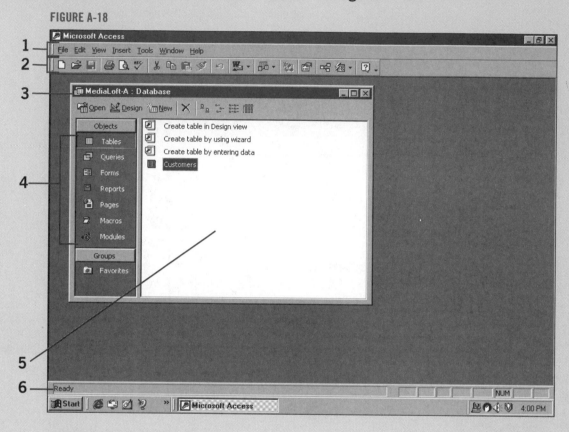

Match each term with the statement that describes it.

7. Objects   **a.** A group of related fields, such as all the demographic information for one customer
8. Table   **b.** A collection of records for a single subject, such as all the customer records
9. Record   **c.** A category of information in a table, such as a customer's name, city, or state
10. Field   **d.** A spreadsheet-like grid that displays fields as columns and records as rows
11. Datasheet   **e.** Seven types of these are contained in an Access database and are used to enter,
                          enhance, and use the data within the database

Select the best answer from the list of choices.

12. Which of the following is NOT a typical benefit of relational databases?
  a. Easier data entry   **c.** Minimized duplicate data entry
  b. Faster information retrieval   **d.** Automatic trend analysis

Practice

13. **Which of the following is NOT an advantage of managing data with a relational database versus a spreadsheet?**
    a. Doesn't require preplanning before data is entered
    b. Allows links between lists of information
    c. Provides greater security
    d. Allows multiple users to enter data simultaneously

14. **The object that holds all of the data within an Access database**
    a. Query
    b. Table
    c. Form
    d. Report

15. **The object that provides an easy-to-use data entry screen**
    a. Table
    b. Query
    c. Form
    d. Report

16. **This displays messages regarding the current database operation**
    a. Status bar
    b. Title bar
    c. Database toolbar
    d. Object tabs

▶ Skills Review

1. **Define database software.**
   a. Identify five disadvantages of using a paper system, such as index cards, to organize database information. Write down your answers to this and the following questions using complete sentences.
   b. Identify five advantages of managing database information in Access versus using a spreadsheet product like Excel.

2. **Learn database terminology.**
   a. Explain the relationship between a field, a record, a table, and a database.
   b. Identify the seven objects of an Access database, and explain the main purpose of each.
   c. Which object of an Access database is most important? Why?

3. **Start Access and open a database.**
   a. Click the Start button, point to Programs, then click Microsoft Access.
   b. Insert your Project Disk into the appropriate disk drive, click the Open an existing file option button, click More Files, then click OK.
   c. In the Open dialog box, choose the correct drive, then open the Recycle-A database file.
   d. Identify the following items. (*Hint*: To create a printout of this screen, press [Print Screen] to capture an image of the screen to the Windows clipboard, start any word-processing program, then click the Paste button. Print the document that now contains a picture of this screen, and identify the elements on the printout.)
   - Database toolbar
   - Recycle-A database window
   - Menu bar
   - Object buttons
   - Objects bar
   - Status bar

4. **View the database window.**
   a. Maximize both the Access window and the Recycle-A Database window.
   b. Click each of the objects, then write down the object names of each type that exist in the Recycle-A database.
   - Tables
   - Queries
   - Reports
   - Pages
   - Macros
   - Modules
   - Forms

5. **Navigate records.**
   a. Open the Clubs table.
   b. Press [Tab] or [Enter] to move through the fields of the first record.
   c. Press [Ctrl][End] to move to the last field of the last record.
   d. Press [Ctrl][Home] to move to the first field of the first record.
   e. Click the Last Record navigation button to quickly move to the Oak Hill Patriots record.

Access 2000

GETTING STARTED WITH ACCESS 2000 ACCESS A-21 ◀

6. Enter records.

a. In the Clubs table, click the New Record button, then add the following records:

Name	Street	City	State	Zip	Phone	Leader	Club Number
EBC Angels	10100 Metcalf	Overland Park	KS	66001	555-7711	Michael Garrett	8
MOT Friends	111 Holmes	Kansas City	MO	65001	555-8811	Aaron Goldstein	9

b. Move the Club Number field from the last column of the datasheet to the first column.

7. Edit records.

a. Change the Name field in the first record from "Jaycees" to "JC Club."

b. Change the Name field in the second record from "Boy Scouts #1" to "Oxford Cub Scouts."

c. Change the Leader field in the fifth record from "Melanie Perry" to "Melanie Griffiths."

d. Enter your name and personal information (make up a club name) as a new record, and enter 99 as the Club Number.

e. Delete the record for Club Number 8.

8. Preview and print a datasheet.

a. Preview the Clubs table datasheet.

b. Use the Page Setup option on the File menu to change the page orientation from portrait to landscape.

c. Print the Clubs table datasheet.

9. Get Help and exit Access.

a. Close the Clubs table object, saving the changes.

b. Close the Recycle-A database.

c. Use Office Assistant to learn more about creating a database.

d. Exit Access.

► Independent Challenges

1. Ten examples of databases are given below. For each example, write a brief answer for the following.

a. What field names would you expect to find in this database?

b. Provide an example of two possible records for each database.

- Telephone directory
- College course offerings
- Restaurant menu
- Cookbook
- Movie listing
- Encyclopedia
- Shopping catalog
- Corporate inventory
- Party guest list
- Members of the House of Representatives

2. You are working with several civic groups in your area to coordinate a community-wide cleanup effort. You have started a database called "Recycle-A" that tracks the clubs, their trash deposits, and the trash centers that are participating in this effort. To complete this independent challenge:

a. Start Access.

b. Open the Recycle-A database from your Project Disk, and determine the number of objects of each type that exist in the database:

- Tables
- Queries
- Reports
- Pages
- Macros
- Modules
- Forms

c. Open the Deposits table, and answer the following questions:
- How many fields does the table have?
- How many records are there in the table?

d. Close the table, then exit Access.

3. You are working with several civic groups in your area to coordinate a community-wide cleanup effort. You have started a database called "Recycle-A" that tracks the clubs, their trash deposits, and the trash centers that are participating in this effort.

To complete this independent challenge:

a. Start Access and open the Recycle-A database from your Project Disk.

b. Add the following records to the Clubs table:

Club Number	Name	Street	City	State	Zip	Phone	Leader
10	Take Pride	222 Switzer St.	Olathe	KS	66001	555-2211	David Reis
11	Cub Scouts #321	333 Ward Pkwy.	Kansas City	MO	65002	555-8811	Daniel Langguth

c. Edit the following records in the Clubs table. The Street field has changed for Club Number 6 and the Phone and Leader fields have changed for Club Number 7.

Club Number	Name	Street	City	State	Zip	Phone	Leader
6	Girl Scouts #1	55 Oak Terrace	Shawnee	KS	68777	555-4444	Jonathan Bacon
7	Oak Hill Patriots	888 Switzer	Overland Park	KS	66444	555-9988	Cynthia Ralston

d. If you haven't already, add your name and personal information (make up a club name) and enter 99 as the Club Number. Print the datasheet.

e. Close the table, close the database, then exit Access.

4. The World Wide Web can be used to collect or research information that is used in corporate databases. MediaLoft often uses their intranet for this purpose. An intranet is a group of connected networks owned by a company or organization that is used for internal purposes. Intranets use internet software to handle the data communications, such as e-mail and Web pages, within an organization. These pages often provide company-wide information. MediaLoft has developed a Web page on the intranet that provides information about their products and customers. Eventually, MediaLoft will tie these Web pages directly to their database so that the information is dynamically tied to their working database. In this exercise, you'll retrieve the new customer information recorded on the intranet Web page, and enter it directly into the MediaLoft-A database.

To complete this independent challenge:

a. Connect to the Internet, and use your browser to go to the Medialoft intranet site at http://www.course.com/illustrated/MediaLoft/

b. Click the link for Our Customers.

c. Print the page that shows the information for the two new customers.

d. Disconnect from the Internet.

e. Start Access and open the MediaLoft-A database.

f. Open the Customers table.

g. Add the new customers to the table. They will become records 30 and 31. Add your name to the table with your personal information as record 32.

h. Review your work, print the datasheet, close the MediaLoft A-database, then exit Access.

► # Visual Workshop

Open the Recycle-A database on your Project Disk. Modify the existing Centers table, and enter a new record using your name as the contact and Center Number 99. The Street field for the first record has changed, the Hazardous field for the first two records has changed, and two new records have been added to the datasheet. See Figure A-19. Print the datasheet.

FIGURE A-19

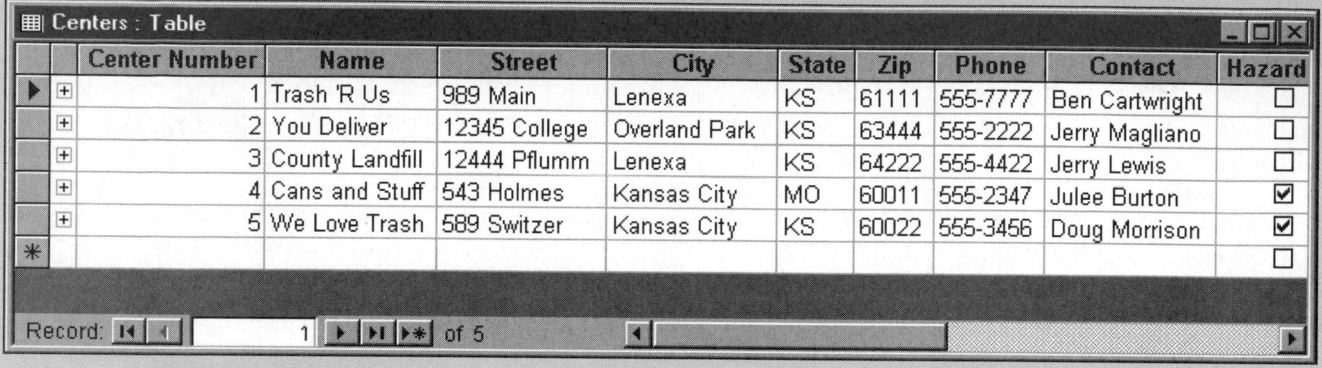

		Center Number	Name	Street	City	State	Zip	Phone	Contact	Hazard
►	+	1	Trash 'R Us	989 Main	Lenexa	KS	61111	555-7777	Ben Cartwright	☐
	+	2	You Deliver	12345 College	Overland Park	KS	63444	555-2222	Jerry Magliano	☐
	+	3	County Landfill	12444 Pflumm	Lenexa	KS	64222	555-4422	Jerry Lewis	☐
	+	4	Cans and Stuff	543 Holmes	Kansas City	MO	60011	555-2347	Julee Burton	☑
	+	5	We Love Trash	589 Switzer	Kansas City	KS	60022	555-3456	Doug Morrison	☑
*										☐

Record: I◄ ◄　1　► ►I ►* of 5

Using
Tables and Queries

Objectives

- MOUS ► **Plan a database**
- MOUS ► **Create a table**
- MOUS ► **Use Table Design view**
- MOUS ► **Format a datasheet**
- MOUS ► **Understand sorting, filtering, and finding**
- MOUS ► **Sort records and find data**
- MOUS ► **Filter records**
- MOUS ► **Create a query**
- MOUS ► **Use Query Design view**

Now that you are familiar with some of the basic Access terminology and features, you are ready to plan and build your own database. Your first task is to create the tables that store the data. Once the tables are created and the data is entered, you can use several techniques for finding specific information in the database, including sorting, filtering, and building queries. ◄━━ John Kim wants to build and maintain a database containing information about MediaLoft's products. The information in the database will be useful when John provides information for future sales promotions.

Planning a Database

The first and most important object in a database is the table object because it contains the **raw data**, the individual pieces of information stored in individual fields in the database. When you design a table, you identify the fields of information the table will contain and the type of data to be stored in each field. Some databases contain multiple tables linked together. John plans his database containing information about MediaLoft's products.

In planning a database it is important to:

Determine the purpose of the database and give it a meaningful name

The database will store information about MediaLoft's music products. You decide to name the database "MediaLoft," and name the first table "Music Inventory."

Determine what reports you want the database to produce

You want to be able to print inventory reports that list the products by artist, type of product (CD or cassette), quantity in stock, and price. These pieces of information will become the fields in the Music Inventory table.

Collect the raw data that will be stored in the database

The raw data for MediaLoft's products might be stored on index cards, in paper reports, and in other electronic formats, such as word-processed documents and spreadsheets. You can use Access to import data from many other electronic sources, which greatly increases your data entry efficiency.

Sketch the structure of each table, including field names and data types

Using the data you collected, identify the field name and data type for each field in each table as shown in Figure B-1. The **data type** determines what type of information you can enter in a field. For example, a field with a Currency data type does accept text. Properly defining the data type for each field helps you maintain data consistency and accuracy. Table B-1 lists the data types available within Access.

Choosing between the text and number data type

When assigning data types, you should avoid choosing "number" for a telephone or zip code field. Although these fields generally contain numbers, they should still be text data types. Consider the following: You may want to enter 1-800-BUY-BOOK in a telephone number field. This would not be possible if the field were designated as a number data type. When you sort the fields, you'll want them to sort alphabetically, like text fields. Consider the following zip codes: 60011 and 50011-8888. If the zip code field were designated as a number data type, the zip codes would be interpreted incorrectly as the values 60,011 and 500,118,888; and sort in that order, too.

FIGURE B-1: Music Inventory table field names and data types

Field Name	Data Type
RecordingID	AutoNumber
RecordingTitle	Text
RecordingArtist	Text
MusicCategory	Text
RecordingLabel	Text
Format	Text
NumberofTracks	Number
PurchasePrice	Currency
RetailPrice	Currency
Notes	Memo

TABLE B-1: Data types

data type	description of data	size
Text	Text information or combinations of text and numbers, such as a street address, name, or phone number	Up to 255 characters
Memo	Lengthy text such as comments or notes	Up to 64,000 characters
Number	Numeric information used in calculations, such as quantities	Several sizes available to store numbers with varying degrees of precision
Date/Time	Dates and times	Size controlled by Access to accommodate dates and times across thousands of years (for example, 1/1/1850 and 1/1/2150 are valid dates)
Currency	Monetary values	Size controlled by Access; accommodates up to 15 digits to the left of the decimal point and 4 digits to the right
AutoNumber	Integers assigned by Access to sequentially order each record added to a table	Size controlled by Access
Yes/No	Only one of two values stored (Yes/No, On/Off, True/False)	Size controlled by Access
OLE Object	Pointers stored that link files created in other programs, such as pictures, sound clips, documents, or spreadsheets	Up to one gigabyte
Hyperlink	Web addresses	Size controlled by Access
Lookup Wizard	Invokes a wizard that helps link the current table to another table (the final data type of the field is determined by choices made in the wizard; a field created with the lookup data type will display data from another table)	Size controlled through the choices made in the Lookup Wizard

Creating a Table

After you plan the structure of the database, your next step is to create the database file itself, which will eventually contain all of the objects such as tables, queries, forms, and reports. When you create a database, first you name it, and then you can build the first table object and enter data. Access offers several methods for creating a table. For example, you can import a table from another data source such as a spreadsheet, or use the Access **Table Wizard**, which provides interactive help to create the field names and data types for each field. John is ready to create the MediaLoft database. He uses the Table Wizard to create the Music Inventory table.

Steps 1 2 3 4

1. **Start Access, click the Blank Access database option button in the Microsoft Access dialog box, then click OK**
   The File New Database dialog box opens.

2. **Type MediaLoft in the File name text box, insert your Project Disk in the appropriate drive, click the Save in list arrow, click the drive, then click Create**
   The MediaLoft database file is created and saved on your Project Disk. The Table Wizard offers an efficient way to plan the fields of a new table.

3. **If the Office Assistant appears on your screen, click Help on the menu bar, click Hide the Office Assistant, then double-click Create table by using wizard in the MediaLoft Database window**
   The Table Wizard dialog box opens, as shown in Figure B-2. The Table Wizard offers 25 business and 20 personal sample tables from which you can select sample fields. The Recordings sample table, which is in the Personal category of tables, most closely matches the fields you want to include in the Music Inventory table.

4. **Click the Personal option button, scroll down and click Recordings in the Sample Tables list box, then click the Select All Fields button** >>
   Your Table Wizard dialog box should look like Figure B-3. At this point, you can change the suggested field names to better match your database.

5. **Click RecordingArtistID in the Fields in my new table list box, click Rename Field, type RecordingArtist in the Rename field text box, then click OK**

6. **Click Next**
   The second Table Wizard dialog box allows you to name the table and determine if Access sets the **primary key field**, a field that contains unique information for each record.

Trouble?

If you don't see all the fields in the table, it is because you have different settings on your monitor. Maximize the window to see all the fields, if necessary.

7. **Type Music Inventory, make sure the Yes, set a primary key for me option button is selected, click Next, click the Modify the table design option button, then click Finish**
   The table opens in **Design view**, shown in Figure B-4, which allows you to add, delete, or modify the fields in the table. The primary **key field symbol** indicates that the RecordingID field has been designated as the primary key field.

FIGURE B-2: Table Wizard

Business and personal categories

Sample tables

Sample fields for the selected table

Select All Fields button

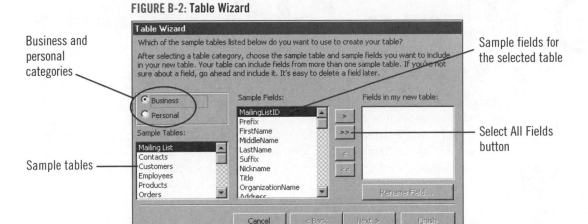

FIGURE B-3: Table Wizard with Recordings table fields

Personal category chosen

Recordings table chosen

RecordingArtistID field

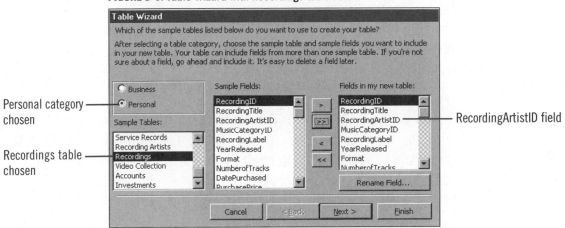

FIGURE B-4: Music Inventory table in Design view

View button

Key field symbol

Field names

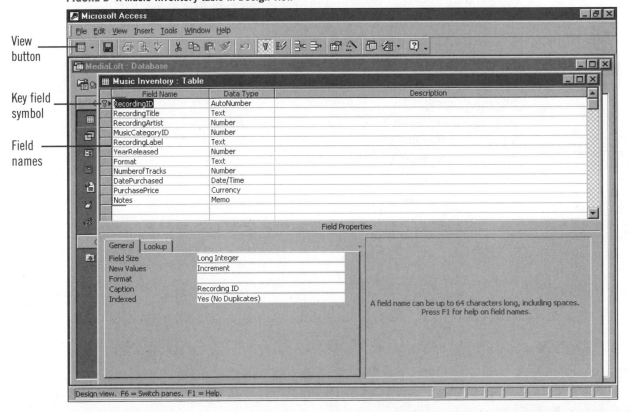

Using Table Design View

Each database object has a **Design view** in which you can modify its structure. The Design view of a table allows you to add or delete fields, add **field descriptions**, or change other field properties. **Field properties** are additional characteristics of a field such as its size or default value. Using the Table Wizard, John was able to create a Music Inventory table very quickly. Now in Design view he modifies the fields to meet his needs. MediaLoft doesn't track purchase dates or release dates, but it does need to store retail price information in the database.

Steps 1 2 3 4

QuickTip

Deleting a field from a table deletes any data stored in that field for all records in the table.

1. In the Music Inventory table's Design view, click **DatePurchased** in the Field Name column, click the **Delete Rows button** 🗗 on the Table Design toolbar, click the **Year Released row selector**, click 🗗 to delete the field, click the **Notes** field, then click the **Insert Rows button** 🗗

   The Year Released and Date Purchased fields are deleted from the table and a new row appears in which you can add the new field name.

2. Type **RetailPrice**, press [Tab], type **C** (for Currency data type), then press [Enter]

   The new field is added to the Music Inventory table, as shown in Figure B-5. The data type of both the RecordingArtist and MusicCategoryID fields should be Text so that descriptive words can be entered in these fields rather than just numbers.

3. Click the **Number** data type in the RecordingArtist field, click the **Data Type list arrow**, click **Text**, click the **Number** data type in the MusicCategoryID field, click the **Data Type list arrow**, then click **Text**

   You must work in the table's Design view to make structural changes to the table.

4. Click to the right of **MusicCategoryID**, press [Backspace] twice, then click the **Save button** 🖫 on the Table Design toolbar

   A description identifies a field and can list the types of data in that field.

5. Click the **MusicCategory Description cell**, then type **classical, country, folk, gospel, jazz, new age, rap, or rock**

   The **field size property** limits the number of characters allowed for each field.

6. Make sure the **MusicCategory** field is still selected, double-click **50** in the Field Size cell, then type **9**

   The longest entry in the MusicCategory field, "classical," is only nine characters. The finished Music Inventory table Design view should look like Figure B-6.

QuickTip

Press [Tab] to move through the RecordingID field (it's an AutoNumber field) and just type the numbers to enter the PurchasePrice and RetailPrice. The Currency format is automatically applied.

7. Click the **Datasheet View button** 🔳 on the Table Design toolbar, click **Yes** to save the table, then type the following record into the new datasheet:

in field:	type:	in field:	type:
Recording ID	[Tab]	Format	CD
Recording Title	No Words	Number of Tracks	12
RecordingArtist	Brickman, Jim	Purchase Price	$10.00
Music Category ID	New Age	RetailPrice	$13.00
Recording Label	Windham Hill	Notes	

   You are finished working with the MediaLoft database for now.

8. Close the Music Inventory table, then close the MediaLoft database

   Data is saved automatically, so you were not prompted to save the record when you closed the datasheet.

FIGURE B-5: Music Inventory table with new RetailPrice field

YearReleased
field deleted

DatePurchased
field deleted

RetailPrice field
added

RetailPrice field is
selected

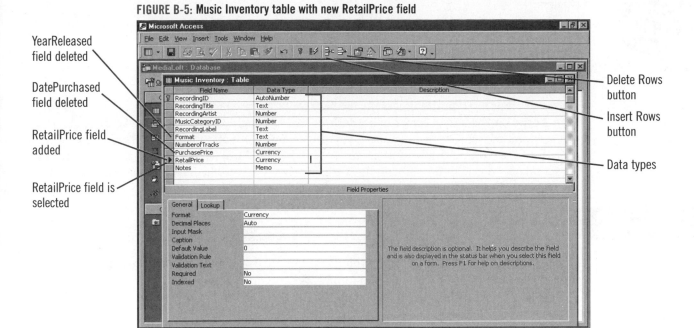

Delete Rows
button

Insert Rows
button

Data types

FIGURE B-6: Description and field size properties for MusicCategory field

Row selector

MusicCategory field
is selected

Field size property
is changed to 9

Field Properties section

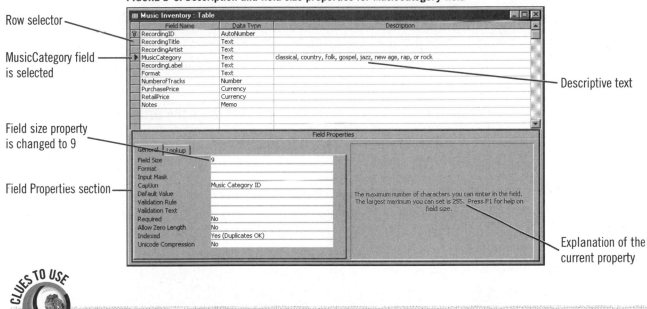

Descriptive text

Explanation of the
current property

Learning about field properties

The properties of a field are the characteristics that define the field. Two properties are required for every field: Field Name and Data Type. Many other properties, such as Field Size, Format (the way the field is displayed on the datasheet), Caption, and Default Value, are defined in the Field Properties section of the table's Design view. As you add more property entries, you are generally restricting the amount or type of data that can be entered in the field, which also increases data entry accuracy. For example, you might change the Field Size property for a State field from the default value of 50 to 2 to eliminate an incorrect entry such as "NYY." The available field properties change depending on the data type of the selected field. For example, there is no Field Size property for a Birth Date field, because Access controls the size of fields with a Date/Time data type. Database designers often insist on field names without spaces because they are easier to reference in other Access objects. The **Caption property**, however, can be used to override the technical field name with an easy-to-read Caption entry when the field name is displayed on datasheets, forms, and reports. When you create a table using the wizard, many fields have Caption properties.

Formatting a Datasheet

Even though the report object is the primary tool to create professional hard copy output from an Access database, you can print a datasheet too. Although you cannot create fancy headings or insert graphic images on a datasheet, you can change the fonts and colors as well as change the gridlines to dramatically change its appearance. ▰▰▰▰ John has been busy entering MediaLoft's music information in the Music Inventory table (which is stored in the MediaLoft-B database). He has also simplified many of the field names. Now he will print the Music Inventory datasheet using new fonts and colors.

Steps 1234

1. Click the **Open button** 📂 on the Database toolbar, select the **MediaLoft-B** database from your Project Disk, then click **Open**
   The Music Inventory table has data that was entered by John Kim.

2. Click **Music Inventory** in the Tables Object window, then click the **Open button** 📖
   Access displays the Music Inventory table, containing 58 records, as shown in Figure B-7. You can change the font and color of the datasheet to enhance its appearance.

3. Click **Format** on the menu bar, click **Font**, click **Comic Sans MS** in the Font list, then click **OK**
   Comic Sans MS is an informal font used for personal correspondence or internal memos. It simulates handwritten text, but is still very readable. You can also change the color and format of the datasheet gridlines.

4. Click **Format** on the menu bar, click **Datasheet**, click the **Gridline Color list arrow**, then click **Red**
   The Sample box in the Datasheet Formatting dialog box displays both the vertical and horizontal gridlines as red.

5. Click the **Border list arrow**, click **Vertical Gridline**, click the **Line Styles list arrow**, click **Transparent Border**, as shown in Figure B-8, then click **OK**
   You removed the vertical gridlines separating the fields. You can also change the left and right margins, and change the page orientation from portrait to landscape to fit all the fields across the page.

6. Click **File** on the menu bar, click **Page Setup**, double-click **1"** in the Top text box, type **0.75**, press **[Tab]**, type **0.75** in the Bottom text box, press **[Tab]**, type **0.75** in the Left text box, press **[Tab]**, type **0.75** in the Right text box, click the **Page tab**, click the **Landscape option button**, then click **OK**
   Print Preview displays your formatted datasheet as it will look when printed.

7. Click the **Print Preview button** 🔍 on the Table Datasheet toolbar to preview the finished product, as shown in Figure B-9
   The red gridlines seem a bit too intense for your printout.

8. Click the **Close button** Close on the Print Preview toolbar, click **Format** on the menu bar, click **Datasheet**, click the **Gridline Color list arrow**, click **Silver**, then click **OK**
   Silver is the default gridline color.

FIGURE B-7: Music Inventory table datasheet

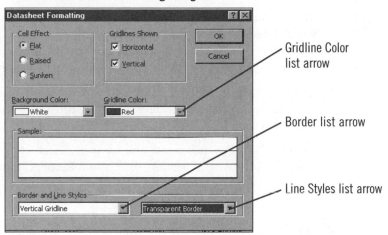

RecordingID	Title	Artist	Category	Label	Format
1	Gravity	Cook, Jesse	New Age	Columbia	CD
2	Come Walk With Me	Adams, Oleta	Gospel	CBS Records	CD
3	Greatest Hits	Winans, BeBe & Cl	Gospel	Benson	Vinyl
4	Tribute	Yanni	New Age	MCA	CD
5	World Café	Tree Frogs	Rap	New Stuff	CD
6	Relationships	Winans, BeBe & Cl	Gospel	Capitol	CD
7	No Words	Brickman, Jim	New Age	Windham Hill	CD
8	God's Property	Nu Nation	Rap	B-Rite Music	Cassette
9	Message	4 Him	Gospel	Benson	CD
10	Sacred Road	Lantz, David	New Age	Narada	Cassette
11	Mariah Carey	Carey, Mariah	Rock	Columbia	CD
12	Ironman Triathlon	Tesh, John	New Age	GTS Records	Cassette
13	Daydream	Carey, Mariah	Rock	Columbia	CD
14	Heartsounds	Lantz, David	New Age	Narada	CD
15	The Roches	Roches, The	Folk	Warner Bros. Reco	Cassette
16	Can We Go Home Now	Roches, The	Folk	Ryko	CD
17	Live at the Red Rocks	Tesh, John	New Age	GTS Records	CD
18	I'll Lead You Home	Smith, Michael	Gospel	Reunion	CD
19	Winter Song	Tesh, John	New Age	GTS Records	CD
20	December	Winston, George	New Age	Windham	CD
21	Time, Love & Tenderness	Bolton, Michael	Rock	Sony Music	CD
22	Autumn	Winston, George	New Age	Windham	Vinyl

Record: 1 of 58

FIGURE B-8: Datasheet Formatting dialog box

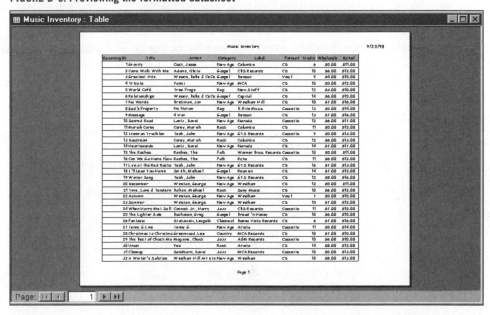

Gridline Color list arrow

Border list arrow

Line Styles list arrow

FIGURE B-9: Previewing the formatted datasheet

Access 2000

Understanding Sorting, Filtering, and Finding

The records of a datasheet are automatically sorted according to the data in the primary key field. Often, however, you'll want to view or print records in an entirely different sort order. Or you may want to display a subset of the records, such as those within the same music category or those below a certain retail price. Access makes it easy to sort, find data, and filter a datasheet with buttons on the Table Datasheet toolbar, summarized in Table B-2. John studies the sort, find, and filter features to learn how to find and retrieve information in his database.

Details

 Sorting refers to reorganizing the records in either ascending or descending order based on the contents of a field. Text fields sort from A to Z, number fields from the lowest to the highest value, and date/time fields from the oldest date to the date furthest into the future. In Figure B-10 the Music Inventory table has been sorted in ascending order on the Artist field. Notice that numbers sort before letters in an ascending sort order.

 Filtering means temporarily isolating a subset of records, as shown in Figure B-11. This is particularly useful because the subset can be formatted and printed just like the entire datasheet. You can produce a listing of all rock music or a listing based on any category, artist, or field in the datasheet. To remove a filter, click the Remove Filter button to view all the records in the datasheet.

 Finding refers to locating a specific piece of data, such as "Amy" or "500," within a field or an entire datasheet, similar to finding text in a word-processing document. The Find and Replace dialog box is shown in Figure B-12. The options in this dialog box are summarized below.

- **Find What:** Provides a text box for your search criteria. For example, you might want to find the text "Amy", "Beatles", or "Capitol Records" in the datasheet.

- **Look In**: Determines whether Access looks for the search criteria in the current field (in this case the Artist field) or in all fields.

- **Match:** Determines whether the search criteria must match the whole field's contents exactly, any part of the field, or the start of the field.

- **More:** Provides more options to limit your search. For example, it allows you to make your search criteria uppercase- or lowercase-sensitive.

- **Replace tab:** Provides a text box for you to specify "replacement text." In other words, you might want to search for every occurrence of "Compact Disc" and replace it with "CD" by entering "Compact Disc" as your search criteria and "CD" as your replacement text.

TABLE B-2: Sort, Filter, and Find buttons

name	button	purpose
Sort Ascending	⬇	Sorts records based on the selected field in ascending order (0 to 9, A to Z)
Sort Descending	⬇	Sorts records based on the selected field in descending order (Z to A, 9 to 0)
Filter By Selection	⬇	Filters records based on selected data and hides records that do not match
Filter By Form	⬇	Filters records based on more than one selection criteria by using the Filter By Form window
Apply Filter or Remove Filter	⬇	Applies or removes the filter
Find	🔍	Searches for a string of characters in the current field or all fields

FIGURE B-10: Records sorted in ascending order by Artist

Records sorted in ascending order by Artist

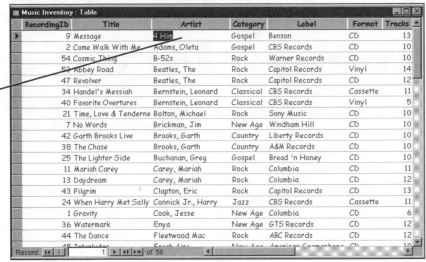

FIGURE B-11: Records filtered by "Rock" category

Sort Ascending button

Sort Descending button

Number of records in filtered subset

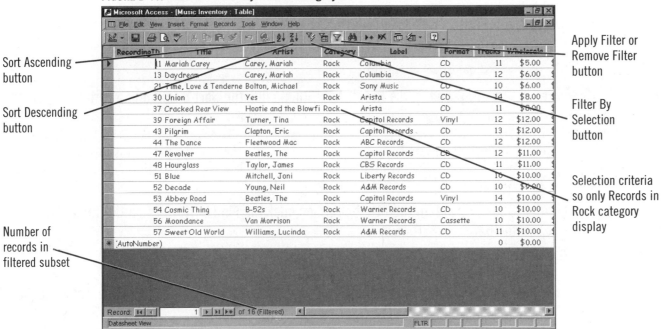

Apply Filter or Remove Filter button

Filter By Selection button

Selection criteria so only Records in Rock category display

FIGURE B-12: Find and Replace dialog box

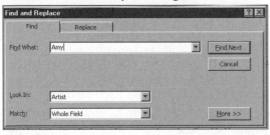

CLUES TO USE

Using wildcards in Find

Wildcards are symbols you can use as substitutes for characters to find information that matches your find criteria. Access uses these wildcards: the asterisk (*) represents any group of characters, the question mark (?) stands for any single character, and the pound sign (#) stands for a single number digit. For example, to find any word beginning with "S," type "s*" in the Find What text box.

Sorting Records and Finding Data

Sorting records and quickly finding information in a database are two powerful tools that help you work more efficiently. ◄━━━ John needs to create several different printouts of the Music Inventory datasheet to satisfy various departments. The Marketing department wants a printout of records sorted by title and artist. The Accounting department wants a printout of records sorted from highest retail price to lowest.

Steps

1. **In the Music Inventory datasheet, click any cell in the Title field, then click the Sort Ascending button** ⊞ **on the Table Datasheet toolbar**
   The records are listed in an A-to-Z sequence based on the data in the Title field, as shown in Figure B-13. Next you'll sort the records according to artist.

2. **Click any cell in the Artist field, then click** ⊞
   The table is sorted alphabetically in ascending order by Artist. You can preview and print a sorted datasheet at any time.

QuickTip

Scroll to the right if necessary to see this field.

3. **Click any cell in the Retail field, then click the Sort Descending button** ⊞ **on the Table Datasheet toolbar**
   The records are sorted in descending order on the value in the Retail field. The CD that sells for the highest retail price, "Skyline Firedance," is listed as the first record. To put the records back in their original order, you can click the key field, RecordingID, and click the Sort Ascending button. Access also lets you find all records based on any search word.

4. **Click any cell in the Title field, then click the Find button** ⊞ **on the Table Datasheet toolbar**
   The Find and Replace dialog box opens. You know MediaLoft will want to find the titles that are going to be hot sellers during the Christmas season.

5. **Type Christmas in the Find What text box, click the Match list arrow, then click Any Part of Field, as shown in Figure B-14**
   Access will find all occurrences of the word "Christmas" in the Title field, whether it is the first, middle, or last part of the title. "Christmas" is the search criteria.

6. **Click Find Next, then if necessary drag the Find and Replace dialog box up and to the right to better view the datasheet**
   If you started the search at the top of the datasheet, "A Family Christmas" is the first title found. You can look for more occurrences of "Christmas."

7. **Click Find Next to find the next occurrence of the word "Christmas," then click Find Next as many times as it takes to move through all the records**
   When no more occurrences of the search criteria "Christmas" are found, Access lets you know that no more matching records can be found.

8. **Click OK when prompted that Access has finished searching the records, then click Cancel to close the Find and Replace dialog box**

FIGURE B-13: Music Inventory datasheet sorted by Title

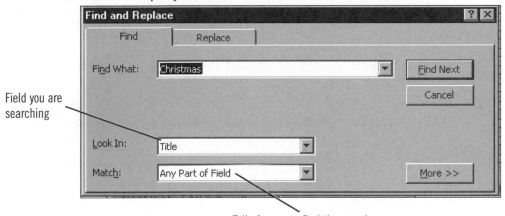

RecordingID	Title	Artist	Category	Label	Format	Tracks
55	A Christmas Album	Grant, Amy	Folk	Reunion Records	CD	11
46	A Family Christmas	Tesh, John	New Age	GTS Records	CD	14
32	A Winter's Solstice	Windham Hill Artists	New Age	Windham	CD	10
53	Abbey Road	Beatles, The	Rock	Capitol Records	Vinyl	14
22	Autumn	Winston, George	New Age	Windham	Vinyl	7
51	Blue	Mitchell, Joni	Rock	Liberty Records	CD	10
16	Can We Go Home Now	Roches, The	Folk	Ryko	CD	11
35	Christmas	Mannheim Steamroller	New Age	Sony Music	CD	11
28	Christmas to Christmas	Greenwood, Lee	Country	MCA Records	CD	10
31	Closeup	Sandborn, David	Jazz	MCA Records	Cassette	10
2	Come Walk With Me	Adams, Oleta	Gospel	CBS Records	CD	10
54	Cosmic Thing	B-52s	Rock	Warner Records	CD	10
37	Cracked Rear View	Hootie and the Blowfi	Rock	Arista	CD	11
13	Daydream	Carey, Mariah	Rock	Columbia	CD	12
52	Decade	Young, Neil	Rock	A&M Records	CD	10
20	December	Winston, George	New Age	Windham	CD	12
26	Fantasia	Stokowski, Leopold	Classical	Buena Vista Records	CD	6
40	Favorite Overtures	Bernstein, Leonard	Classical	CBS Records	Vinyl	5
39	Foreign Affair	Turner, Tina	Rock	Capitol Records	Vinyl	12

Record: 1 of 58

Records are sorted in ascending order by Title

FIGURE B-14: Specify "Christmas" as the search criteria in the Title field

Find and Replace

Find | Replace

Find What: Christmas

Find Next

Cancel

Field you are searching

Look In: Title

Match: Any Part of Field

More >>

Tells Access to find the search criteria anywhere in the selected field

CLUES TO USE

Sorting on more than one field

The telephone book sorts records by last name (**primary sort field**) and when ties occur on the last name (for example, two "Smiths"), it further sorts the records by first name (**secondary sort field**). Access allows you to sort by more than one field using the query object, which you will learn more about later in this unit. Queries allow you to specify more than one sort field in Query Design view, evaluating the sort orders from left to right (the leftmost sort field is the primary sort field).

Filtering Records

Sorting allows you to reorder all the records of a datasheet. Filtering the datasheet displays only those records that match criteria. **Criteria** are rules or limiting conditions you set. For example, you may want to show only those records where the Category field is equal to "Rap," or where the PurchasePrice field is less than $10. Once you have filtered a datasheet to display a subset of records, you can still sort the records and find data just as if you were working with the entire datasheet. To make sure the Filter By Form grid is clear of any previous entries, you should click the Clear Grid button ▣. ✐ The Accounting department asked John for a printout of cassettes with a retail price of $15 or more. John uses the datasheet's filter buttons to answer this request.

Steps

1. **In the Music Inventory datasheet, click the RecordingID field, click the Sort Ascending button ☷ on the Table Datasheet toolbar, click any occurrence of Cassette in the Format field, then click the Filter By Selection button ☷ on the Table Datasheet toolbar**
   Twelve records are selected, as shown in Figure B-15. Filter By Selection is a fast and easy way to filter the records for an exact match (that is, where Format field value is *equal to* Cassette). To filter for comparative data and to specify more complex criteria (for example, where PurchasePrice is *equal to* or *greater than* $15), you must use the Filter By Form feature. See Table B-3 for more information on comparison operators.

QuickTip

If you click the Field List arrow, you can pick an entry from a list of existing entries in that field.

2. **Click the Filter By Form button ☷ on the Table Datasheet toolbar, click the Retail field, then type >=15**
   The finished Filter By Form window is shown in Figure B-16. The previous Filter By Selection criteria, "Cassette" in the Format field, is still valid in the grid. Access distinguishes between text and numeric entries by placing quotation marks around text entries. You can widen a column to display the entire criteria. Filter By Form is more powerful than Filter By Selection because it allows you to use comparison operators such as >=. Filter By Form also allows you to enter criteria for more than one field at a time where *both* criteria must be "true" in order for the record to be shown in the resulting datasheet.

3. **Click the Apply Filter button ☷ on the Filter/Sort toolbar, then scroll to the right to display the Retail field**
   Only two records are true for both criteria, as shown in Figure B-17. The Record Navigation buttons in the lower-left corner of the datasheet display how many records are in the filtered subset. You can remove the current filter to view all the records in the datasheet at any time by clicking the Remove Filter button.

4. **Click the Remove Filter button ☷ on the Table Datasheet toolbar**
   Be sure to remove existing filters before you apply a new filter or you will end up filtering the existing subset of records versus the entire datasheet. Next find all selections produced under the "A&M Records" recording label.

5. **Click any cell in the Label field, click ☷, A&M Records is selected as the Label entry, then click ☷**
   Using both the sort and filter buttons, you quickly found the five records that met the "A&M Records" criteria.

6. **Close the datasheet, then click Yes if prompted to save the changes to the Music Inventory table**
   Any filters applied to a datasheet will be removed the next time you open the datasheet, but the sort order will be saved.

FIGURE B-15: Music Inventory datasheet filtered for "Cassette" records

12 records are selected

All records have Cassette in Format field

FIGURE B-16: Filter By Form grid

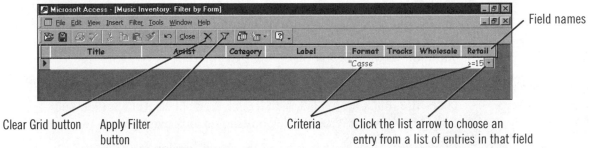

Field names

Clear Grid button   Apply Filter button   Criteria   Click the list arrow to choose an entry from a list of entries in that field

FIGURE B-17: Results of Filter By Form

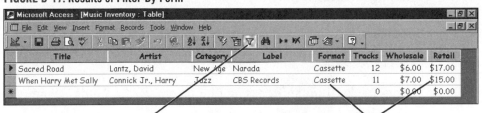

Filter is applied and the Apply Filter button becomes the Remove Filter button

Both records have Cassette in the Format field and all records have a Retail value >=15

TABLE B-3: Comparison operators

operator	description	expression	meaning
>	Greater than	>500	Numbers greater than 500
>=	Grealer than or equal to	>=500	Numbers greater than or equal to 500
<	Less than	<"Bunin"	Names from A through Bunim, but not Bunin
<=	Less than or equal to	<="Calloway"	Names from A through, and including, Calloway
<>	Not equal to	<>"Cyclone"	Any name except for Cyclone

CLUES TO USE

Searching for blank fields

Is Null and **Is Not Null** are two other types of common criteria. Is Null criteria will find all records where no entry has been made in the field.

Is Not Null will find all records where there is any entry in the field, even if the entry is 0. Primary key fields cannot have a null entry.

Creating a Query

A **query** is a database object that creates a datasheet of specified fields and records from one or more tables. It displays the answer to a "question" about the data in your database. You can edit, navigate, sort, find, and filter a query's datasheet just like a table's datasheet. Because a query datasheet is a subset of data, however, it is similar to a filter, but much more powerful. One of the most important differences is that a query is a saved object within the database, which means that it does not need to be recreated each time you want to see that particular subset of data. A **filter** is a temporary view of the data whose criteria is discarded when you remove the filter or close the datasheet. Table B-4 compares the two. ⬛━━ John uses a query to correct data in the table and then find all of the music selections in the "country" category.

Steps

1. **Click Queries on the Objects bar, then double-click Create query by using wizard**
   The Simple Query Wizard dialog box opens, allowing you to choose the table or query which contains the fields you want to display in the query. You select the fields in the order you want them to appear on the query datasheet.

QuickTip

You also can double-click a field to move it from the Available Fields list to the Selected Fields list.

2. **Click Category in the Available Fields list, click the Select Single Field button ▸, click Title, click ▸, click Artist, click ▸, click Tracks, then click ▸**
   The Simple Query Wizard dialog box should look like Figure B-18.

3. **Click Next, click Next to accept the Detail option in the next dialog box, accept the title Music Inventory Query, make sure the Open the query to view information option button is selected, then click Finish**
   The query's datasheet opens, as shown in Figure B-19, with all 58 records, but with only the four fields that you requested in the query wizard. You can use a query datasheet to edit or add information.

QuickTip

The sort, filter, and find buttons work the same way whether you are working with a query or table datasheet.

4. **Double-click 10 in the Tracks cell for record 7, "No Words", then type 11**
   This record is now correct in the database.

5. **Click the Design View button 🖾 on the Query Datasheet toolbar**
   The **Query Design view** opens, showing you a list of fields in the Music Inventory table in the upper portion of the window, and the fields you have requested for the query in the **query design grid** in the lower portion of the window.

6. **Click the Criteria cell for the Category field, then type country, as shown in Figure B-20**
   Query Design view is the view in which you add, delete, or change the order of fields, sort the records, or add criteria to limit the number of records shown in the resulting datasheet. Any change made in Query Design view is saved with the query object.

7. **Click the Datasheet View button 🖾 on the Query Design toolbar**
   The resulting datasheet has four records that match the criteria "country" in the Category field. You can save a query with a name that accurately describes the resulting datasheet.

QuickTip

The only time you need to save changes in an Access database is when you make structural changes to an object in Design view.

8. **Click File on the menu bar, click Save As, type Country Music in the Save Query 'Music Inventory Query' To text box, click OK, then close the query datasheet**
   Both the Music Inventory Query and Country Music queries are saved in this database as objects that you can access in the MediaLoft-B database window.

The available fields come from this object

FIGURE B-18: Simple Query Wizard dialog box

Select Single Field button

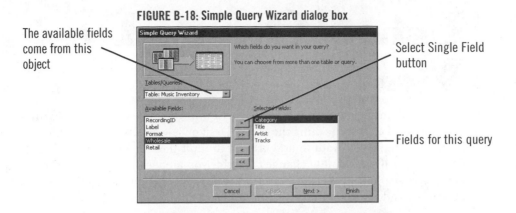

Fields for this query

FIGURE B-19: Music Inventory Query datasheet

Design View button

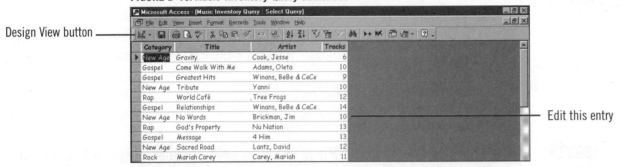

Edit this entry

FIGURE B-20: Query Design view

Datasheet View button

Music Inventory field list

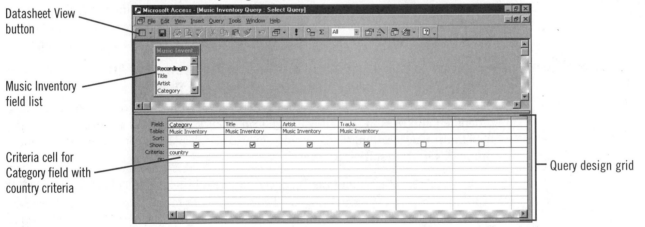

Criteria cell for Category field with country criteria

Query design grid

TABLE B-4: Queries vs. filters

characteristics	filters	queries
Are saved as an object in the database	No	Yes
Can be used to select a subset of records in a datasheet	Yes	Yes
Can be used to select a subset of fields in a datasheet	No	Yes
Its resulting datasheet can be used to enter and edit data	Yes	Yes
Its resulting datasheet can be used to sort, filter, and find records	Yes	Yes
Is commonly used as the source of data for a form or report	No	Yes
Can calculate sums, averages, counts, and other types of summary statistics across records	No	Yes
Can be used to create calculated fields	No	Yes

Using Query Design View

Every object in the database has a Design view in which you change the structure of the object. You can build a query by using the Query Design view directly or let the Query Wizard help you. In either case, if you want to add criteria to limit the number of records that you view in the datasheet, or if you want to change the fields you are viewing, you must use the query's Design view. ◤ John wants the Country Music query to also display the Retail field. In addition, he wants to add the folk music records and sort all the records according to the recording artist.

Steps 1234

1. Click the **Country Music query** in the MediaLoft-B Database window, click the **Design button** 🗹 in the database window, then click the **Restore button** 🗗 (if the window is maximized)
Query Design view opens, displaying the current fields and criteria for the Country Music query. To add fields to the query, you can drag the fields from the upper field list and place them in any order in the grid.

Trouble?
You may have to scroll through the Music Inventory field list to display the Retail field.

2. Click the **Retail field** in the Music Inventory field list, then drag the **Retail field** to the **Tracks Field cell** in the query design grid
The Query Design view now looks like Figure B-21. The Retail field is added to the query design grid between the Artist and Tracks fields. When you dropped the Retail field into the fourth column position of the query design grid, the Tracks field moved to the right to make room for the new field. You can also change the order of existing fields in the query design grid.

QuickTip
To remove fields from the query design grid, click the field selector, then press [Delete].

3. In the second column, click **Title**, click the **Title list arrow**, click **Artist**, click **Artist** in the third column, click the **Artist list arrow**, then click **Title**
You have switched the order of the Title and Artist fields. You can also move fields by dragging them left and right in the query design grid by clicking the field selector, and dragging the field to the new location. The query design grid also displays criteria that limit the number of records in the resulting datasheet.

4. Click the **or: criteria cell** under the "country" criteria of the Category field, then type **folk**
This additional criteria expression will add the folk selections to the current country selections. You also can enter Or criteria in one cell of the query design grid by entering "country" or "folk," but using two rows of the query design grid inherently joins the criteria in an Or expression.

5. Click the **Sort cell** for the Artist field, click the **Artist Sort list arrow**, then click **Ascending**
The final Query Design view, as shown in Figure B-22, will find all records that match the Category criteria for "country" or "folk" and sort the records in ascending order by Artist. Notice that text criteria in the query design grid are surrounded by quotation marks (as were filter criteria), but that you did not need to type these characters.

6. Click the **Datasheet view button** 🃏 on the Query Design toolbar
Eight records are displayed in both the country and folk music categories, sorted in ascending order by Artist, as shown in Figure B-23.

7. Click **File** on the menu bar, click **Save As**, type **Country and Folk**, click **OK**, then click the **Print button** 🖨 on the Query Datasheet toolbar

8. Close the query datasheet, close the MediaLoft-B database, then exit Access

Scroll bar for Music Inventory field list

FIGURE B-21: Query Design view with new field, Retail

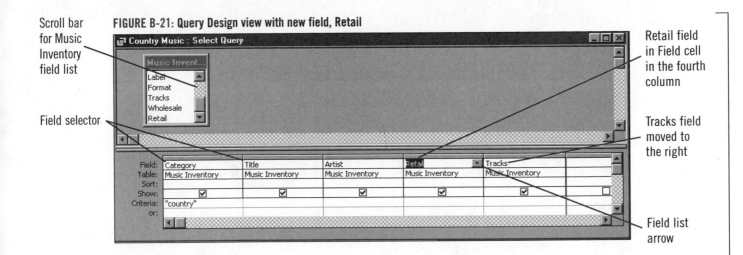

Field selector

Retail field in Field cell in the fourth column

Tracks field moved to the right

Field list arrow

Field order of Artist and Title fields is changed

FIGURE B-22: Adding Or criteria and specifying a sort order

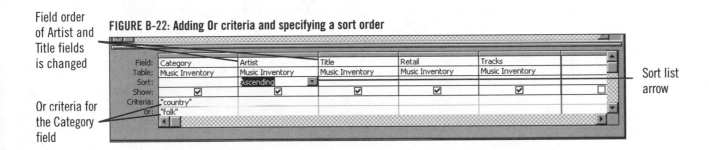

Or criteria for the Category field

Sort list arrow

FIGURE B-23: Final query datasheet

Only Country or Folk records are displayed

Records are sorted in ascending order by Artist

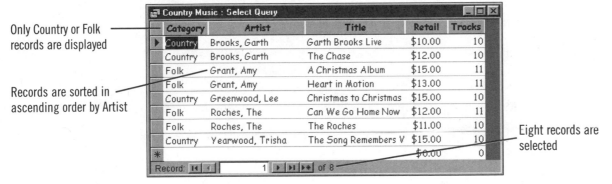

Eight records are selected

Understanding And and Or criteria

Criteria placed on different rows of the query design grid are considered Or criteria. In other words, a record may be true for *either* row of criteria in order for it to be displayed on the resulting datasheet. Placing additional criteria in the *same* row, however, is considered the And criteria. For example, if "folk" were in the Category Criteria cell and >10 in the Retail Criteria cell, *both* criteria must be true in order for the record to be displayed in the resulting datasheet.

Practice

▶ Concepts Review

Label each element of the Select Query window shown in Figure B-24.

FIGURE B-24

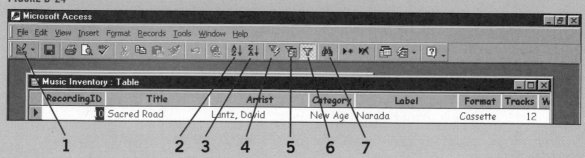

1   2 3   4   5   6 7

Match each term with the statement that describes it.

8. **Primary key**
9. **Table Wizard**
10. **Filter**
11. **Data type**
12. **Query**

a. Determines what type of data can be stored in each field
b. Provides interactive help to create the field names and data types for each field
c. A database object that creates a datasheet of specified fields and records from one or more tables
d. A field that contains unique information for each record
e. Creates a temporary subset of records

Select the best answer from the list of choices.

13. **Which data type would be best for a field that was going to store birth dates?**
    a. Text
    b. Number
    c. AutoNumber
    d. Date/Time
14. **Which data type would be best for a field that was going to store Web addresses?**
    a. Text
    b. Memo
    c. OLE
    d. Hyperlink
15. **Which data type would be best for a field that was going to store telephone numbers?**
    a. Text
    b. Number
    c. OLE
    d. Hyperlink
16. **Each of the following is true about a filter, *except***
    a. It creates a temporary datasheet of records that match criteria.
    b. The resulting datasheet can be sorted.
    c. The resulting datasheet includes all fields in the table.
    d. A filter is automatically saved as an object in the database.
17. **Sorting refers to**
    a. Reorganizing the records in either ascending or descending order.
    b. Selecting a subset of fields and/or records to view as a datasheet from one or more tables.
    c. Displaying only those records that meet certain criteria.
    d. Using Or and And criteria in the query design grid.

18. **Which criteria would be used in a Category field to find all music except that in the rap category?**
    a. /=/"rap"   c. NULL "rap"
    b. <>"rap"   d. IS NULL "rap"

 Skills Review

1. Plan a database.

a. Plan a database that will contain the names and addresses of physicians. You can use the local yellow pages to gather the information.

b. On paper, sketch the Table Design view of a table that will hold this information. Write the field names in one column and the data types for each field in the second column.

2. Create a table.

a. Start Access and use the Blank Access database option to create a database. Save the file as "Doctors" on your Project Disk.

b. Use the Table Wizard to create a new table.

c. Make sure the Business option button is selected. In the Sample Tables list, click Contacts.

d. In the Sample Fields list box, choose each of the fields in the following order for your table: ContactID, FirstName, LastName, Address, City, StateOrProvince, PostalCode, Title.

e. Rename the StateOrProvince field as "State."

f. Name the table "Addresses," and allow Access to set the primary key field.

g. Click the Modify the table design option button in the last Table Wizard dialog box, then click Finish.

3. Use Table Design view.

a. In the first available blank row, add a new field called "PhoneNumber" with a Text data type.

b. Change the Field Size property of the State field from 20 to 2.

c. Insert a field named "Suite" with a Text data type between the Address and City fields.

d. Add the description "M.D." or "D.O." to the Title field.

e. Save and close the Addresses table, then close the Doctors database, but don't exit Access.

4. Format a datasheet.

a. Open the Doctors-B database from your Project Disk. Open the Doctor Addresses table datasheet.

b. Change the font to Arial Narrow, and the font size to 9.

c. Change the gridline color to black, and change the vertical gridline to a transparent border.

d. Change the page orientation to landscape and all of the margins to 0.5". Preview the datasheet (it should fit on one page), then print it.

5. Understand sorting, filtering, and finding.

a. On a sheet of paper, identify three ways that you might want to sort an address list, such as the Doctor Addresses datasheet. Be sure to specify both the field you would sort on and the sort order (ascending or descending).

b. On a sheet of paper, identify three ways that you might want to filter an address list, such as the Doctor Addresses datasheet. Be sure to specify both the field you would filter on and the criteria that you would use.

6. Sort records and find data.

a. Sort the Doctor Addresses records in ascending order on the Last field, then list the first two doctors on paper.

b. Sort the Doctor Addresses records in descending order on the Zip field, then list the first two doctors on paper.

c. Find the records in which the Title field contains "D.O." How many records did you find?

d. Find the records where the Zip field contains "64012." How many records did you find?

Access 2000

7. Filter records.
a. In the Doctor Addresses datasheet, filter the records for all physicians with the Title "D.O."

b. In the Doctor Addresses datasheet, filter the records for all physicians with the title "M.D." in the "64012" zip code, then print the datasheet.

8. Create a query.
a. Use the Query Wizard to create a new query based on the Doctor Addresses table with the following fields: First, Last, City, State, Zip.

b. Name the query "Doctors in Missouri," then view the datasheet.

c. In Query Design view, add the criteria "MO" to the State field, then view the datasheet.

d. Change Mark Garver's last name to Garvey.

9. Use Query Design view.
a. Modify the Doctors in Missouri query to include only those doctors in Kansas City, Missouri. Be sure that the criteria is in the same row so that both criteria must be true for the record to be displayed.

b. Save the query with the name "Doctors in Kansas City Missouri." Print the query results, then close the query datasheet.

c. Modify the Doctors in Kansas City Missouri query so that the records are sorted in ascending order on the last name, and add "DoctorNumber" as the first field in the datasheet.

d. Print and save the sorted query's datasheet, then close the datasheet.

e. Close the Doctors-B database and exit Access.

▶ Independent Challenges

1. You want to start a database to track your personal video collection.
To complete this independent challenge:

a. Start Access and create a new database called "Movies" on your Project Disk.

b. Using the Table Wizard, create a table based on the Video Collection sample table in the personal category with the following fields: MovieTitle, YearReleased, Rating, Length, DateAcquired, PurchasePrice.

c. Rename the YearReleased field as "Year" and the PurchasePrice field as "Price."

d. Name the table "Video Collection," and allow Access to set a primary key field.

e. Modify the Video Collection table in Design view with the following changes:
  • Change the Rating field size property to 4.
  • Change the Length field to a Number data type.
  • Change the DateAcquired field name to DatePurchased.
  • Add a field between Rating and Length called "PersonalRating" with a Number data type.
  • In the description of the PersonalRating field, type: My personal rating on a scale from 1 (bad) to 10 (great).

f. Save and close the Video Collection table, and close the Movies database.

2. You work for a marketing company that sells medical supplies to doctors' offices.
To complete this independent challenge:

a. Open the Doctors-B database on your Project Disk, then open the Doctors Addresses table datasheet.

b. Filter the records to find all those physicians who live in Grandview, then print the filtered datasheet.

c. Sort the records by last name, change the font size to 12, resize the columns so all the data within each column is visible, change the page orientation to landscape, then print the datasheet.

d. Using the Query Wizard, create a query with the following fields: First, Last, Phone.

e. Name the query "Telephone Query." Sort the records in ascending order by last name, then print the datasheet.

f. Add the Title field to the third field position, then delete the First field. Save and close the query.

g. Modify the Telephone Query so that the State field is added to the fourth field position. Add criteria so that only those physicians in Missouri are shown on the resulting datasheet.

h. Print, save, and close the query. Close the Doctors-B database, then exit Access.

3. You want to create a database to keep track of your personal contacts.
To complete this independent challenge:

a. Start Access and create a new database called "People" on your Project Disk.

b. Using the Table Wizard, create a table based on the Addresses sample table in the Personal category with the following fields: FirstName, LastName, SpouseName, Address, City, StateOrProvince, PostalCode, EmailAddress, HomePhone, Birthdate.

c. Name the table Contact Info, allow Access to set the primary key field, and choose the Enter data directly into the table option in the last Table Wizard dialog box.

d. Enter at least five records into the table, making sure that two people have the same last name. Use your name for one of the records. You do not have to enter real names and addresses into the other records.

e. Press [Tab] to move through the Contact InfoID field.

f. Sort the records in ascending order by last name.

g. Adjust the column widths, change the datasheet margins, change the paper orientation, and make other adjustments, as necessary, to print the five records on one page. Print

h. Using the Query Wizard, create a query with the following fields from the Contact Info table in this order: LastName, FirstName, Birthdate.

i. Name the query Birthday List, and in Query Design view, sort the records in ascending order by LastName and then by FirstName.

j. Save the query as Sorted Birthday List, then view the query.

k. Change the Birthdate field to 8/20/58 for one of the records in the query datasheet.

l. Print the query's datasheet, close the query, then close the People database and exit Access.

4. MediaLoft has developed a Web site that provides information about their products and allows viewers to vote for their favorite music collections. In this exercise, you will print the Web page from the MediaLoft intranet site that records the People's choice awards. Then you will enter that information in the database, and create a query that displays only the top records.

a. Connect to the Internet, and use your browser to go to the MediaLoft intranet site at http://www.course.com/illustrated/medialoft

b. Click the link for Products to go to the Web page summarizing the most popular music selection in several categories as determined by a recent vote of customers.

c. Print the People's Choice Web page, then disconnect from the Internet.

d. Open the MediaLoft-B database, and then open the Music Inventory table in Design view.

e. Add a field called PeoplesChoice at the end of the field list with a Yes/No data type.

f. Find the six records listed on the People's Choice Web page (*Hint*: Use the Find and Sort buttons). Then place a checkmark in the PeoplesChoice field in your database for the six records to indicate that they were contest winners.

g. Using the Query Wizard, create a query that is based on the Music Inventory table with the following fields: Category, Title, Artist, Retail, PeoplesChoice.

h. Show all the Detail records, name the query "Peoples Choice Query," then modify the query so that only those records with "Yes" in the PeoplesChoice field are displayed.

i. Save and print the Peoples Choice Query datasheet.

j. Close the Peoples Choice Query, close the MediaLoft-B database, then exit Access.

Open the MediaLoft-B database and create a query based on the Music Inventory table that displays the datasheet

Visual Workshop

Open the MediaLoft-B database and create a query based on the Music Inventory table that displays the datasheet shown in Figure B-25. Notice that only the Jazz category is displayed and that the records are sorted in a descending order on the Retail field. Save the query as "Jazz Selections" in the MediaLoft-B database.

FIGURE B-25

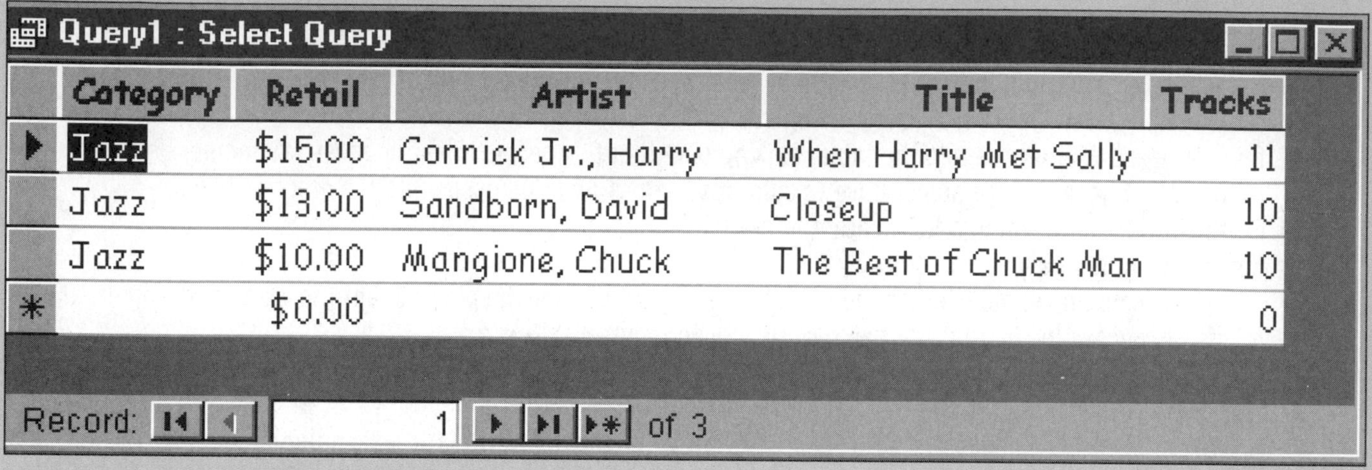

Category	Retail	Artist	Title	Tracks
Jazz	$15.00	Connick Jr., Harry	When Harry Met Sally	11
Jazz	$13.00	Sandborn, David	Closeup	10
Jazz	$10.00	Mangione, Chuck	The Best of Chuck Man	10
*	$0.00			0

Record: 1 of 3

Using

Forms

Objectives

► **Plan a form**

► **Create a form**

► **Move and resize controls**

► **Modify labels**

► **Modify text boxes**

► **Modify tab order**

► **Enter and edit records**

► **Insert an image**

A **form** is an Access database object that allows you to arrange the fields of a record in any layout. Although the datasheet view of a table or query can be used to navigate, edit, and enter new information, all of the fields for one record are sometimes not visible unless you scroll left or right. A form fixes that problem by using the screen to show the fields of only one record at a time. Forms are often the primary object used to enter, edit, and find data. ➤ More people are becoming excited about the MediaLoft music inventory database. They have asked John Kim to create a form to make it easier to access, enter, and update this important inventory data.

Planning a Form

Properly organized and well-designed forms make a tremendous difference in the productivity of the end user. Since forms are the primary object used to enter and edit data, time spent planning a form is time well spent. Forms are often built to match a **source document** (for example, an employment application or a medical history form) to facilitate fast and accurate data entry. Now, however, it is becoming more common to type data directly into the database rather than first recording it on paper. Form design considerations, such as clearly labeled fields and appropriate formatting, are important. Other considerations include how the user tabs from field to field, and what type of **control** is used to display the data. See Table C-1 for more information on form controls. ✎ John considers the following form design considerations when planning his Music Inventory form.

 Determine the overall purpose of the form

Have a good understanding of what information you need to gather through the form. This purpose often becomes the form's title such as "Music Inventory Entry Form."

 Determine the underlying record source

The **record source** is either a table or query object, and contains the fields and records that the form will display.

 Gather the source documents used to design your form, or sketch the form by hand if a paper form does not exist

When sketching the form, be sure to list all the fields and instructions you want the form to display.

 Determine the best type of control to use for each element on the form

Figures C-1 and C-2 show examples of several controls. **Bound controls** display data from the underlying record source and are also used to edit and enter new data. **Unbound controls** do not change from record to record and exist only to clarify or enhance the appearance of the form.

TABLE C-1: Form Controls

name	used to:	bound or unbound
Label	Provide consistent descriptive text as you navigate from record to record	Unbound
Text box	Display, edit, or enter data for each record from an underlying record source	Bound
List box	Display a list of possible data entries	Bound
Combo box	Display a list of possible data entries for a field, and also provide text box for an entry from the keyboard; a "combination" of the list box and text box controls	Bound
Tab control	Create a three-dimensional aspect to a form so that controls can be organized and displayed by clicking the "tabs"	Unbound
Check box	Display "yes" or "no" answers for a field; if the box is "checked" it displays "yes" information	Bound
Toggle button	Display "yes" or "no" answers for a field; if the button is "pressed," it displays "yes" information	Bound
Option button	Display a limited list of possible choices for field	Bound
Bound image control	Display OLE data, such as a picture	Bound
Unbound image control	Display picture or clip art that doesn't change as you navigate from record to record	Unbound
Line and Rectangle controls	Draw lines and rectangles on the form	Unbound
Command button	Provide an easy way to initiate a command or run a macro	Unbound

FIGURE C-1: Sample Form Controls

Tab controls

Option group

Labels

List box

Combo box

Text boxes

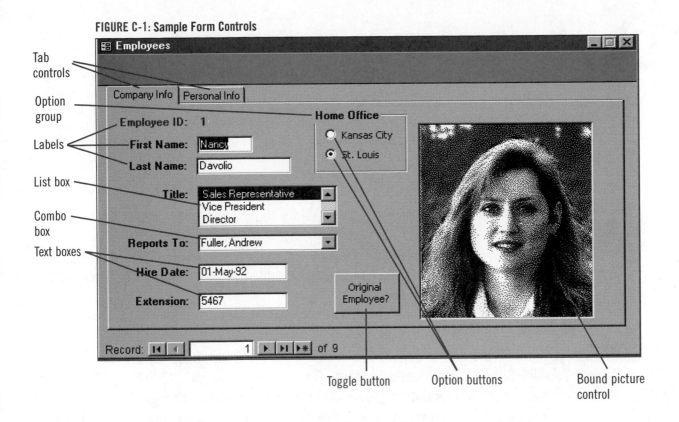

Toggle button   Option buttons   Bound picture control

FIGURE C-2: Sample Form Controls

Unbound image

Rectangle

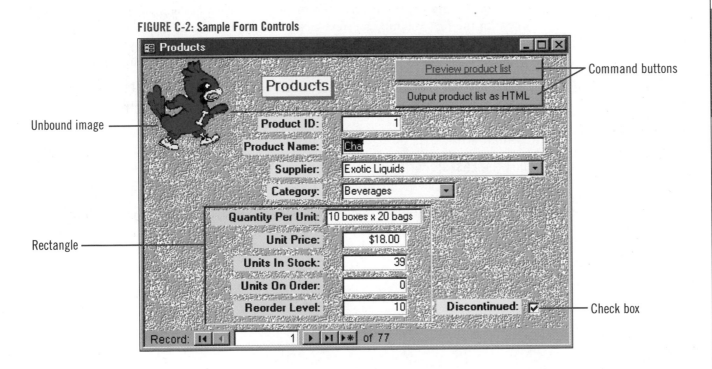

Command buttons

Check box

Creating a Form

You can create a form from scratch using **Form Design view**, or you can use the **Form Wizard** to create an initial form object that can be modified later if needed. The Form Wizard provides options for selecting fields, an overall layout, a style, and a form title. ▓▬▬ John created a sketch and made some notes on how he'd like the final Music Inventory form arranged, shown in Figure C-3. He uses the Form Wizard to get started.

Steps

1. Start Access, click the **Open an existing file option button**, then open the **MediaLoft-C** database from your Project Disk
   This MediaLoft-C database contains an enhanced Music Inventory table. John added more fields and records.

> **QuickTip**
> To hide the Office Assistant, click Help on the menu bar, then click Hide Office Assistant.

2. Click **Forms** on the Objects bar in the MediaLoft-C Database window, then double-click **Create form by using wizard**
   The Music Inventory table includes all of the fields required in the Music Inventory form.

3. Click the **Select All Fields button** >> , click **Next**, click the **Columnar layout option button**, click **Next**, click the **Standard** style, click **Next**, then click **Finish** to accept the name **Music Inventory** for the form
   The Music Inventory form opens in **Form view**, as shown in Figure C-4. Descriptive labels appear in the first column, and text boxes that display data from the underlying records appear in the second column. A check box control displays the yes/no data in the PeoplesChoice field. You can enter, edit, find, sort, and filter records using the form.

> **QuickTip**
> Sort, filter, and find buttons work the same way in a form as a datasheet, except that a form generally shows only one record at a time.

4. Click the **Artist text box**, click the **Sort Ascending button** ▲₂▼ on the Form View toolbar, then click the **Next Record button** ▶ to move to the second record
   The "Adams, Oleta" record is second when the records are sorted in ascending order by recording artist.

5. Click the **Last Record button** ▶❘ on the Music Inventory form
   Neil Young's "Decade" is the last record when the records are sorted in ascending order.

6. Click the **Close button** on the Music Inventory form title bar to close the form
   The new Music Inventory form object appears in the Forms section of the MediaLoft-C Database window.

CLUES TO USE

Using AutoForm

You can quickly create a form by clicking a table or query object in the database window, and then clicking the New Object:AutoForm button ▣ on the Database toolbar. AutoForm offers no prompts or dialog boxes; it instantly creates a form that displays all the fields in the previously chosen table or query using the same options as those you chose the last time you used the Form Wizard.

FIGURE C-3: Sketch of Music Inventory form

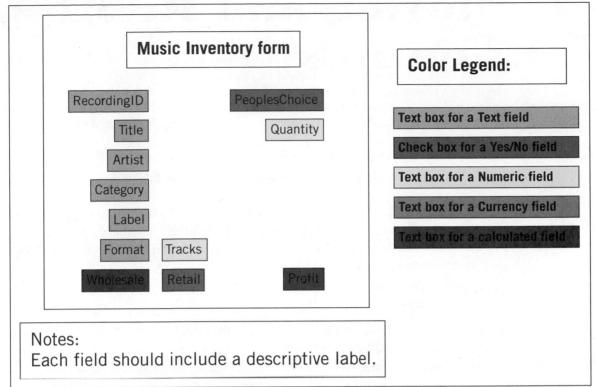

Notes:
Each field should include a descriptive label.

FIGURE C-4: Music Inventory form

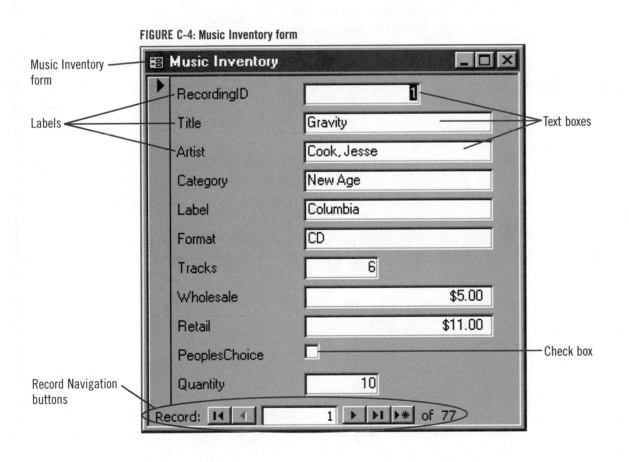

Moving and Resizing Controls

After you create a form, you can modify the size, location, and appearance of existing controls in Form Design view. Form Design view also allows you to add or delete controls. ✎ John moves and resizes the controls on the form to better match his original design.

1. Click the **Music Inventory form**, click the **Design button** 🖉 in the MediaLoft-C Database window, then click the **Maximize button** to maximize the Design view of the Music Inventory form

   The Design view of the Music Inventory form opens. The **Toolbox toolbar** contains buttons that allow you to add controls to the form. The **field list** contains the fields in the underlying object. You can toggle both of these screen elements on and off as needed. Widening the form gives you more room to reposition the controls.

2. Click the **Toolbox button** 🛠 on the Form Design toolbar to toggle it off (if necessary), click the **Field List button** 🗐 to toggle it off (if necessary), place the pointer on the right edge of the form, then when the pointer changes to ↔, drag the right edge to the **6"** mark on the horizontal ruler

   The form is expanded so that it is 6" wide, as shown in Figure C-5. Before moving, resizing, deleting, or changing a control in any way, you must select it.

3. Click the **PeoplesChoice check box**

   Squares, called **sizing handles**, appear in the corners and on the edges of the selected control. When you work with controls, the mouse pointer shape is very important. Pointer shapes are summarized in Table C-2.

4. Place the pointer on the **selected control**, when the pointer changes to ✋, drag the control so that the left edge of the label is at the **4"** mark on the horizontal ruler and the bottom edge is aligned with the **RecordingID text box**

   The text boxes appear as white rectangles in this form. When you move a bound control, such as a text box or check box, the accompanying unbound label control to its left moves with it. The field name for the selected control appears in the Object list box.

5. Select and move the **Quantity** and **Tracks text boxes** using the ✋ pointer to match their final locations as shown in Figure C-6

   Resizing controls also improves the design of the form.

6. Click the **Retail text box**, then use the ↔ pointer to drag the middle-right edge sizing handle left to the **2"** mark, click the **Wholesale text box**, then drag the middle-right edge sizing handle left to the **2"** mark

   Moving and resizing controls requires great concentration and mouse control. Don't worry if your screen doesn't *precisely* match the next figure, but *do* make sure that you understand how to use the move and resize mouse pointers used in Form Design view. Precision and accuracy are naturally developed with practice, but even experienced form designers regularly rely on the Undo button.

7. Click the **Form View button** 🖽 on the Form Design toolbar, click the **Artist text box**, click the **Sort Descending button** ⬇, then click the **Sort Ascending button** ⬆ on the Form View toolbar

   Your screen should look like Figure C-7.

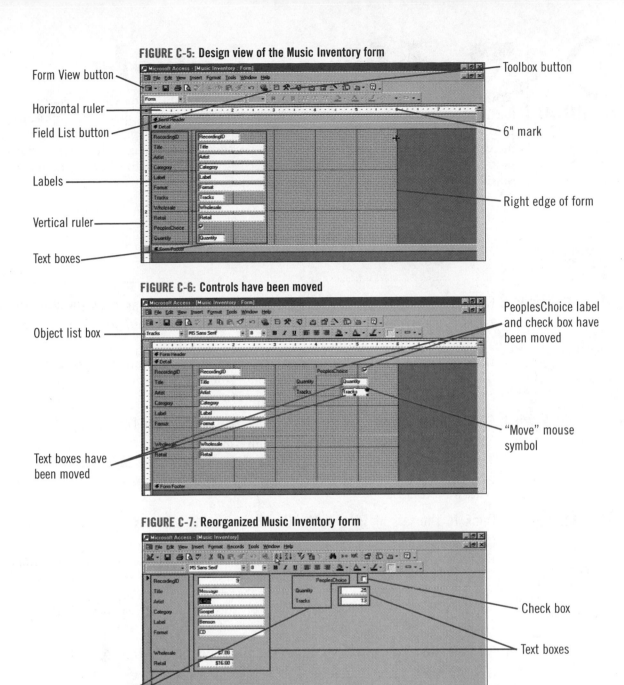

FIGURE C-5: Design view of the Music Inventory form

Form View button
Horizontal ruler
Field List button
Labels
Vertical ruler
Text boxes

Toolbox button
6" mark
Right edge of form

FIGURE C-6: Controls have been moved

Object list box

Text boxes have been moved

PeoplesChoice label and check box have been moved

"Move" mouse symbol

FIGURE C-7: Reorganized Music Inventory form

Check box

Text boxes

Labels

TABLE C-2: Form Design view mouse pointer shapes

shape	when does this shape appear?	action
▸	When you point to any nonselected control on the form; it is the default mouse pointer	Single-clicking with this mouse pointer *selects* a control
✋	When you point to the edge of a selected control (but not when you are pointing to a sizing handle)	Dragging this mouse pointer moves all selected controls
☝	When you point to the larger sizing handle in the upper-left corner of a selected control	Dragging this mouse pointer *moves only the single control* where pointer is currently positioned, not other controls that may also be selected
↔ ↕ ↖ ↗	When you point to any sizing handle (except the larger one in the upper-left corner)	Dragging this mouse pointer *resizes* the control

Modifying Labels

When you create a form with the Form Wizard, it places a label to the left of each text box with the field's name. Often, you'll want to modify those labels to be more descriptive or user friendly. You can modify a label control by directly editing it in Form Design view, or you can make the change in the label's property sheet. The **property sheet** is a comprehensive listing of all **properties** (characteristics) that have been specified for that control. ◀━━ John modifies the Music Inventory form's labels to be more descriptive.

Steps 1 2 3 4

Trouble?

If you double-click a label, you will open its property sheet. Close the property sheet by clicking its Close button, then single-click the label again.

1. Click the **Design View button** ▦ on the Form View toolbar, click the **RecordingID label** to select it, click between the **g** and **I** in the RecordingID label, then press **[Spacebar]** to insert a space

   Directly editing labels in Form Design view is tricky because you must select the label and then precisely click where you want to edit it. You can also open the label's property sheet and modify the Caption property to change the displayed text.

2. Click the **Title label**, click the **Properties button** ▦ on the Form Design toolbar, then click the **Format tab**, as shown in Figure C-8

   The Caption property controls the text displayed by the label control, and the property can be found on either the Format or the All tabs. The All tab is an exhaustive list of all the properties for a control.

Trouble?

Be sure to modify the Title label control and not the Title text box control. Text box controls must reference the *exact* field name in order to display the data within that field.

3. Click to the left of **Title** in the Caption property text box, type **Recording**, press **[Spacebar]**, then click ▦ to toggle the property sheet off

   Don't be overwhelmed by the number of properties available for each control on the form. Over time, you may want to learn about most of these properties, but in the beginning, you'll be able to make the vast majority of the property changes through menu and toolbar options rather than by accessing the property sheet itself. Labels can be aligned so that they are closer to their respective text boxes.

4. Click the **Recording ID label**, then click the **Align Right button** ▦ on the Formatting (Form/Report) toolbar

   The Recording ID label is now much closer to its associated text box. See Table C-3 for a list of techniques to quickly select several controls so that you can apply alignment and formatting changes to many controls simultaneously.

5. Click the **0.5"** mark on the horizontal ruler to select the first column of controls, as shown in Figure C-9, then click ▦

   All the labels in the first column are right-aligned and next to their text boxes.

6. Click the **Save button** ▦ on the Form Design toolbar, then click the **Form View button** ▦ on the Form Design toolbar

   The Music Inventory form is saved, and you can see that the labels are close to the data in the first column.

FIGURE C-8: Looking at a label's property sheet

Recording ID label has been changed

Title label is chosen

Caption property

Properties button

The property sheet title bar tells you what type of control you are working with

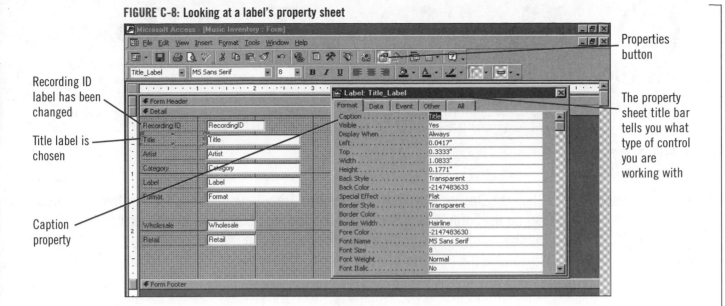

FIGURE C-9: Selecting several labels at the same time

Clicking the 0.5" mark on the ruler

All labels in the first column are selected

Formatting (Form/Report) toolbar

Align Right button

TABLE C-3: Selecting more than one control

technique	description
Click, [Shift]+click	Click a control, then press and hold [Shift] while clicking other controls; each one will be selected
Drag a selection box	If you drag a selection box (an imaginary box you create by dragging the pointer in Form Design view), every control that is in or touched by the edges of the box will be selected
Click in the ruler	If you click in either the horizontal or vertical ruler you will select all controls that intersect the selection line (an imaginary line you create by clicking the ruler)
Drag in the ruler	If you drag through either the horizontal or vertical ruler you will select all controls that intersect the selection line as it is dragged through the ruler

Modifying Text Boxes

Access 2000

Text boxes are generally used to display data from underlying fields and are therefore *bound* to that field. You can also use a text box as a **calculated control** which is not directly bound to a field but rather uses information from a field to calculate an answer. ✎ John wants the Music Inventory form to calculate the profit for each record. He uses a text box calculated control to find the difference between the Retail and Wholesale fields.

1. Click the **Design View button** 🔲 on the Form View toolbar, click the **Toolbox button** 🔧 on the Form View toolbar, click the **Text Box button** [ab] on the Toolbox toolbar, the pointer changes to ⁺[ab], click just below the Retail text box on the form, then if necessary move the new text box and label control to align with the controls above it

Your screen should look like Figure C-10. Adding a new text box *automatically* added a new label with the default caption "Text22:". You can access the text box's property sheet to bind it to an underlying field or expression, or you can create the calculated expression directly in the text box.

2. Click **Unbound** in the new text box, type **=[Retail]-[Wholesale]**, then press **[Enter]**

When referencing field names within an expression, you *must* use square brackets and type the field name exactly as it appears in the Table Design view. You do not need to worry about uppercase and lowercase letters. The label for any expression should be descriptive.

3. Click the **Text22: label** to select it, click the **Text22: label** again to edit it, double-click **Text22**, type **Profit** as the new caption, then press **[Enter]**

The calculated text box control and associated label are modified.

4. Click the **Form View button** 🔳 to view your changes, click the **Ascending Sort button** ⏬ on the Form View toolbar

Your screen should look like Figure C-11. The first record is $5 wholesale and sells for $11.00 retail so the profit is calculated as $6. You can use Form Design view to make a few more changes to clarify the form.

5. Click 🔲, click the **Calculated text box**, then click the **Properties button** 📋 on the Form Design toolbar

By default, the values in text boxes that contain numeric and currency fields are right-aligned. Text boxes that contain fields with other data types or those that start as unbound controls are left-aligned. Monetary values should be right-aligned and display with a dollar sign and cents.

6. Click the **Format tab** in the Text Box property sheet, click the **Format property text box**, click the **Format property list arrow**, scroll and click **Currency**, click the **Text Align property text box**, scroll and click the **Text Align property list arrow**, then click **Right**

7. Click the **Properties button** 📋, switch the position of the **Retail and Wholesale text boxes**, move and align the **Profit label**, resize the **calculated text box** (as shown in Figure C-12), then click the **Form View button** 🔳

The calculated profit value should display as $6.00 and be right-aligned within the text box.

Trouble?

The Toolbox toolbar may be floating or docked on the edge of your screen. Drag the title bar of a floating toolbar or the top edge of a docked toolbar to move it to a convenient location.

Trouble?

The number in the caption "Text22" varies depending on how many controls you add to the form.

Trouble?

If your calculated control did not work, return to Design view, click the calculated control, press [Delete], then repeat steps 1 through 4.

Trouble?

Properties are not listed in alphabetical order so you may have to scroll up or down the property sheet to find the Format and Text Align properties.

FIGURE C-10: Adding a calculated text box

Toolbox button

Toolbox toolbar

Click to add a text box control

New label

New text box

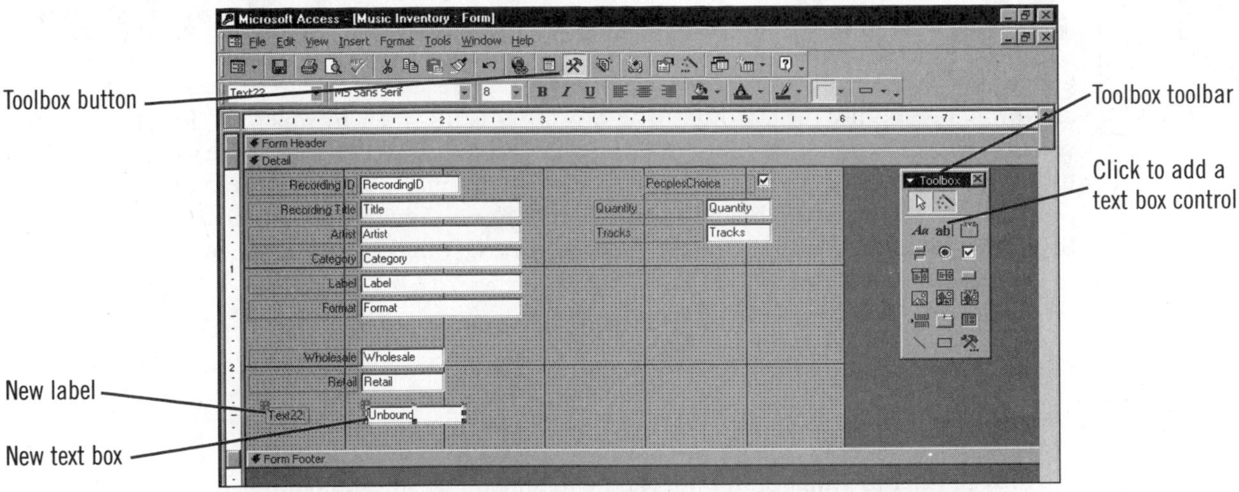

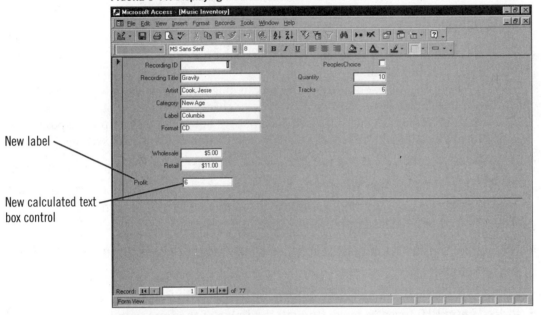

FIGURE C-11: Displaying a calculated text box

New label

New calculated text box control

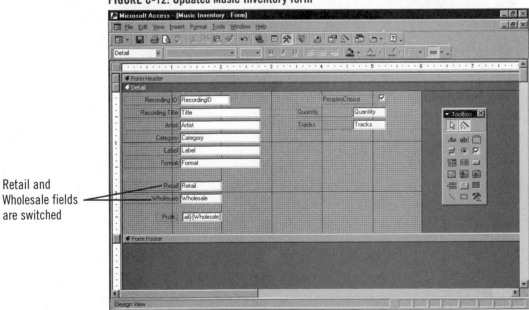

FIGURE C-12: Updated Music Inventory form

Retail and Wholesale fields are switched

Access 2000

Modifying Tab Order

Once all of the controls have been added, moved, and resized on the form, you'll want to check and probably modify the tab order. The **tab order** is the order in which the **focus** (the active control) moves as you press [Tab] in Form view. Since the form is the primary object by which users will view, edit, and enter data, careful attention to tab order is essential to maintain their productivity and satisfaction with the database. John checks the tab order of the Music Inventory form, then changes the tab order as necessary in Form Design view.

Steps

QuickTip

You can also press [Enter] to move the focus from field to field on a form.

1. **Press [Tab] 11 times watching the focus move through the bound controls of the form**
   Currently, focus moves back and forth between the left and right columns of controls. For efficient data entry, you want the focus to move down through the first column of text boxes before moving to the second column.

2. **Click the Design View button** ✍ **on the Form View toolbar, click View on the menu bar, then click Tab Order**
   The Tab Order dialog box opens in which you can drag fields up or down to change their tab sequence. The Tab Order dialog box allows you to change the tab order of controls in three sections: Form Header, Detail, and Form Footer. Right now, all of the controls are positioned in the form's Detail section. See Table C-4 for more information on form sections.

3. **Click the Retail row selector in the Custom Order list, drag it up to position it just below Format, click the Wholesale row selector, drag it under Retail, click the Tracks row selector, then drag it under Quantity as shown in Figure C-13**
   With the change made, test the new tab order.

4. **Click OK in the Tab Order dialog box, then click the Form View button** ▦ **on the Form Design toolbar**
   Although nothing visibly changes on the form, the tab order is different.

5. **Press [Enter] 10 times to move through the fields of the form with the new tab order**
   You should now be moving through all of the text boxes of the first column, with the exception of the calculated field, before you move to the second column.

6. **Click the Save button** 🖫 **on the Form View toolbar**

FIGURE C-13: Tab Order dialog box

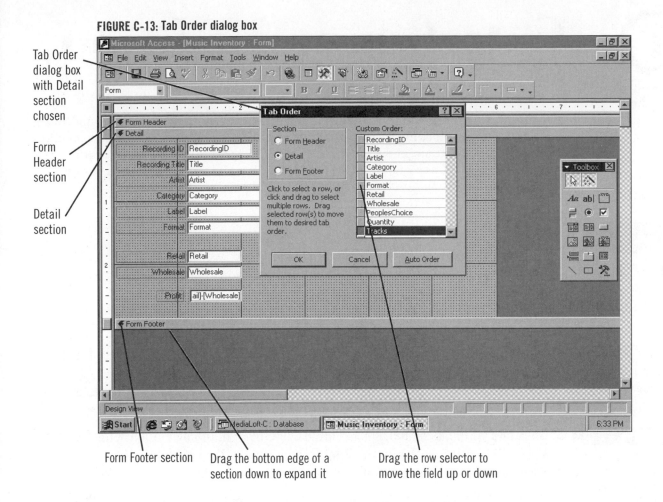

Tab Order dialog box with Detail section chosen

Form Header section

Detail section

Form Footer section

Drag the bottom edge of a section down to expand it

Drag the row selector to move the field up or down

Access 2000

TABLE C-4: Form sections

section	description
Form Header	Controls placed in the Form Header print only once at the top of the printout; by default, this section is not "opened" in Form Design view, but can be expanded by dragging its bottom edge in Form Design view.
Detail	Controls placed in the Detail section print once for every record in the underlying table or query object; all controls created by the Form Wizard are placed in this section
Form Footer	Controls placed in the Form Footer print only once at the end of the printout; by default, this section is not "opened" in Form Design view, but it can be expanded by dragging its bottom edge down in Form Design view

Entering and Editing Records

The most important reasons for using a form are to find, enter, or edit records to the underlying object. You can also print a form, but you must be careful because printing a form often produces a very long printout because of the vertical orientation of the fields. ▄▄▄ John uses the Music Inventory form to add a new record to the underlying Music Inventory table. Then he prints the form with the data for only the new record.

QuickTip
A New Record button is also on the Navigation buttons.

1. **Click the New Record button ▶* on the Form View toolbar**
A new, blank record is displayed. The text "(AutoNumber)" appears in the Recording ID field, which will automatically increment when you begin to enter data. The Specific Record box indicates the current record number.

QuickTip
To enter a check in a check box press [Spacebar].

2. **Click the Recording Title text box, type The Dance, then enter the rest of the information shown in Figure C-14**
Notice that the Profit text box shows the calculated result of $4.00. The new record is stored as record 78 in the Music Inventory table.

Trouble?
Don't click the Print button on the Form View toolbar because *all* of the records in the underlying object will print.

3. **Click File on the menu bar, click Print to open the Print dialog box, click the Selected Record(s) option button in the Print Range section, then click OK**
Forms are also often used to edit existing records in the database.

4. **Click the Recording Title text box, click the Find button 🔍 on the Form View toolbar to open the Find and Replace dialog box, type Mermaid Avenue in the Find What text box, then click Find Next**
Record 77 appears behind the Find and Replace dialog box, as shown in Figure C-15.

5. **Click Cancel in the Find and Replace dialog box, press [Tab] five times to go to the Retail field, type 20, then press [Tab]**
Editing either the Wholesale or Retail fields automatically updates the calculated Profit field. Forms are also a great way to filter the records to a specific subset.

6. **Click Pop in the Category text box, then click the Filter By Selection button 🔽 on the Form View toolbar**
Twelve records were found that matched the "Pop" criteria. Previewing the records helps to determine how many pages the printout would be.

7. **Click the Print Preview button 🔍 on the Form View toolbar**
Since about three records print on a page, your printout would be four pages long.

8. **Click the Close button on the Print Preview toolbar, then click the Remove Filter button 🔽 on the Form View toolbar so that all 78 records in the Music Inventory table are available**

FIGURE C-14: Entering a new record into a form

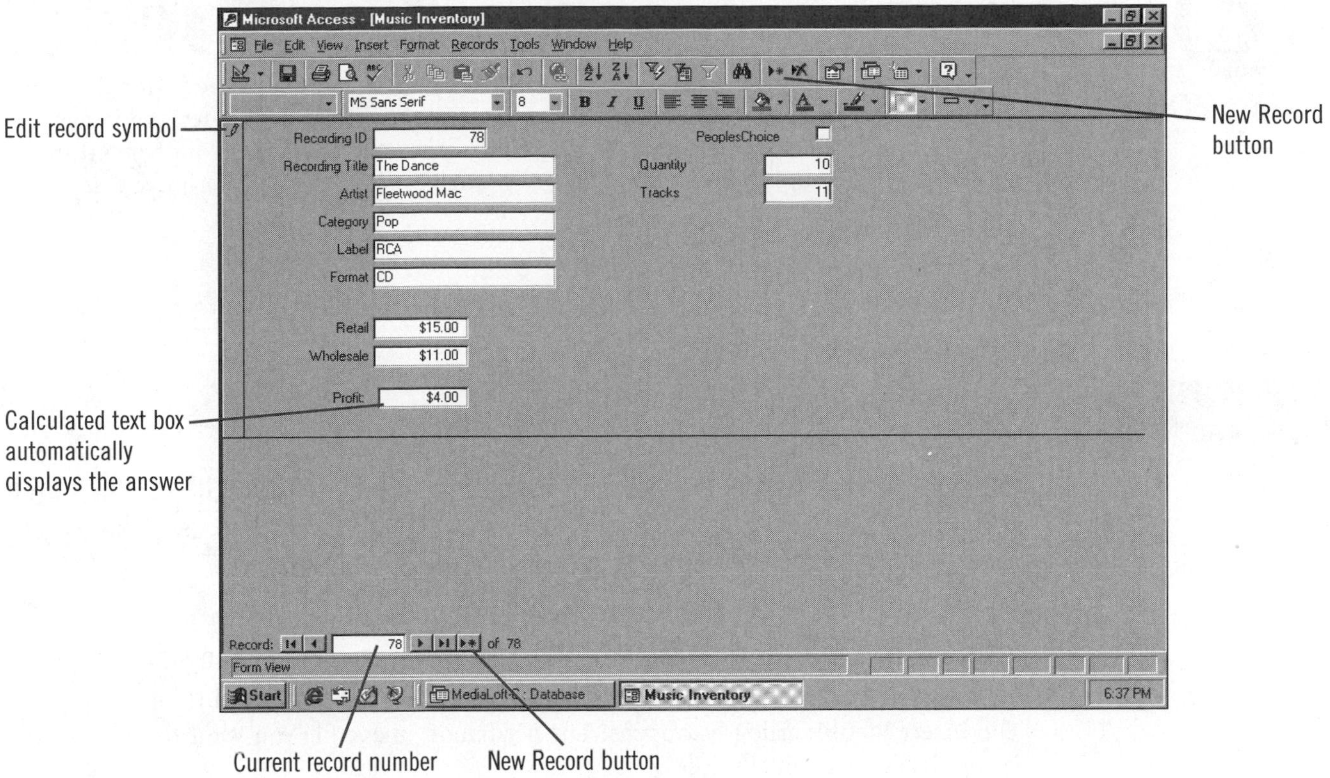

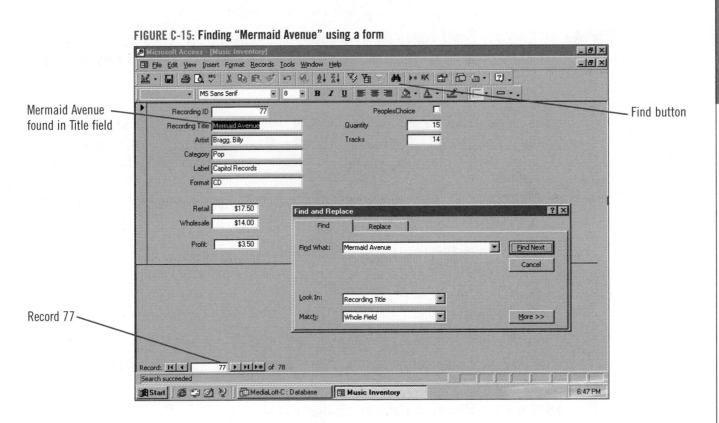

Edit record symbol ——

New Record button

Calculated text box automatically displays the answer

Current record number   New Record button

FIGURE C-15: Finding "Mermaid Avenue" using a form

Mermaid Avenue found in Title field

Find button

Record 77

Inserting an Image

Graphic images, such as pictures, a logo, or clip art, can add style and professionalism to a form. If you add a graphic image as an unbound image to the Form Header, the image will appear at the top of the form in Form view and once at the top of the printout when printing records through a form. ➤ John adds the MediaLoft logo and a descriptive title to the Form Header section.

Steps

1. Click the **Design View button** 🖼 on the Form View toolbar, place the pointer on the bottom edge of the Form Header, the pointer changes to ✚, then drag the bottom of the Form Header section to the **1"** mark on the vertical ruler
   The Form Header section is open.

2. Click the **Image button** 🖼 on the Toolbox toolbar, the pointer changes to ⁺🖼, then click in the **Form Header section** at the **1"** mark on the horizontal ruler
   The Insert Picture dialog box opens. The MediaLoft image file you want to insert in the Form Header is on the Project Disk.

3. Click the **Look in list arrow**, click the drive containing your Project Disk, click **smallmedia**, then click **OK**
   The MediaLoft logo appears in the Form Header, surrounded by handles, as shown in Figure C-16. Form header titles add a finishing touch to a form.

   QuickTip
   If you need your name on the printed solution, enter your name as a label below the MediaLoft Music label.

4. Click the **Label button** 🅰 on the Toolbox toolbar, the pointer changes to ⁺A, click to the right of the **MediaLoft logo** in the Form Header section, type **MediaLoft Music**, then press **[Enter]**
   Labels can be formatted to enhance the appearance on the form.

5. Click the **Font Size list arrow**, click **24**, point to the **upper-right resizing handle**, then drag the ↗ pointer so that the label **MediaLoft Music** is completely displayed
   If you double-click a label's sizing handle, the label will automatically adjust to display the entire caption.

6. Click the **Form View button** 🖾 on the Form Design toolbar
   You can go directly to a specific record by typing the record number in the specific record box.

7. Click in the **specific record box** on the Record Navigation buttons, type **11**, then press **[Enter]**
   Compare your form with Figure C-17.

8. Click **File** on the menu bar, click **Print**, click the **Selected Record(s) option button**, then click **OK**

9. Click the **Close button** on the Music Inventory form, then click **Yes** to save any changes if necessary

10. Close the MediaLoft-C database, then exit Access

FIGURE C-16: Adding an image to the Form Header section

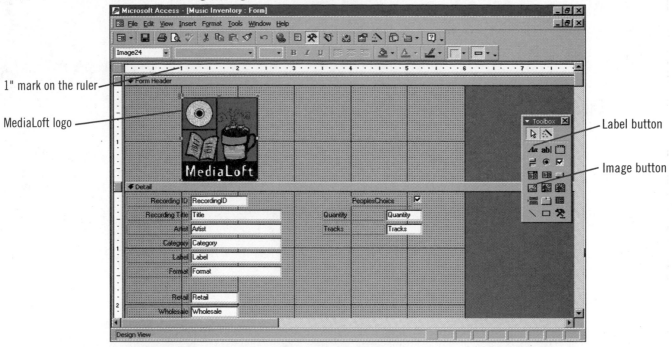

1" mark on the ruler

MediaLoft logo

Label button

Image button

FIGURE C-17: The final Music Inventory form

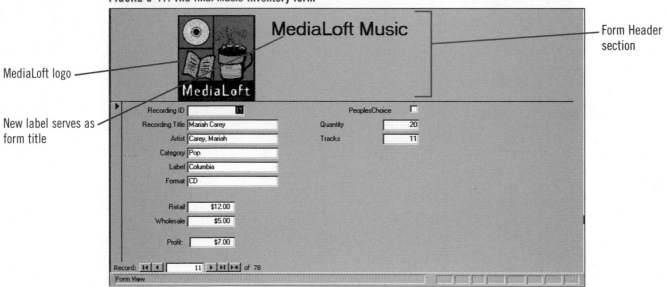

MediaLoft logo

New label serves as form title

Form Header section

Access 2000

Creating a hyperlink from an image

Once an image is added to a form, you can convert it to a hyperlink by using its property sheet to modify the control's **Hyperlink Address** property in Form Design view. Depending on what you enter for the Hyperlink Address property, clicking the hyperlinked image in Form view opens another file, Access object, Web address, or e-mail address. For example, C:\Colleges\JCCCDescriptions.doc is the Hyperlink Address property entry to link a Word document at the specified drive and folder location; http://www.jccc.net creates a link between the image and the specified Web address.

Practice

▶ Concepts Review

Label each element of the Form Design window shown in Figure C-18.

FIGURE C-18

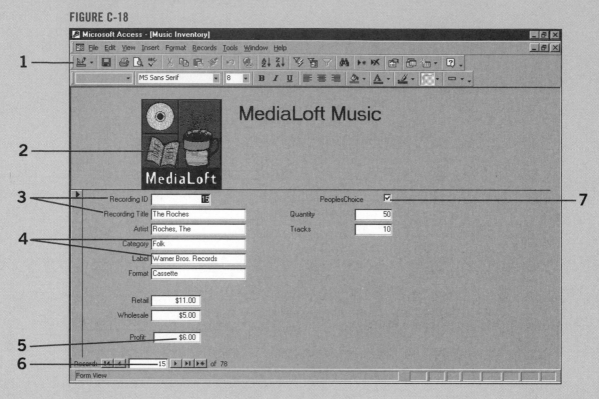

Match each term with the statement that describes it.

8. Sizing handles
9. Detail section
10. Bound control
11. Tab order
12. Form
13. Calculated control

a. An Access database object that allows you to arrange the fields of a record in any layout; you use it to enter, edit, and delete records
b. Displays data from a field in the underlying record source
c. Black squares that appear in the corners and edges of the selected control
d. The way in which the focus moves from one bound control to the next
e. Uses a text box and an expression to display an answer
f. Controls placed here print once for every record in the underlying table or query object

Select the best answer from the list of choices.

14. Every element on a form is called a
    a. Property.
    b. Control.
    c. Piece.
    d. Handle.

15. The pointer used to resize a control is
    a. ✛
    b. ↔
    c. ✋
    d. ☝

16. The most common bound control is the
    a. Label.
    b. Text box.
    c. Combo box.
    d. Check box.

17. The most common unbound control is the
    a. Label.
    b. Text box.
    c. Combo box.
    d. Image.

18. The _____ view is used to modify form controls.
    a. Form
    b. Datasheet
    c. Print Preview
    d. Design

▶ Skills Review

1. Plan a form.

a. Plan a form to use for the data entry of business contacts by looking at several business cards.

b. Write down the organization of the fields on the form. Determine what type of control you will use for each bound field.

c. Identify the labels you would like to display on the form.

2. Create a form.

a. Start Access and open the Membership-C database from your Project Disk.

b. Click the Forms button in the Membership-C Database window, then double-click the Create form by using wizard option.

c. Base the form on the Contacts table, and include all of the fields.

d. Use a Columnar layout, a Standard style, and title the form "Contact Entry Form."

e. Display the form with data.

3. Move and resize controls.

a. Open and maximize the Design View window for the Contact Entry Form.

b. Widen the form so that the right edge is at the 6" mark on the horizontal ruler.

c. Move the LNAME text box and corresponding label to the right of the FNAME text box.

d. Move the DUESOWED and DUESPAID text boxes and corresponding labels to the right of the address controls.

e. Resize the PHONE and ZIP text boxes to be the same size as the CITY text box.

f. Move the PHONE text box and corresponding label between the FNAME and COMPANY controls.

4. Modify labels.

a. Right align all of the labels.

b. Modify the FNAME label to FIRST NAME, the LNAME label to LAST NAME, the DUESOWED label to DUES OWED, and the DUESPAID label to DUES PAID.

5. Modify text boxes.

a. Add a new text box below the DUESPAID text box.

b. Type the expression =[DUESOWED]-[DUESPAID] in the new unbound text box. (*Hint*: Remember that you must use the *exact field names* in a calculated expression.)

c. In the property sheet for the new calculated control, change the Format property to Currency.

d. Right align the new calculated text boxes.

e. Change the calculated text box label from Text20: to BALANCE.

f. Move and resize the new calculated control and label so that it is aligned beneath the DUESOWED and DUES-PAID controls.

6. Modify tab order.

a. Change the Tab order so that pressing [Tab] moves the focus through the text boxes in the following order: FNAME, LNAME, PHONE, COMPANY, STREET, CITY, STATE, ZIP, DUESOWED, DUESPAID, BALANCE text box

7. Enter and edit records.

a. Use the Contact Entry Form to enter the following new records:

	FIRST NAME	LAST NAME	PHONE	COMPANY	STREET
Record 1	Jane	Eagan	555-1166	Cummins Construction	1515 Maple St.
Record 2	Mark	Daniels	555-2277	Motorola	1010 Green St.

	CITY	STATE	ZIP	DUES OWED	DUES PAID
1 con't.	Fontanelle	KS	50033-	$50.00	$25.00
2 con't.	Bridgewater	KS	50022-	$50.00	$50.00

b. Print the Mark Daniels record.

c. Find the Lois Goode record, enter IBM in the Company text box, then print that record.

d. Filter for all records with a Zip entry of 64145. How many records did you find?

e. Sort the filtered 64145 zip code records in ascending order by Last Name, then print the first one.

8. Insert an image.

a. In Form Design view, expand the Form Header section to the 1" mark on the vertical ruler.

b. Use the Image control to insert the handin1.bmp file found on your Project Disk in the Form Header.

c. Centered and below the graphic file, add the label MEMBERSHIP INFORMATION in a 24-point font. Be sure to resize the label so that all of the text is visible.

d. Add your name as a label in the Form Header section.

e. View the form using the Form view.

f. Print the selected record.

g. Close the form, close the database, then exit Access.

▶ Independent Challenges

1. As the office manager of a cardiology clinic, you need to create a new patient data entry form. To complete this independent challenge:

a. Open the Clinic-C database from your Project Disk.

b. Using the Form Wizard, create a form that includes all the fields in the Demographics table, using the Columnar layout and Standard style. Title the form "Patient Entry Form."

c. In Form Design view, widen the form to the 6" mark, then move the DOB, Gender, Ins Code, and Entry Date controls to a second column to the right of the existing column. DOB should be next to Last Name.

d. Switch the positions of the State and Zip controls.

e. Modify the Medical Record Number label to MR Number, the Address 1 label to Address, the DOB label to Birthday, and the Ins Code label to Insurance.

f. Change the tab order so State is above Zip.

g. Use the newly created form to add a record using your own personal information. Enter 2000 for the MR Number, BCBS for the Insurance, and 2/1/00 for the Entry Date.

h. Print the form with the new record you just added about yourself.

i. Close the Patient Entry Form, close the Clinic-C database, then exit Access.

2. As office manager of a cardiology clinic you want to build a form that quickly calculates a height to weight ratio value based on information in the Outcomes Data table.

To complete this independent challenge:

a. Open the Clinic-C database from your Project Disk.

b. Using the Form Wizard, create a form based on the Outcomes Data table with only the following fields: MR#, Height, and Weight.

c. Use the Columnar layout and Standard style, and name the form "Height to Weight Ratio Form."

d. In Design view, widen the form to the 4" mark on the horizontal ruler, then add a text box to the right half of the form.

e. Close the Field list if necessary.

f. Enter the expression =[Height]/[Weight] in the unbound text box.

g. Modify the calculated expression's label from Text6: (the number may vary) to Ratio.

h. Resize the Ratio label so that it is closer to the calculated expression control, then right-align the Ratio label.

i. Change the format property of the calculated control to Fixed.

j. Open the form header and enter your name as a label.

k. View the form.

l. Print the form for the record for MR# 006494.

m. Sort the records in descending order by Height, then print the record with the tallest height entry.

n. Close the Height to Weight Ratio Form, close the Clinic-C database, then exit Access.

3. As office manager of a cardiology clinic you want to build a form to enter new insurance information.

To complete this independent challenge:

a. Open the Clinic-C database from your Project Disk.

b. Using the Form Wizard, create a form based on the Insurance Company Information table, and include all of the fields.

c. Use the Columnar layout, Standard style, and accept the default title for the form "Insurance Company Information."

d. Change the label Insurance Company Name to just "Insurance Company."

e. Resize the State text box so that it is the same size as the City text box.

f. Expand the Form Header section, and add the graphic image Medical.bmp found on your Project Disk to the left side of the Form Header section.

g. Add a label "Insurance Entry Form" and another for your name to the right of the medical clip art in the Form Header section.

h. Increase the size of the Insurance Entry Form label to 18 points. Resize the label to display the entire caption.

i. Switch to Form view, then find and print the Cigna record.

j. Filter for all records with a State entry of KS. Print those records.

k. Close the Insurance Company Information Form, close the Clinic-C database, then exit Access.

4. As a new employee in the Market Research department for MediaLoft, you use the World Wide Web to find information on competitors' Web sites, specifically as it relates to Web-based forms.

To complete this independent challenge:

a. Connect to the Internet, use your browser to go to the MediaLoft intranet site at http://www.course.com/illustrated/ MediaLoft, then click the link for the Research Center.

b. Click the link for www.amazon.com, and explore its Web site until you find a Web-based form that requests information about you as a customer or an order that you'd like to place. Print that online form.

c. Use the MediaLoft Research Center to find the home pages of at least three other Internet-based book and/or music stores.

d. Find and print one Web-based data entry form from each of the three sites that you found.
(*Note*: You may have to pretend that you are actually making an online purchase in order to view and print these forms, so be sure to cancel the transaction if you do not intend to purchase any products. Never enter credit card or payment information if you are not serious about finalizing the sale.)

e. Disconnect from the Internet.

f. Draw a sketch to design a form that MediaLoft can use to take orders online. You can use the Music Inventory table in the MediaLoft database as your guide for product information.

g. List all the fields, the data types, and any labels and images for your order form.

Access 2000

► Visual Workshop

Using the Clinic-C database, create the form based on the Demographics table, as shown in Figure C-19. Notice that the label "Patient Form" is 24 points and has been placed in the Form Header section. The clip art, medstaff.bmp, can be found on the Project Disk. The image has been placed on the right side of the Detail section, and many controls had to be resized in order for it to fit. Also notice that the labels are right-aligned. You also need to correct the gender entry for this record.

FIGURE C-19

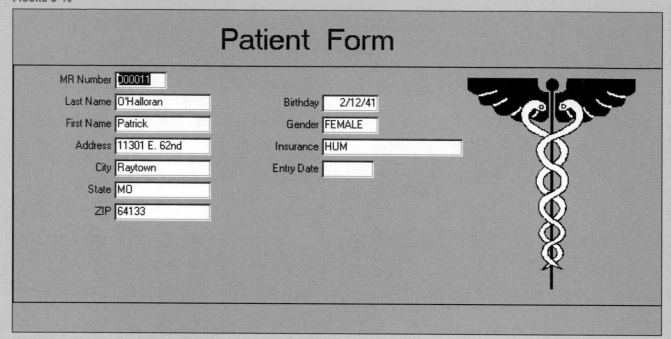

Using

Reports

Objectives

- [MOUS] ▶ **Plan a report**
- [MOUS] ▶ **Create a report**
- [MOUS] ▶ **Group records**
- [MOUS] ▶ **Change the sort order**
- [MOUS] ▶ **Modify an expression**
- [MOUS] ▶ **Align controls**
- [MOUS] ▶ **Format controls**
- ▶ **Create mailing labels**

A **report** is an Access object used to create printouts. You cannot enter or edit data through a report. Although data displayed in a report can be viewed on the screen, it is usually sent to a printer. Access reports can be based on the fields and records of either a table or a query object, can include extensive formatting embellishments such as clip art and lines, and can include professional headers and footers. Reports can also include meaningful calculations such as subtotals on groups of records. John Kim wants to produce reports that he can distribute to MediaLoft employees who do not yet have access to the MediaLoft database.

Planning a Report

Without clear communication, the accuracy and integrity of information being discussed can be questioned, misinterpreted, or obscured. Hard copy reports are often the primary tool used to communicate database information at meetings, with outsiders, and with top executives. Although the **Report Wizard** can help you create an initial report object that you can later modify, the time spent planning your report not only increases your productivity but also ensures that the overall report meets its intended objectives. John has been asked to provide several reports on a regular basis to the MediaLoft executives. He plans his first report that summarizes inventory quantities within each music category.

John uses the following guidelines to plan his report:

Identify a meaningful title for the report

The title should clearly identify the purpose of the report and be meaningful to those who will be reading the report. The title is created with a label control placed in the **Report Header** section. **Sections** are the parts of the report that determine where a control will display on the report. See Table D-1 for more information on report sections. Just like forms, every element on a report is a control.

Determine the information (the fields and records) that the report will show

You can base a report on a table, but usually you create a query to gather the specific fields from the one or more tables upon which to base the report. Of course, using a query also allows you to set criteria to limit the number of records displayed by the report.

Determine how the fields should be laid out on the report

Most reports display fields in a horizontal layout across the page, but you can arrange them in any way you want. Just as in forms, bound text box controls are used on a report to display the data stored in the underlying records. These text boxes are generally placed in the report **Detail** section.

Determine how the records should be sorted and/or grouped within the report

In an Access report, the term **grouping** refers to sorting records *plus* providing a section before the group of records called the **Group Header** section and a section after the group of records called the **Group Footer** section. These sections include additional controls that often contain calculated expressions such as a subtotal for a group of records. The ability to group records is extremely powerful and only available through the report object.

Identify any other descriptive information that should be placed at the end of the report or at the top or bottom of each page

You will use the **Report Footer**, **Page Header**, and **Page Footer** sections for these descriptive controls. John has sketched his first report in Figure D-1.

FIGURE D-1: Sketch of the Quantities Report

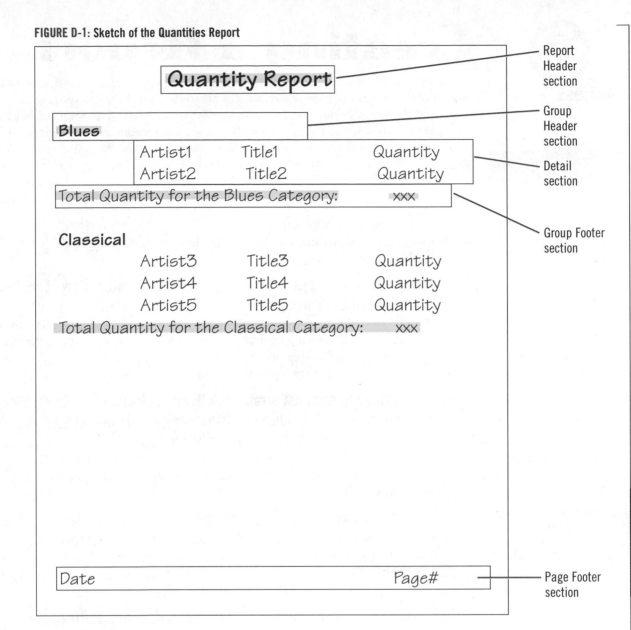

Quantity Report — Report Header section

Blues — Group Header section

| Artist1 | Title1 | Quantity |
| Artist2 | Title2 | Quantity |

Detail section

Total Quantity for the Blues Category: xxx — Group Footer section

Classical

Artist3	Title3	Quantity
Artist4	Title4	Quantity
Artist5	Title5	Quantity

Total Quantity for the Classical Category: xxx

Date   Page# — Page Footer section

TABLE D-1: Report sections

section	where does this section print?	which controls are most commonly placed there?
Report Header	At the top of the first page of the report	Label controls containing the report title; can also include clip art, a logo image, or a line separating the title from the rest of the report
Page Header	At the top of every page (but below the report header on page one)	Descriptive label controls often acting as column headings for text box controls in the Detail section
Group Header	Before every group of records	Text box control for the field by which the records are grouped
Detail	Once for every record	Text box controls for the rest of the fields
Group Footer	After every group of records	Text box controls containing calculated expressions, such as subtotals or counts, for the records in that group
Page Footer	At the bottom of every page	Text box controls containing page number or date expression
Report Footer	At the end of the entire report	Text box controls containing expressions such as grand totals or counts that calculate an answer for all of the records in the report

Creating a Report

You can create reports in Access in **Report Design view**, or you can use the **Report Wizard** to help you get started. The Report Wizard asks questions that guide you through the initial development of the report, similar to the Form Wizard. In addition to questions about which object the report is based, which fields you want to view in the report, and the style and layout of the report, the Report Wizard also asks how you want report records to be grouped and sorted. John uses the Report Wizard to create the Quantities Report he planned on paper.

1. Start Access, click the **Open an existing file option button**, then open the **MediaLoft-D** database from your Project Disk

   This database contains an enhanced Music Inventory table and several queries from which you will base your reports.

2. Click **Reports** on the Objects bar in the MediaLoft-D Database window, then double-click **Create report by using wizard**

   The Report Wizard dialog box opens. You'll use the Selection Quantities query for this report. Another way to quickly create a report is by selecting a table or query, clicking the New Object list arrow on the Database toolbar and then selecting AutoReport. AutoReport, however, does not give you a chance to review the options provided by the Report Wizard.

3. Click the **Tables/Queries list arrow**, click **Query: Selection Quantities**, click **Category** in the Available Fields list, click the **Select Single Field button** > , click **Title**, click > , click **Artist**, click > , click **Quantity**, then click >

   The first dialog box of the Report Wizard should look like Figure D-2. The Report Wizard also asks grouping and sorting questions that determine the order and amount of detail provided on the report.

   > **Trouble?**
   > You can always click Back to review previous dialog boxes within a wizard.

4. Click **Next**, click **Next** to move past the grouping levels question, click the **first sort order list arrow** in the sort order dialog box, then click **Category**

   At this point you have not specified any grouping fields, but specified that you want the fields sorted by Category. You can use the Report Wizard to specify up to four sort fields in either an ascending or descending sort order for each field.

5. Click **Next**, click **Next** to accept the **Tabular** layout and **Portrait** orientation, click **Corporate** for the style, click **Next**, type **Quantities Report** for the report title, verify that the **Preview the report option button** is selected, then click **Finish**

   The Quantities Report opens in Print Preview, as shown in Figure D-3. It is very similar to the sketch created earlier. Notice that the records are sorted by the Category field.

Why reports should be based on queries

Although you can use the first dialog box of the Report Wizard to select fields from different tables without first creating a query to collect those fields into one object, it is not recommended. If you later decide that you want to add more fields to the report or limit the number of records in the table, you will find it very easy to add fields or criteria to an underlying query object to meet these new needs. To accomplish this same task without using an intermediary query object requires that you change the properties of the report itself, which most users find more difficult.

FIGURE D-2: First Report Wizard dialog box

Base the report on the Selection Quantities query

Select Single Field button

Fields selected for the report

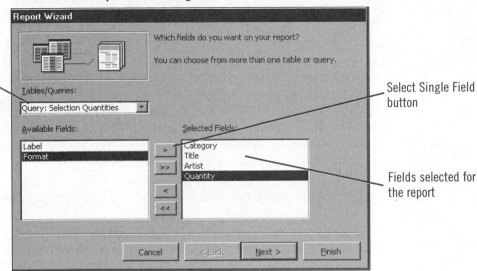

Report Header

Page Header

FIGURE D-3: Quantities Report in Print Preview

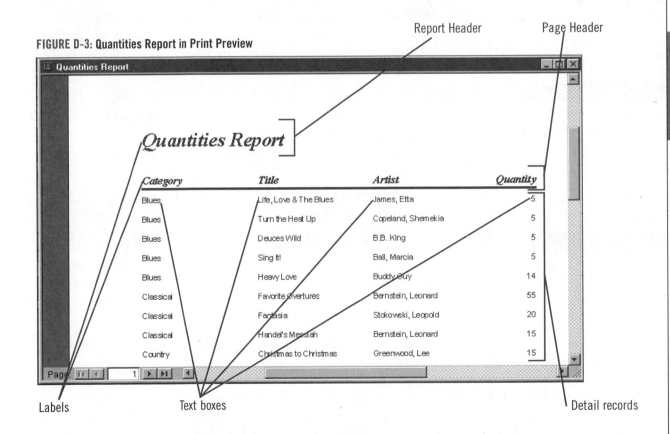

Labels

Text boxes

Detail records

Grouping Records

Grouping refers to sorting records on a report *plus* providing an area above and below the group of records in which additional controls can be placed. These two sections of the report are called the Group Header and Group Footer. You can create groups on a report through the Report Wizard, or you can change an existing report's grouping and sorting fields in Report Design view. Just as with forms, you make all structural changes to a report in the object's Design view.
John wants to group the Quantities Report by Category instead of simply sorting it by Category. In addition, he wants to add controls to the Group Header and Group Footer to clarify and summarize information within the report.

Steps

Trouble?

If a property has a predetermined set of options, a list arrow will display when you click that property's text box in the property sheet.

1. Click the **Design View button** on the Print Preview toolbar to switch to Report Design view, as shown in Figure D-4
   Report Design view shows you the sections of the report as well as the controls within each section. Labels and text boxes are formatted similarly in Report Design view. You can click a control and then click the Properties button to view the title bar of the property sheet to determine the nature of a control. Report Design view is where you change grouping and sort fields.

2. Click the **Sorting and Grouping button** on the Report Design toolbar, click the **Group Header text box**, click the **Group Header list arrow**, click **Yes**, click the **Group Footer text box**, click the **Group Footer list arrow**, then click **Yes**
   Specifying "Yes" for the Group Header and Group Footer properties opens those sections of the report in Report Design view.

3. Click to close the dialog box, click the **Category text box** in the Detail section, then drag the **textbox** with the pointer directly up into the Category Header section
   By placing the Category text box in the Category Header, it will print once for each new group rather than once for each record. You can add calculated subtotal controls for each category of records by placing a text box in the Category Footer section.

QuickTip

The Field list, Toolbox toolbar, and property sheet may or may not be visible, but you can turn them on and off by clicking their respective toggle buttons. You can move them by dragging their title bars.

4. If the Toolbox toolbar is not visible, click the **Toolbox button** on the Report Design toolbar, click the **Text Box button** on the Toolbox toolbar, then click in the **Category Footer section** directly below the Quantity text box
   Your screen should look like Figure D-5. You can use the label and text box controls in the Category Footer section to describe and subtotal the Quantity field respectively.

5. Click the **Text13: label** in the Category Footer section to select it, double-click **Text13**, type **Subtotal**, then press **[Enter]**

Trouble?

If you double-click the edge of a control, you open the control's property sheet.

6. Click the **unbound text box control** in the Category Footer section to select it, click the **unbound text box control** again to edit it, then type **=sum([Quantity])**
   The expression that calculates the sum of the Quantity field is now in the unbound text box control. Calculated expressions start with an equal sign. When entering an expression, the field name must be referenced exactly and surrounded by square brackets.

7. Click the **Print Preview button** on the Report Design toolbar, then scroll through the report as necessary
   The new report that groups and summarizes records by Category appears, as shown in Figure D-6. Since the Category text box was moved to the Category Header section, it prints only once per group of records. Each group of records is trailed by a Group Footer that includes the Subtotal label as well as a calculated field that subtotals the Quantity field.

8. Click **Close** on the Print Preview toolbar, click the **Save button**, then click the **Quantities Report Close button** to close the report
   The Quantities Report is now an object in the MediaLoft-D Database window.

FIGURE D-4: Quantities Report Design view

Field List button

Toolbox button

Sorting and Grouping button

Properties button

Sections

Labels

Toolbox toolbar

Text boxes

Field list

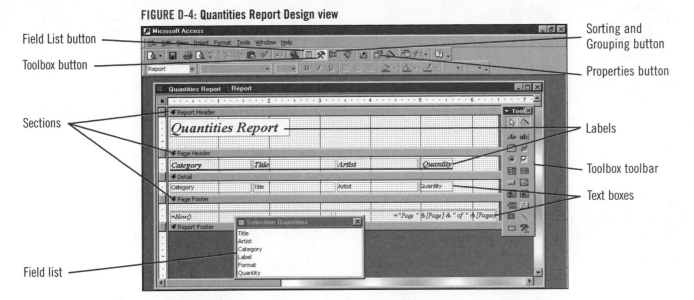

FIGURE D-5: Adding controls to the group footer section

Text Box button

Category Header

Category text box moved up from Detail section into Category Header section

New text box

Category Footer

New label

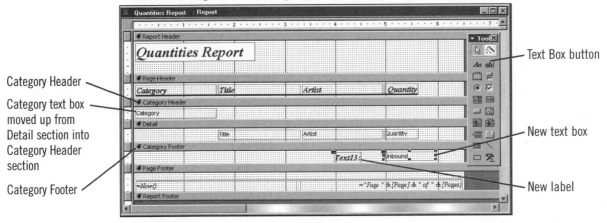

FIGURE D-6: The Quantities Report grouped by Category

Report Header

Page Header

Group Header (Category is the grouping field)

Detail

Group Footer (Category is the grouping field)

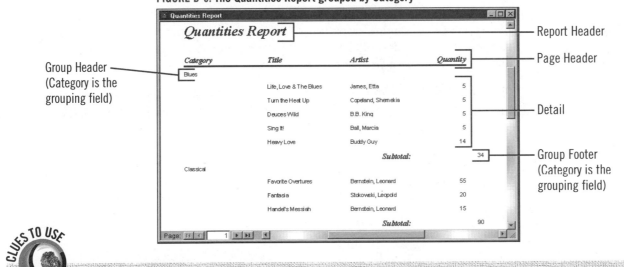

Adding a field to a report

Clicking the Field List button 🔲 on the Report Design toolbar toggles the field list of the underlying table or query object. To add a field from this list to the report, simply drag it from the Field list to the appropriate position on the report. This action creates both a label control that displays the field name and a text box control that displays the value of the field from the underlying records.

Access 2000

Changing the Sort Order

Grouping records is really just sorting them with the additional ability to create a Group Header or Group Footer section on the report. The grouping field acts as a primary sort field. You can define further sort fields too. When you further sort records within a group, you order the Detail records according to a particular field. The Report Wizard prompts you for group and sort information at the time you create the report, but you can also group and sort an existing report by using the Sorting and Grouping dialog box in Report Design view. ◢◣◥ John wants to modify the Quantities Report so that the Detail records are sorted by the Artist field within the Category group.

Steps 1234

1. **Click the Quantities Report in the MediaLoft-D Database window, then click the Design button** 🖳
   The Quantities Report opens in Report Design view.

2. **Click the Sorting and Grouping button** 🖽 **on the Report Design toolbar, click the second row Field/Expression text box, click the Field/Expression list arrow, then click Artist**
   The Sorting and Grouping dialog box looks like Figure D-7. There is no Sorting and Grouping indicator in the Artist row selector. Both the Group Header and Group Footer Group properties are "No" which indicates that the Artist field is providing a sort order only.

3. **Click** 🖽 **to toggle the Sorting and Grouping dialog box off, then click the Print Preview button** 🔍 **on the Report Design toolbar**
   Part of the report is shown in Print Preview, as shown in Figure D-8. You can use the buttons on the Print Preview toolbar to view more of the report.

4. **Click the One Page button** ▣ **on the Print Preview toolbar to view one miniature page, click the Two Pages button** ▦ **to view two miniature pages, click the Multiple Pages button** ▦ **, then drag to 1x4 Pages in the grid as shown in Figure D-9**
   The Print Preview window displays the four pages of the report in miniature. Regardless of the zoom magnification of the pages, however, you can click the **Zoom pointer** 🔍 to quickly toggle between two zoom magnifications.

5. **Point to the last subtotal on the last page of the report with the** 🔍 **pointer, click to read the number 92, then click again to return the report to its former four-page magnification level**

6. **Click the Close button on the Print Preview toolbar, then click the Save button** 💾 **on the Report Design toolbar**

FIGURE D-7: Specifying a sort order

Sorting and Grouping indicator

Ascending sort order

Grouping sections are turned off for the Artist field

Field/Expression list arrow

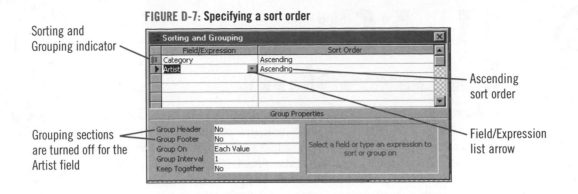

FIGURE D-8: The Quantities Report sorted by Artist

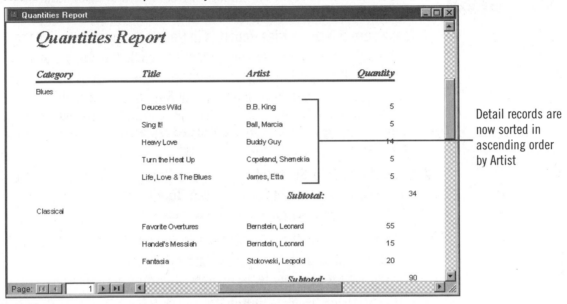

Detail records are now sorted in ascending order by Artist

FIGURE D-9: Print Preview

One Page button

Two Pages button

Multiple Pages button

Drag to 1x4 Pages

Currently viewing two pages

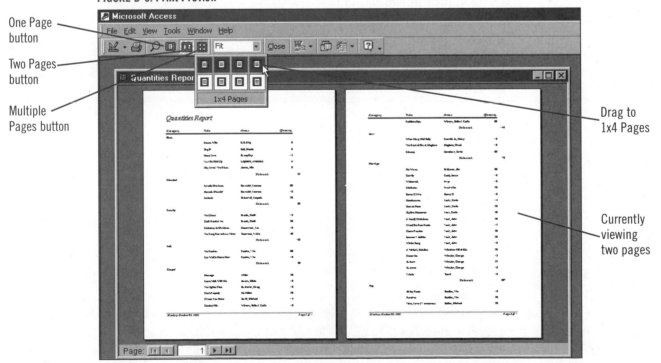

Modifying an Expression

An **expression** is a combination of fields, operators (such as +, -, / and *) and functions that result in a single value. A **function** is a built-in formula provided by Access that helps you quickly create a calculated expression. See Table D-2 for examples of common expressions that use Access functions. Notice that every calculated expression starts with an equal sign, and when it uses a function, the arguments for the function are placed in parentheses. **Arguments** are the pieces of information that the function needs to create the final answer. Calculated expressions are entered in text box controls. ➤ John adds a calculated expression to the Quantities Report that uses the Count function to count the number of records within each music category.

Steps

1. Make sure the Quantities Report is in Report Design view, click the **=Sum([Quantity])**
   text box in the Category Footer section, click the **Copy button** 🖺 on the Report
   Design toolbar, click in a **blank area** in the left part of the Category Footer section,
   then click the **Paste button** 🖺 on the Report Design toolbar
   The text box and accompanying label are copied and pasted, as shown in Figure D-10.
   Modifying a copy of the existing calculated expression control helps reduce errors and saves
   on keystrokes.

2. Click the copied **Subtotal label** in the Category Footer section to select it, double-
   click **Subtotal** to select the text, type **Count**, then press **[Enter]**
   The label is only descriptive text. The text box is the control that actually calculates the count.

3. Click the copy of the **=Sum([Quantity]) text box** to select it, double-click **Sum** to
   select it, type **count**, then press **[Enter]**
   The expression now counts the number of records in each group.

4. Click the **Print Preview button** 🖺 on the Report Design toolbar to view the updated
   report, click the **One Page button** 🖺 on the Print Preview toolbar, then scroll and
   zoom as shown in Figure D-11

FIGURE D-10: Copying and pasting a calculated control

Copy button

Paste button

New label control

New text box control

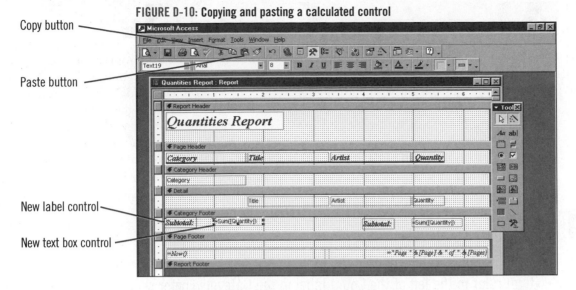

FIGURE D-11: Previewing the Count calculated control

New label control

New text box control

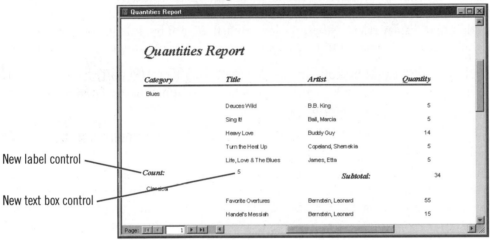

TABLE D-2: Common Access expressions

category	sample expression	description
Arithmetic	=[Price]*1.05	Multiplies the Price field by 1.05 (adds 5% to the Price field)
Arithmetic	=[Subtotal]+[Shipping]	Adds the value of the Subtotal field to the value of the Shipping field
Page Number	=[Page]	Displays the current page number, such as 5, 6, or 10
Page Number	="Page "&[Page]	Displays the word "Page," a space, and the current page number, such as Page 5, Page 6, or Page 10
Text	=[FirstName]&" "&[LastName]	Displays the value of the FirstName and LastName fields in one control separated by a space
Text	=Left([ProductNumber],2)	Uses the **Left** function to display the first two characters in the ProductNumber field
Aggregate	=Avg([Freight])	Uses the **Avg** function to display an average of the values in the Freight field
Aggregate	=Count([FirstName])	Uses the **Count** function to display the number of records that contain an entry in the FirstName field
Aggregate	=Sum([Tracks])	Uses the **Sum** function to display the total value from the Tracks field
Date	=Date()	Uses the **Date** function to display the current date in the form of mm-dd-yy, such as 10-23-00 or 11-14-01

Aligning Controls

Once the information that you want to present has been added to the appropriate section of a report, you may also want to rearrange the data on the report. By aligning controls in columns and rows, you can present your information so it is easier to understand. There are several **alignment** commands that are important to understand. You can left-, right-, or center-align a control *within its own border*, or you can align the edges of controls *with respect to one another*. ◄▬▬ John aligns several controls on the Quantities Report to improve the readability and professionalism of the report. His first task is to right-align all of the controls in the Category Footer.

Steps

1. Click the **Design View button** on the Print Preview toolbar, then click in the vertical ruler to the left of the Count label in the Category Footer section
   All four controls in the Category Footer section are selected. Text boxes that display numeric fields are right-aligned by default; the labels and text boxes you added in the Category Footer section that display calculated expressions are left-aligned by default. You can use the same techniques for selecting controls in Report Design view as you did in Form Design view.

2. Click the **Align Right button** on the Formatting (Form/Report) toolbar
   Your screen should look like Figure D-12. Now the information displayed by the control is right-aligned within the control.

3. With the four controls still selected, click **Format** on the menu bar, point to **Align**, then click **Bottom**
   The bottom edges of the four controls are now aligned with respect to one another. The Align command on the Format menu refers to aligning controls with respect to one another. The Alignment buttons on the Formatting toolbar refer to aligning controls within their own borders. You can also align the right or left edges of controls in different sections.

4. Click the **Quantity label** in the Page Header section, press and hold [Shift], click the **Quantity text box** in the Detail section, click the **=Sum([Quantity])** text box in the Category Footer section, release [Shift], click **Format** on the menu bar, point to **Align**, then click **Right**
   The right edges of the Quantity label, Quantity text box, and Quantity calculated controls are aligned. With the edges at the same position and the information right-aligned within the controls, the controls form a perfect column on the final report. You can extend the line in the Page Header section to better define the sections on the page.

Trouble?

Don't drag beyond the 6"
mark or the printout will be
wider than one sheet of paper.

5. Click the **blue line** in the Page Header section, press and hold [Shift], point to the **right sizing handle**, when the pointer changes to ↘, drag the handle to the **6" mark**, then release [Shift]
   By pressing [Shift] when you draw or resize a line, the line remains perfectly horizontal as you drag it left or right.

6. Click the **Print Preview button** on the Report Design toolbar, then scroll and zoom
   Your screen should look like Figure D-13.

FIGURE D-12: Working with the alignment buttons

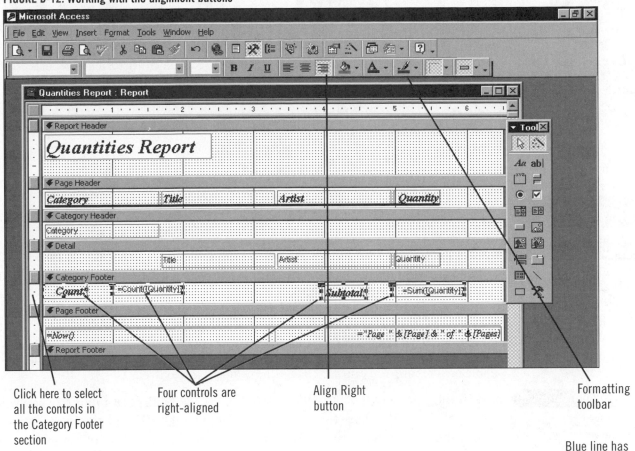

Click here to select
all the controls in
the Category Footer
section

Four controls are
right-aligned

Align Right
button

Formatting
toolbar

FIGURE D-13: Controls are aligned

Blue line has
been widened

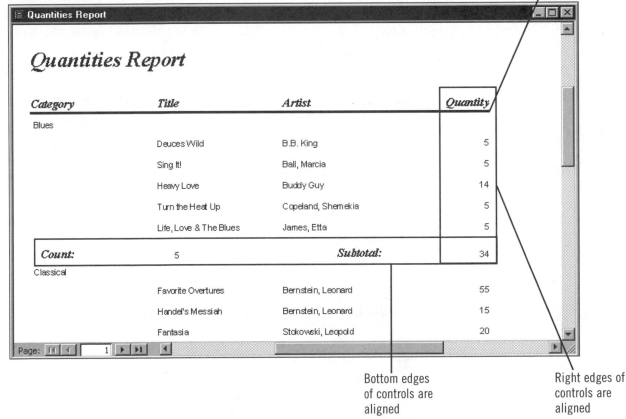

Bottom edges
of controls are
aligned

Right edges of
controls are
aligned

Formatting Controls

Formatting refers to enhancing the appearance of the information. Table D-3 lists several of the most popular formatting commands which can be used with either forms or reports. Although the Report Wizard provides many formatting embellishments on a report, you often want to improve upon the report's appearance to fit your particular needs. ✏ John doesn't feel that the music category information is prominent on the report, so he wants to format that control to change its appearance.

Steps

1. Click the **Design View button** 🖾 on the Print Preview toolbar, click the **Toolbox button** 🛠 to toggle it off, then click the **Category text box** in the Category Header section
   Before you can format any control, it must be selected.

2. Click the **Font size list arrow** on the Formatting (Form/Report) toolbar, click **11**, then click the **Bold button** 🄱
   Increasing the font size and applying bold are common ways to make information more visible on a report. You can also change the colors of the control.

3. With the Category text box still selected, click the **Font/Fore Color list arrow** 🄰▾, then click the **Red box** (third row, first column on the left), as shown in Figure D-14
   Many buttons on the Formatting (Form/Report) toolbar include a list arrow that you can click to reveal a list of choices. When you click the color list arrow, a palette of available colors is displayed. You can change the background color of the Category text box using the palette.

4. With the Category text box still selected, click the **Fill/Back Color list arrow** 🎨▾, then click the **light gray box** (fourth row, first column on the right)
   When you print colors on a black and white printer, they become various shades of gray. So unless you always print to a color printer, be careful about relying too heavily on color formatting, especially background shades that often become solid black boxes when printed on a black and white printer or fax machine. Fortunately, Access allows you to undo your last command if you don't like the change you've made. You must pay close attention, however, because you can only undo your very last command.

5. With the Category text box still selected, click the **Undo button** ↶ on the Report Design toolbar to remove the background color, click the **Line/Border Color list arrow** ✎▾, then click the **blue box** (second row, third column from right)

6. Click the **Print Preview button** 🔍 on the Report Design toolbar
   The screen should look like Figure D-15.

7. Click **File** on the menu bar, click **Print**, type **1** in the From text box, type **1** in the To text box, click **OK**, then click **Close** on the Print Preview toolbar
   The first page of the report is printed.

8. Click the **Save button** 💾, then close the Quantities Report

FIGURE D-14: Working with color formats

Bold button

Fill/Back Color button

Font/Fore Color button

Category text box is selected

Line/Border Color button

Blue

Light gray

Red

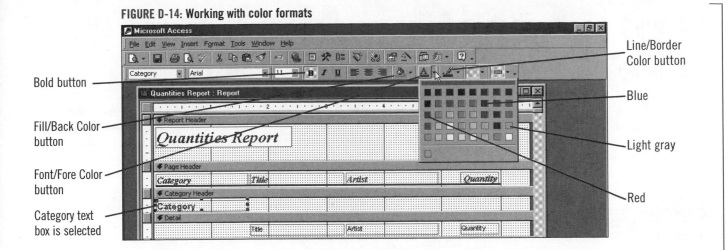

FIGURE D-15: Formatted Quantities Report

Category text box has been formatted

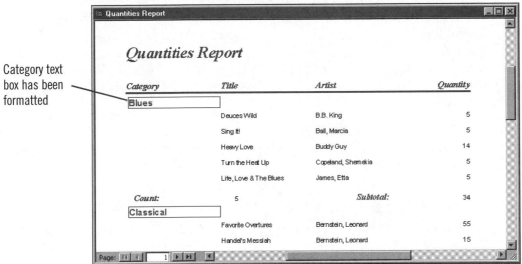

TABLE D-3: Popular formatting commands

button	button name	description
B	Bold	Toggles bold on or off for the selected control(s)
I	Italic	Toggles italics, on or off for the selected control(s)
U	Underline	Toggles underline on or off for the selected control(s)
≡	Align Left	Left-aligns the selected control(s) within its own border
≡	Center	Center-aligns the selected control(s) within its own border
≡	Align Right	Right-aligns the selected control(s) within its own border
🖍 ▾	Fill/Back Color	Changes the background color of the selected control(s)
A ▾	Font/Fore Color	Changes the text color of the selected control(s)
✐ ▾	Line/Border Color	Changes the border color of the selected control(s)
☐ ▾	Line/Border Width	Changes the style of the border of the selected control(s)
▭ ▾	Special Effect	Changes the special visual effect of the selected control(s)

Access 2000

Creating Mailing Labels

Mailing Labels are used for many business purposes such as identifying paper folders and providing addresses for mass mailings. Once you enter raw data into your Access database, you can easily create mailing labels from this data using the **Label Wizard**. John has been asked to create labels for the display cases in the MediaLoft stores with the Artist and Title fields only. The labels are to be printed in alphabetical order by Artist and then by Title. John uses the Label Wizard to get started.

Trouble?

If you don't see Avery, click English units of measure, click the Filter by manufacturer list arrow, then click Avery.

1. Click **Reports** on the Objects bar in the MediaLoft-D Database window, click the **New button** , click **Label Wizard** in the New Report dialog box, click the **Choose the table or query where the object's data comes from list arrow**, click **Music Inventory**, then click **OK**

   The Label Wizard dialog box opens requesting that you specify information about the characteristics of the label, as shown in Figure D-16. Avery 5160 labels are one of the most popular sizes. Avery 5160 label sheets have three columns and ten rows of labels for a total of 30 labels per page.

2. Click **5160**, then click **Next**

   The next wizard dialog box allows you to change the font, font size, and other text attributes. Larger fonts will be easier to read and will fit on this label since there are only two fields of information.

Trouble?

If your system doesn't have the Comic Sans MS font, choose another font appropriate for music labels.

3. Click the **Font size list arrow**, click **11**, click the **Font name list arrow**, scroll and click **Comic Sans MS** (a sample appears in the Sample box), then click **Next**

   The next wizard dialog box, which shows you the prototype label, allows you choose which fields you want to include in each label as well as their placement. Any spaces or punctuation that you want on the label must be entered from the keyboard. Also, if you want to put a field on a new line, you must press [Enter] to move to a new row of the prototype label.

QuickTip

You can double-click the field name in the Available Fields list to move it to the Prototype label list.

4. Click **Artist**, click the **Select Single Field button** , press [Enter], click **Title**, then click

   Your screen should look like Figure D-17.

5. Click **Next**

   The next wizard dialog box asks about sorting.

6. Double-click **Artist** for your primary sort field, double-click **Title** for your secondary sort field, then click **Next**

   You should give your labels a descriptive name.

7. Type **Artist-Title Labels** to name the report, click **Finish**, then click the **Zoom pointer** to see a full page of labels

   The labels should look like Figure D-18.

8. Click **Close** on the Print Preview toolbar to see the Artist-Title Labels report in Design view, click the **Save button** , then click the **Print button**

9. Click **File** on the menu bar, then click **Exit** to exit Access

FIGURE D-16: Label Wizard

Avery 5160
label type

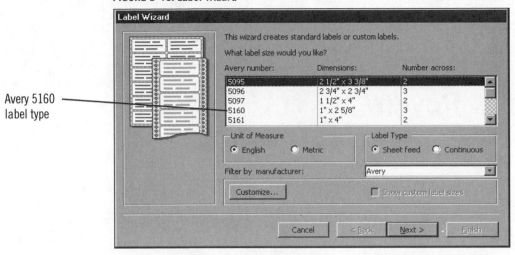

FIGURE D-17: The prototype label

Select Single Field
button

Artist field

Title field

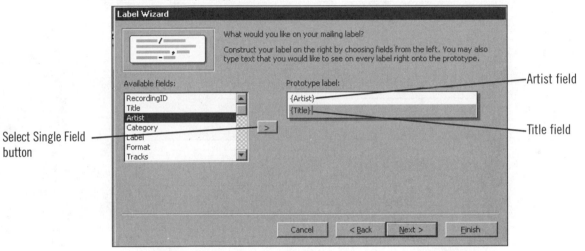

FIGURE D-18: The Artist-Title Labels report

Labels are
3 columns by
10 rows on
each page

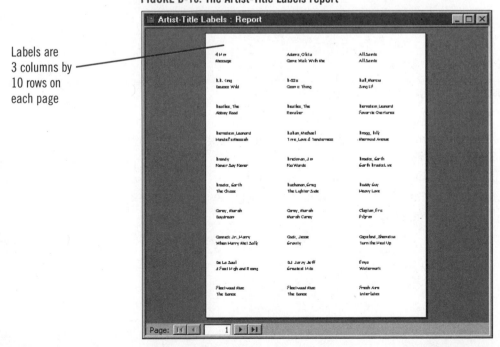

Practice

▶ Concepts Review

Label each element of the Report Design window shown in Figure D-19.

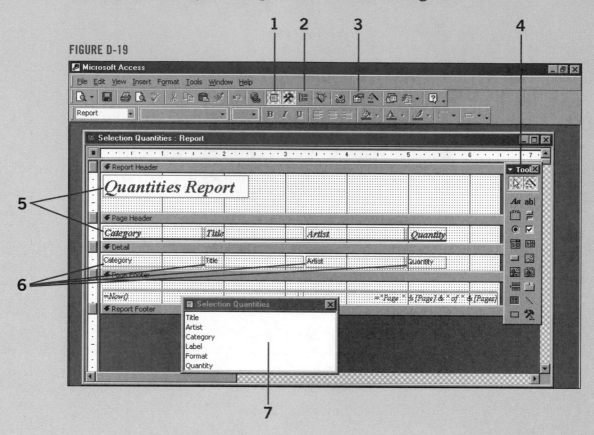

FIGURE D-19

Match each term with the statement that describes it.

8. Function	a. Part of the report that determines where a control will display on the report
9. Section	b. Sorting records *plus* providing a section before and after the group of records
10. Detail section	c. An Access object used to create paper printouts
11. Report	d. Enhancing the appearance of the information
12. Formatting	e. A built-in formula provided by Access that helps you quickly create a calculated expression
13. Grouping	f. Prints once for every record

Select the best answer from the list of choices.

14. Press and hold which key to select more than one control in Report Design view?
    a. [Ctrl]
    b. [Alt]
    c. [Shift]
    d. [Tab]

15. Which type of control is most likely found in the Detail section?
    a. Label
    b. Text box
    c. Combo box
    d. List box

16. Which type of control is most likely found in the Page Header section?
    a. Label
    b. Combo box
    c. Command button
    d. Bound image

17. A calculated expression is most often found in which report section?
    a. Report Header
    b. Detail
    c. Formulas
    d. Group Footer

18. Which of the following would be the appropriate expression to count the number of records using the FirstName field?
    a. =Count(FirstName)
    b. =Count[FirstName)
    c. =Count{FirstName}
    d. =Count([FirstName])

19. To align the edges of several controls with respect to one another, you use the alignment commands on the
    a. Formatting toolbar.
    b. Standard toolbar.
    c. Print Preview toolbar.
    d. Format menu.

▶ Skills Review

1. Plan a report.

a. Pretend that you are looking for a job. Plan a report to use for tracking job opportunities. To gather the raw data for your report, find a newspaper with job listings in your area of interest.

b. Identify the Report Header, Group Header, and Detail sections of the report by using sample data based on the following information:

- The title of the report should be "Job Opportunity Report."
- The records should be grouped by job title. For example, if you are interested in working with computers, job titles might be "Computer Operator" or "Computer Analyst." Include at least two job title groupings in your sample report.
- The Detail section should include information on the company, contact, and telephone number for each job opportunity.

2. Create a report.

a. Start Access and open the Club-D database on your Project Disk.

b. Use the Report Wizard to create a report based on the Contacts table.

c. Include the following fields for the report:
STATUS, FNAME, LNAME, DUESOWED, DUESPAID

d. Do not add any grouping or sorting fields.

e. Use the Tabular layout and Portrait orientation.

f. Use a bold style and title the report "Contact Status Report."

g. Preview the first page of the new report.

3. Group records.

a. In Report Design view, open the Sorting and Grouping dialog box, and group the report by the STATUS field in ascending order. Open both the Group Header and Group Footer sections, then close the dialog box.

b. Move the STATUS text box in the Detail section up to the left edge of the STATUS Header section.

c. Preview the first page of the new report.

4. Change the sort order.

a. In Report Design view, open the Sorting and Grouping dialog box, then add LNAME as a sort field in ascending order immediately below the STATUS field.

b. Preview the first page of the new report.

5. Modify an expression.

a. In Report Design view, add a text box control in the STATUS Footer section directly below the DUESOWED text box in the Detail section.

b. Delete the accompanying label to the left of the unbound text box.

c. Add a text box control in the STATUS Footer section directly below the DUESPAID text box in the Detail section.

d. Delete the accompanying label to the left of the unbound text box by clicking the label, then pressing [Delete].

e. Add an unbound label to the report header, and type your name as the label.

f. Modify the text boxes so that they subtotal the DUESOWED and DUESPAID fields respectively. The calculated expressions will be =Sum([DUESOWED]) and =Sum([DUESPAID]).

g. Preview both pages of the report, then print both pages of the report.

6. Align controls.

  a. In Report Design view, right-align the new calculated controls in the STATUS Footer section.

  b. Select the DUESOWED text box in the Detail section, and the =Sum([DUESOWED]) calculated expression in the STATUS Footer, then right-align the controls with respect to one another.

  c. Select the DUESPAID text box in the Detail section, and the =Sum([DUESPAID]) calculated expression in the STATUS Footer, then right-align the controls with respect to one another.

7. Format controls.

  a. Select the two calculated controls in the STATUS Footer, click the Properties button, then change the Format property on the Format tab to Currency. Close the property sheet.

  b. Select the STATUS text box in the STATUS Header section, change the font size to 12 points, bold and italicize the control, then change the background color to bright yellow.

  c. Preview the report, check the new totals, save the report, print it, then close the report.

8. Create mailing labels.

  a. Use the Label Wizard and the Contacts table to create mailing labels using Avery 5160 labels.

  b. The text should be formatted as Arial, 10 points, Light font weight, black, with no italic or underline attributes.

  c. The prototype label should be organized as follows:

    FNAME LNAME

    COMPANY

    STREET

    CITY, STATE ZIP

  d. Sort the labels by the ZIP field.

  e. Name the report "Mailing Labels."

  f. Print the first page of the labels, save the report, then close it.

  g. Exit Access.

► Independent Challenges

1. You have been hired to create several reports for a physical therapy clinic.
To complete this independent challenge:

a. Start Access and open the Therapy-D database from your Project Disk.

b. Using the Report Wizard, create a report using all of the fields from the Location Financial Query.

c. View your data by Survey, group by Street, sort in ascending order by PatientLast, and sum both the AmountSent and AmountRecorded fields.

d. Use the Stepped layout, Portrait orientation, and Soft Gray style.

e. Name the report "Location Financial Report."

f. Modify the AmountSent and AmountRecorded labels in the Page Header section to "Sent" and "Recorded" respectively.

g. Change the font/fore color of the labels in the Page Header section to bright blue.

h. Widen the Street text box label in the Street Header section to twice its current size, and change the border color to bright blue.

i. Save and print the report.

j. Exit Access.

2. You have been hired to create several reports for a physical therapy clinic.
To complete this independent challenge:

a. Start Access and open the Therapy-D database from your Project Disk.

b. Using the Report Wizard, create a report using all of the fields from the Therapist Satisfaction Query except for the Initials and First fields.

c. View the data by Survey. Do not add any grouping levels and do not add any sorting levels.

d. Use the Tabular layout, Portrait orientation, and Casual style.

e. Title the report "Therapist Satisfaction Report," then print the report.

f. In Report Design view, group the report by Last, and open both the Group Header and Group Footer sections.

g. Further sort the records by PatientLast.

h. Move the Last text box from the Detail section up into the Last Header section.

i. Remove bold from all of the labels in the Page Header section.

j. Add text boxes in the Last Footer section directly below the Courtesy and Knowledge text boxes in the Detail section. Enter the calculated controls =Avg([Courtesy]) and =Avg([Knowledge]) respectively. Delete their accompanying labels, and resize the new calculated controls so that they are a little narrower than the Courtesy and Knowledge text boxes in the Detail section.

k. Open the property sheet for the two new calculated controls, and change the Format property on the Format tab to "Fixed."

l. Right-align the two new calculated controls within their own borders. Also, align the right edge of the =Avg([Courtesy]) control with respect to the Courtesy text box in the Detail section. Right-align the edges of the =Avg([Knowledge]) and Knowledge text boxes with respect to each other.

m. Align the top edges of the new calculated controls.

n. Drag the right edge of the report to the left so the report is 6½" wide (if necessary).

o. Save, preview, and print the report.

p. Exit Access.

3. Use the knowledge and skills that you have acquired about Access to create an attractive report that includes information about colleges and universities that offer programs in computer science. Create a database containing this information, and then design a report that displays the data. Gather information from libraries, friends, and the Web to enter into the database.

To complete this independent challenge:

a. Start Access and create a new database called "Colleges" on your Project Disk. Include any fields you feel are important, but make sure you include the institution's name, state, and whether it is a 4- or 2-year school.

b. Find information on schools that offer programs in computer science. If you are using the Web, use any available search engines.

c. Compile a list of at least 15 institutions, and enter the 15 records into a table named "Computer Science Schools."

d. Create a report that includes all the fields in the table Computer Science Schools, and group by the field that contains the information on whether it is a 4- or 2-year school.

e. Sort the records in ascending order by the state, then by the institution's name.

f. Use an appropriate style and title for your report. Insert your initials at the end of the report title so you can identify it.

g. Save, preview, and print the report.

h. Exit Access.

4. As an assistant in the marketing department at MediaLoft, you are often asked to create mailing labels for the MediaLoft store locations. You have decided to create a small database that stores information about the stores so that you can quickly create the labels using the Label Wizard.

To complete this independent challenge:

a. Start Access and create a new database on your Project Disk called "MediaLoft Locations."

b. Connect to the Internet, use your browser to go to the MediaLoft intranet site at http://www.course.com/illustrated/MediaLoft, then click the About link for the page with the MediaLoft store locations.

c. Print the Web page that displays the store locations.

d. Disconnect from the Internet, and switch to the Access window.

e. Create a table called "Stores" with the following fields (each field's data type should be Text): StoreName, Street, City, State, Zip, Phone

f. Using the Stores datasheet, type each store location into the database. Pay close attention to capitalization and spelling.

g. Using the Label Wizard, create mailing labels with the store address information on Avery 5160 labels.

h. Format the label with any decorative font, a 12-point font size, and bright red text.

i. Use the following label prototype:
StoreName
Street
City, State Zip

j. Name the label report "Store Address Labels," and print the report.

k. Save and close the report, then exit Access.

Access 2000

► Visual Workshop

Use the Club-D database on your Project Disk to create the report based on the CONTACTS table shown in Figure D-20. The Report Wizard and the Corporate style were used to create this report. Note that the records are grouped by the CITY field and sorted within each group by the LNAME field. A calculated control that counts the number of records is displayed in the Group Footer.

FIGURE D-20

Membership by City

CITY	LNAME	FNAME	PHONE
Bridgewater			
	Daniels	Mark	555-2277
Count: 1			
Fontanelle			
	Eagan	Jane	555-1166
Count: 1			
Industrial Airport			
	Braven	Mary	555-7002
Count: 1			
Kansas City			
	Alman	Jill	555-6931
	Bouchart	Bob	555-3081
	Collins	Christine	555-3602
	Diverman	Barbara	555-0401
	Duman	Mary Jane	555-8844
	Eahle	Andrea	555-0401
	Eckert	Jay	555-7414
	Hammer	Mike	555-0365
	Hubert	Holly	555-6004
	Mackintosh	Helen	555-9414
	Mayberry	Mitch	555-0401
	Olson	Marcie	555-1388
	Parton	Jeanette	555-8773
	Walker	Shirley	555-0403
Count: 14			

Modifying
a Database Structure

Objectives

- ▶ **Examine relational databases**
- ▶ **Plan related tables**
- ▶ **Create related tables**
- ▶ **Define Text field properties**
- ▶ **Define Number and Currency fields**
- ▶ **Define Date/Time and Yes/No fields**
- ▶ **Define field validation properties**
- ▶ **Create one-to-many relationships**

In this unit, you will add new tables to an existing database and link them in one-to-many relationships to create a relational database. You will also modify several field properties such as field formatting and field validation to increase data entry accuracy. ▰ David Dumont, director of training at MediaLoft, has created an Access database to track the courses attended by MediaLoft employees. Courses include hands-on computer classes, business seminars, and self-improvement workshops. Because a single-table database will not meet all of his needs, he will use multiple tables of data and link them together to create a relational database.

Examining Relational Databases

A **relational database** is a collection of related tables that share information. The goals of a relational database are to satisfy dynamic information management needs and to eliminate duplicate data entry wherever possible.  MediaLoft employees have tried to track course attendance using a Training database in a single Access table called "Attendance Log," as shown in Figure E-1. Although only four records are shown in this sample, David sees a data redundancy problem because there are multiple occurrences of the same employee and same course information. He knows that data redundancy in one table is a major clue that the database needs to be redesigned. Therefore, David studies the principles of relational database design.

 A relational database is based on multiple tables of data. Each table should be based on only one subject

Right now the Attendance Log table in the Training database contains three subjects: Courses, Attendance, and Employees. Therefore, you have to duplicate several fields of information in this table every time an employee takes a course. Redundant data in one table creates a need for a relational database.

 Each record in a table should be uniquely identified with a key field or key field combination

A **key field** is a field that contains unique information for each record. Typically, an employee table contains an Employee Identification (EmployeeID) field to uniquely identify each employee. Often, the Social Security Number (SSN) field serves this purpose. Although using the employee's last name as the key field might accommodate a small database, it is a poor choice because the user cannot enter two employees with the same last name.

 Tables in the same database should be related, or linked, through a common field in a one-to-many relationship

To tie the information from one table to another, a single field of data must be common to each table. This common field will be the key field in one of the tables, creating the "one" side of the relationship; the field data will be listed "many" times in the other table, creating a **one-to-many relationship**. Table E-1 shows common examples of one-to-many relationships between two database tables.

Attendance Log

Course Description	Prerequisite	Date	Employee
Internet Fundamentals	Computer Fundamentals	2/7/2000	Maria Abbott
Internet Fundamentals	Computer Fundamentals	2/7/2000	Lauren Alber
Introduction to Access	Computer Fundamentals	3/6/2000	Maria Abbott
Introduction to Access	Computer Fundamentals	3/6/2000	Lauren Alber

Redundant data is shaded the same color

Redundant data is shaded the same color

Access 2000

TABLE E-1: One-to-many relationships

table on "one" side of relationship	table on "many" side of relationship	linking field	description
Products	Sales	ProductID	A ProductID field must have a unique entry in a Products table, but will be listed many times in a Sales table as multiple copies of that item are sold
Customers	Sales	CustomerID	A CustomerID field must have a unique entry in a Customers table, but will be listed many times in a Sales table as multiple sales are recorded for the same customer
Employees	Promotions	EmployeeID	An EmployeeID field must have a unique entry in an Employees table, but will be listed many times in a Promotions table as the employee is promoted over time
Vendors	Products	VendorID	A VendorID field must have a unique entry in a Vendors table, but will be listed many times in the Products table if multiple products are purchased from the same vendor

Access 2000

Planning Related Tables

Careful planning is crucial to successful relational database design and creation. Duplicated data is not only error-prone and inefficient to enter, but it also limits the query and reporting capabilities of the overall database. After studying the concepts of solid relational database design, David is ready to apply those concepts and redesign MediaLoft's Training database. He uses the following steps to move from a single table of data to the powerful relational database capabilities provided by Access.

Details

List all of the fields of data that need to be tracked

Typically, these fields are already present in existing tables or paper reports. Still, it is a good idea to document each field in order to examine all fields at the same time. This is the appropriate time to determine if there are additional fields of information that do not currently exist on any report that should be tracked. David lists the fields he wishes to track, including fields about employee information, course information, and attendance information.

Group fields together in subject matter tables

The new MediaLoft training database will track courses attended by employees. It will contain three tables: Courses, Employees, and Attendance. David organizes the fields he listed under their appropriate table name.

Identify key fields that exist in tables

Each table should include a key field or key field combination in order to uniquely identify each record. David will use the SSN field in the Employees table, the CourseID field in the Courses table, and an automatically incrementing (AutoNumber data type) LogID field in the Attendance table to handle this requirement.

Link the tables with a one-to-many relationship via a common field

By adding an SSN field to the Attendance table, David creates a common field in both the Employees and Attendance tables that can serve as the link between them. Similarly, by adding a CourseID field to the Attendance table, David creates a common field in both the Attendance and Courses tables that can serve as the link. For a valid one-to-many relationship, the linking field must be designated as the key field in the "one" side of the one-to-many relationship. The final sketch of David's redesigned relational database is shown in Figure E-2.

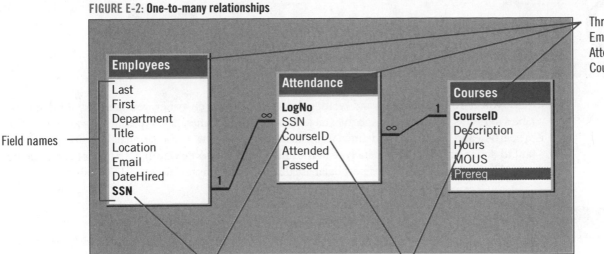

FIGURE E-2: **One-to-many relationships**

Field names

Linking SSN field

Linking CourseID field

Three tables:
Employees,
Attendance,
Courses

Identifying key field combinations

Identifying a single key field may be difficult in some tables. Examine, for instance, a table that records employee promotions over time that includes three fields: employee number, date, and pay rate. None of the fields individually could serve as a valid key field because none are restricted to unique data. The employee number and date together, however, could serve as a valid **key field combination** because an employee would get promoted only once on any given date; uniquely identifying the record.

Creating Related Tables

Once you have developed a valid relational database design on paper, you are ready to define the tables in Access. All characteristics of a table including field names, data types, field descriptions, field properties, and key fields are defined in the table's **Design view**. In a relational database, it is important to define the length and data type of the linking field the same way in both tables to create a successful link. Using his new database design, David creates the Attendance table.

Steps

1. **Start Access and open the Training-E database on your Project Disk**
   The Courses and Employees tables already exist in the database.

2. **Click Tables on the Objects Bar if it is not already selected, then click the New Table button 📖 in the Training-E database window**
   You will enter the fields for the Attendance table directly into the table's Design view.

3. **Click Design View in the New Table dialog box, then click OK**
   Field names should be as short as possible, but long enough to be descriptive. The field name entered in a table's Design view is used as the default name for the field in all later queries, forms, and reports.

> **QuickTip**
> Press [Enter] or [Tab] to move to the next column in a table's Design view window.

4. **Maximize the Table1: Table window, type LogNo, press [Enter], type a to select the AutoNumber Data Type, then press [Enter] twice to bypass the Description column and move to the second row**
   The LogNo is a unique number used to identify each record in the Attendance table (each occurrence of an employee taking a course). The AutoNumber data type, which automatically sequences each new record with the next available integer, works well for this field. When entering data types, you can type the first letter of the data type; for example, type "T" for Text, "D" for Date/Time, or "C" for Currency. You can also click the Data Type list arrow, then select the data type from the list.

5. **Type the other fields, entering the data types as shown in Table E-2**
   Field descriptions entered in a table's Design view are optional. In Datasheet view, the description of a field appears in the status bar, and therefore provides further clarification about what type of data should be entered in the field. The SSN field will serve as the linking field between the Attendance and Employee tables. The CourseID field will serve as the linking field between the Attendance and Courses tables. You are not required to use the same field name in both tables, but doing so makes it easier to understand the link between the related tables later.

6. **Click LogNo in the Field Name column, then click the Primary Key button 🔑 on the Table Design toolbar**
   The LogNo field serves as the primary key field in this table.

7. **Click the Save button 💾 on the Table Design toolbar, type Attendance in the Table Name text box in the Save As dialog box, then click OK**
   The completed Table Design view for the Attendance table is shown in Figure E-3.

8. **Click the Attendance: Table Design Close Window button**
   The Attendance table is now displayed as a table object in the Training-E database window.

FIGURE E-3: Design view for the Attendance table

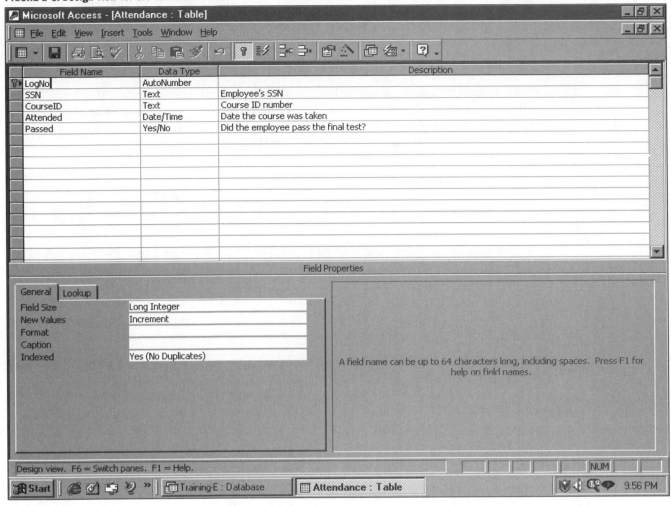

TABLE E-2: Additional fields for the Attendance Table

field name	data type	description
SSN	Text	Employee's SSN
CourseID	Text	Course ID number
Attended	Date/Time	Date the course was taken
Passed	Yes/No	Did the employee pass the final test?

Comparing linked tables to imported tables

A **linked table** is a table created in another database product, or another program such as Excel, that is stored in a file outside the open database. You can add, delete, and edit records in a linked table from within Access, but you can't change its structure. An **imported table** creates a copy of the information from the external file and places it in a new Access table in your database.

Access 2000

Access 2000

Defining Text Field Properties

Field properties are the characteristics that apply to each field in a table, such as field size, default value, or field formats. Modifying these properties helps ensure database accuracy and clarity because they restrict the way data is entered and displayed. You modify field properties in Table Design view. ▰▰▰ David decides to make field property changes to several text fields in the Employees table. He modifies the size and format properties.

Steps

1. Click the **Tables button** on the Objects bar in the database window if it is not already selected, click the **Employees table**, then click the **Design button** 🔲 in the Training-E database window

   The Employees table opens in Design view. The Field Properties panel (the lower half of the Table Design view window) changes to display the properties of the selected field, which depend on the field's data type. For example, when a field with a Text data type is selected, the Field Size property is visible. However, when a field with a Date/Time data type is selected, Access controls the Field Size property, so the property is not displayed. Most field properties are optional, but if they require an entry, Access provides a default value.

2. Click the **SSN field name**, look at the Field properties, then click each of the **field names** while viewing the Field Properties panel

QuickTip

Fifty is the default field size for a text field.

3. Click the **Last field name**, double-click **255** in the **Field Size text box** in the Field Properties, then type **30**

   Changing this property to 30 should accommodate even the longest entry for Last Name.

QuickTip

Press [F6] to quickly move between the upper and lower panels of Table Design view.

4. Change the **Field Size property** to **30** for the following Field Names: **First**, **Department**, **Title**, **Location**, and **Email**

   Changing the Field Size property to **30** for each of these text fields in this table should accommodate all the entries. The **Input Mask property** controls both the values that users can enter into a text box control and provides a visual guide for users as they enter data.

Trouble?

Insert the Office 2000 CD to install the Input Mask Wizard if necessary.

5. Click the **SSN field name**, click the **Input Mask text box** in the Field Properties panel, click the **Build button** 🔲 to start the Input Mask Wizard, click **Yes** to save the table, then click **Yes** when warned about losing data

QuickTip

You can enter the Input Mask directly in the field properties.

6. Click **Social Security Number** in the Input Mask list, click **Next**, click **Next** to accept **000-00-0000** as the default input mask, click **Next** to accept the option to store the data **without the symbols in the mask**, then click **Finish**

   The Design view of the Employees table should now look like Figure E-4. Notice that the SSN field is chosen, and the Field Properties panel displays the Input Mask property.

7. Click the **Save button** 🔲 on the Table Design toolbar, then click the **Datasheet View button** 🔲 on the Table Design toolbar

8. Maximize the datasheet, press **[Tab]** seven times to move to the SSN field for the first record, then type **115774444**

   The SSN Input Mask property creates an easy-to-use visual pathway to facilitate accurate data entry. See Table E-3 for more information on Text field properties.

9. Close the Employees table

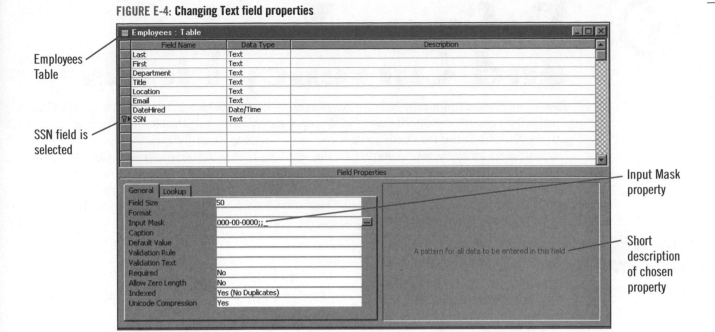

FIGURE E-4: Changing Text field properties

Employees Table

SSN field is selected

Input Mask property

Short description of chosen property

TABLE E-3: Common Text field properties

property	description	sample field name	sample property entry
Field Size	Controls how many characters can be entered into the field	State	2
Format	Controls how information will be displayed and printed < forces all characters to *display* lowercase even though the data is stored in the same way it was entered > forces all characters to *display* uppercase even though the data is stored in the same way it was entered @ requires that an entry be made & does not require that an entry be made	State	>
Input Mask	Provides a pattern for data to be entered; contains three parts separated by semicolons	Phone	(999)000-0000;1;_
Caption	A label used to describe the field. When a Caption property isn't entered, the field name is used to describe the field	Emp#	Employee Number
Default Value	Value that is automatically entered in the given field for new records	City	Kansas City
Required	Determines if an entry is required for this field	LastName	Yes

CLUES TO USE

Defining input mask property parts

Input mask properties contain three parts. The first part controls what type of data can be entered and how it will be displayed: 9 represents an optional number; 0 represents a required number, ? represents an optional letter; L represented a required letter. The second part determines whether all displayed characters (such as dashes in the SSN field) are stored in the field, or just the entry. The 0 (zero) entry stores all characters. The 1 (one) entry stores only the entered characters. The third part determines which character Access will display for the space where a character is typed in the input mask. Common entries are the asterisk (*), underscore (_), or pound sign (#).

Defining Number and Currency Fields

Even though some of the properties for Number and Currency fields are the same as for Text fields, each field type has its own specific list of valid properties. Numeric and Currency fields have very similar properties because they both contain numbers. One important difference, however, is that a Currency field limits the user's control over the field size. Therefore, you would use a Currency field to prevent rounding off during calculations. A Currency field is accurate to fifteen digits to the left of the decimal point and four digits to the right. ✐ The Courses table contains both a Number field (Hours), and a Currency field (Cost). David modifies the properties of these two fields.

Steps

1. **Click the Courses table, click the Design button ⊠ in the Training-E database window, then click the Hours field**
   The Field Size property for a Number field defaults to Long Integer. See Table E-4 for more information on common Number field properties.

QuickTip

Choosing Byte and Integer field sizes for numeric fields lowers the storage requirements for that field. Byte allows entries only from 0 to 255.

2. **Click the Field Size text box in the Field Properties, click the Field Size list arrow, then click Byte**

3. **Click the Cost field, click the Decimal Places text box in the Field Properties, click the Decimal Places list arrow, then click 0**
   Your screen should look like Figure E-5. Because all of MediaLoft's courses are priced at a round dollar value, there is no need to display zero cents in each field entry.

4. **Click the Save button 🖫 on the Table Design toolbar, then click the Datasheet View button ▦ on the Table Design toolbar**
   Since none of the entries in any of the fields were longer than the new field size entries, you won't lose any data.

5. **Press [Tab] twice to move to the Hours field for the first record, type 1000, then press [Tab]**
   Because 1,000 is larger than the Byte field size for the Hours field will allow, you are cautioned with an Access error message indicating that the value isn't valid for this field.

6. **Click OK, press [Esc] to remove the inappropriate entry in the Hours field, then press [Tab] three times to move to the Cost field**
   The Cost field currently displays all data rounded to the nearest dollar.

7. **Type 199.75 in the Cost field, then press [↓]**
   Because this field has been formatted to display no cents, remainders are rounded to the nearest dollar and $200 is displayed in the datasheet. Even though remainders of cents are rounded when displayed on the datasheet, 199.75 is the actual value stored in the field. Formatting does not change the actual data, but only the way it is displayed.

8. **Close the Courses table**

FIGURE E-5: Changing Currency and Number field properties

Courses table —

Cost field is — chosen

Decimal Places — property

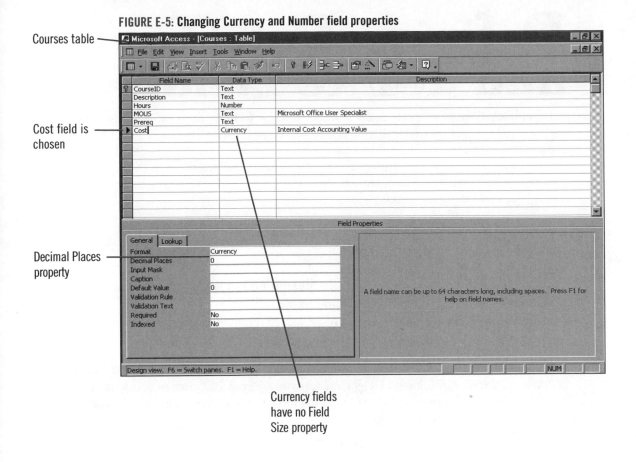

Currency fields have no Field Size property

TABLE E-4: Common numeric and currency field properties

property	description	sample field name	sample property entry
Field size (Number field only)	Determines the largest number that can be entered in the field, as well as the type of data (e.g. integer or fraction) • Byte stores numbers from 0 to 255 (no fractions) Integer stores numbers from −32,768 to 32,767 (no fractions) • Long Integer stores numbers from −2,147,483,648 to 2,147,483,647 (no fractions) • Single stores numbers (including fractions with six digits to the right of the decimal point) times 10 to the −38th to +38th power • Double stores numbers (including fractions with over 10 digits to the right of the decimal point) in the range of 10 to the −324th to +324th power	Quantity	Integer
Decimal Places	The number of digits to the right of the decimal separator	Dues	0

Defining Date/Time and Yes/No Fields

A Date field's Format property is designed specifically to show dates in just about any format such as January 5, 2003; 05-Jan-03; or 1/5/2003. Many of a Date field's other properties such as Input Mask, Caption, and Default Value are very similar to Text and Number field types. David wants the database to display all Date fields with four digits for the year, so there is no confusion regarding the century. He will also ensure that the Yes/No field is displayed as a check box versus a text entry of "Yes" or "No."

Steps

1. **Click the Attendance table, click the Design button** in the Training-E database window, then click the **Attended field name**
   You want the dates of attendance to display as 01/17/2000 instead of as 1/17/00. You must work with the Attended field's Format property.

2. **Click the Format text box** in the Field Properties, then click the **Format list arrow**
   Although several predefined Date/Time formats are available, none matches the format you want. To define a custom format, enter symbols that represent how you want the date to appear in the Format property text box.

3. **Type mm/dd/yyyy, then press [Enter]**
   The updated Format property for the Attended field shown in Figure E-6 forces the date to appear with two digits for the month, two digits for the day, and four digits for the year. The parts of the date will be separated by forward slashes. You want the Passed field to display a check box for this control. The Display Control property is on the Lookup tab.

4. **Click the Passed field name, click the Lookup tab** in the Field Properties, click the **Display Control textbox**, then click the **Display Control property's list arrow**
   A Yes/No field may appear as a check box in which "checked" equals "yes" and "unchecked" equals "no," as a text box that displays "yes" or "no," or as a combo box that displays "yes" and "no" in the drop-down list.

5. **Click Check Box in the Display Control list**
   The linking SSN field in the Attendance table must be the same data type and size as it is in the Employees table.

6. **Click the SSN field, click the General tab** in the Field Properties, click the **Input Mask text box**, click the **Build button**, click **Yes** to save the table, click **Social Security Number** in the Input Mask Wizard dialog box, click **Next,** click **Next,** click **Finish,** click the **Datasheet View button** on the Table Design, then click **Yes** when prompted
   Entering records tests the property changes.

7. **Press [Tab]** to move to the SSN field, type **115774444,** press **[Tab],** type **Comp1,** press **[Tab],** type **1/31/00,** press **[Tab],** then press **[Spacebar]**
   Your screen should look like Figure E-7. Double-check that the SSN and Attended fields are formatting correctly too.

8. **Press [Enter],** press **[Tab]** to move through the LogNo field, type **222334444,** press **[Tab],** type **Comp1,** press **[Tab],** type **1/31/00,** press **[Tab],** then press **[Spacebar]**

FIGURE E-6: Changing Date/Time field properties

Attendance table

Attended field is chosen

Custom Format property change is made

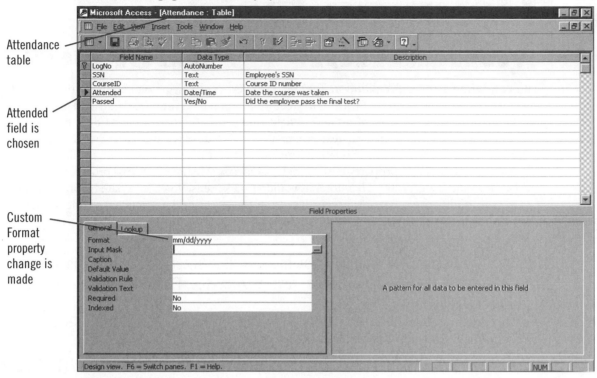

FIGURE E-7: Testing field property changes

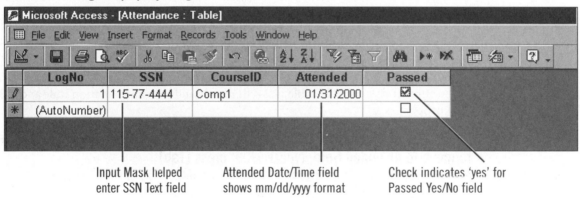

Input Mask helped
enter SSN Text field

Attended Date/Time field
shows mm/dd/yyyy format

Check indicates 'yes' for
Passed Yes/No field

Planning for the 21st century

The default Format property (General) for a Date/Time field assumes that dates entered as 1/1/30 to 12/31/99 are twentieth-century dates (1930–1999), and those entered as 1/1/00 to 12/31/29 are twenty-first century dates (2000–2029). If you wish to enter dates outside these ranges, you must enter all four digits of the date.

Defining Field Validation Properties

The **Validation Rule** and **Validation Text** field properties can help you eliminate unreasonable entries by establishing criteria for the entry before it is accepted into the database. For example, the Validation Rule property of a Gender field might be modified to allow only two entries: "male" or "female." The Validation Text property is used to display a message when a user tries to enter data that doesn't pass the Validation Rule property for that field. Without a Validation Rule entry, the Validation Text property is meaningless. ◀━━ MediaLoft started providing in-house courses on January 17, 2000. Therefore, it wouldn't make sense to enter a date before that time. David will modify the validation properties of the Date field in the Attendance table to prevent the entry of incorrect dates.

Steps

1. Click the **Design View button** 🔛 on the Table Datasheet toolbar, click the **Attended field**, click the **Validation Rule text box** in the Field Properties, then type **>=1/17/2000**

   This property forces all course dates to be greater than or equal to 1/17/2000. See Table E-5 for more examples of Validation Rule expressions.

2. Click the **Validation Text text box**, then type **Date must be on or after 1/17/2000**

   The Validation Text property will appear in a dialog box to explain to the user why a field entry that doesn't pass the Validation Rule criteria cannot be accepted. The Design view of the Attendance table should now look like Figure E-8. Access changed the entry in the Validation Rule property to appear as >=#1/17/00#. Pound signs (#) are used to surround date criteria. Access assumes that years entered with two digits in the range 30 and 99 refer to the years 1930 through 1999, whereas digits in the range 00 and 29 refer to the years 2000 through 2029. If you wish to indicate a year outside these ranges, you must enter all four digits of the year.

3. Click the **Save button** 💾 on the Table Design toolbar, then click **Yes** when asked to test the existing data

   Because all dates in the Attended field are more recent than 1/17/00, there are no date errors in the current data, and the table is saved. You should test the Validation Rule and Validation Text properties.

4. Click the **Datasheet View button** on the Table Design toolbar, press **[Tab]** three times to move to **Attended field**, type **1/1/99**, press **[Tab]**

   Because you tried to enter a 1999 date in the Attended field of the Attendance datasheet, the Validation rule that you entered appears in a dialog box. See Figure E-9.

5. Click **OK** to close the Validation Rule dialog box

   You know that the Validation Rule and Validation Text properties work properly.

6. Press **[Esc]** to reject the invalid date entry

7. Close the Attendance table

FIGURE E-8: Using the Validation properties

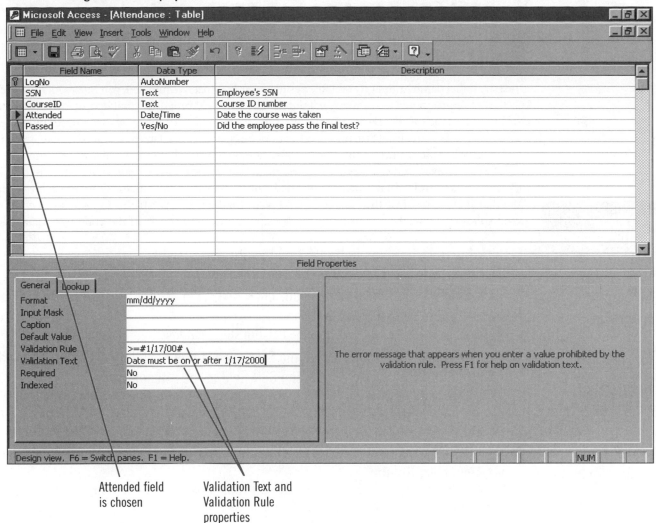

Attended field is chosen

Validation Text and Validation Rule properties

FIGURE E-9: Validation Rule dialog box

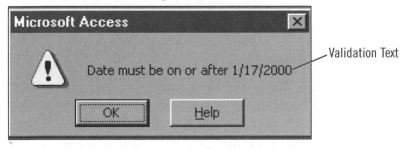

Validation Text

TABLE E-5: Validation Rule expressions

data type	validation rule expression	description
Number or Currency	>0	The number must be positive
Number or Currency	>10 And <100	The number must be between 10 and 100
Number or Currency	10 Or 20 Or 30	The number must be 10, 20, or 30
Text	"IA" Or "NE" Or "MO"	The entry must be IA, NE, or MO
Date/Time	>=#1/1/93#	The date must be on or after 1/1/1993
Date/Time	>#1/1/80# And <#1/1/90#	The date must be between 1/1/1980 and 1/1/1990

Creating One-to-Many Relationships

Once the initial database design and table design phase have been completed, you must link the tables together in appropriate one-to-many relationships. Some field properties that do not affect how the data is stored (such as the Format property), can be changed after the tables are linked, but other properties (such as the Field Size property), cannot be changed once tables are linked. Therefore, it is best to complete all of the table and field design activities before linking the tables. Once the tables are linked, however, you can design queries, reports, and forms with fields from multiple tables. David's initial database sketch revealed that the SSN field will link the Employee table to the Attendance table and that the CourseID field will link the Courses table to the Attendance table. David will now define the one-to-many relationships between the tables of the Training-E database.

QuickTip

If the Show Table dialog box is not open, click the Show Table button 🔄 on the Relationships toolbar.

1. Click the Relationships button 🔳 **on the Database toolbar**

The Show Table dialog box opens and lists all three tables in the Training-E database.

2. Click Employees on the Tables tab, click Add, click Attendance, click Add, click Courses, click Add, then click Close

All three tables have been added to the Relationships window.

QuickTip

To display all of a table's field names, drag the bottom border of the table window until all fields are visible. Drag the table's title bar to move the field list.

3. Maximize the window, click SSN in the Employees table Field List, then drag the SSN field from the Employees table to the SSN field in the Attendance table

Dragging a field from one table to another in the Relationships window links the two tables with the chosen field and opens the Edit Relationships dialog box as shown in Figure E-10. **Referential integrity** helps ensure data accuracy.

4. Click the Enforce Referential Integrity check box in the Edit Relationships dialog box, then click Create

The **one-to-many line** shows the linkage between the SSN field of the Employees table and the Attendance table. The "one" side of the relationship is the unique SSN for each record in the Employees table. The "many" side of the relationship is identified by an infinity symbol pointing to the SSN field in the Attendance table. The CourseID field will link the Courses table to the Attendance table.

QuickTip

To delete a table or relationship from the Relationships window, click the table or relationship line and press [Delete].

5. Click the CourseID field in the Courses table, then drag it from the Courses table to the CourseID field in the Attendance table

6. Click the Enforce Referential Integrity check box, then click Create

The finished Relationships window should look like Figure E-11. Print the Relationships window to show structural information including table names, field names, key fields, and relationships between tables.

7. Click File on the menu bar, click Print Relationships, click the Print button 🖨 **on the Print Preview toolbar, click the Close Window button, click Yes to save the report, click OK to accept the default report name, click the Relationships Window Close button, then click Yes to save changes**

When tables are related with one-to-many relationships, their datasheets will show an **expand button**, to the left of the record that can be clicked to show related records in a **sub-datasheet**. When the related records appear, the expand button becomes a **collapse button**, which can be clicked to close the related records window.

8. Double-click the Courses table, then click the Comp1 Expand button 🔳

Your screen should look like Figure E-12.

9. Close the Training-E database, then exit Access

FIGURE E-10: **Edit Relationships dialog box**

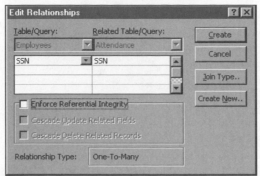

FIGURE E-11: **Final Relationships window**

"Many" side of one-to-many relationship

"One" side of one-to-many relationship

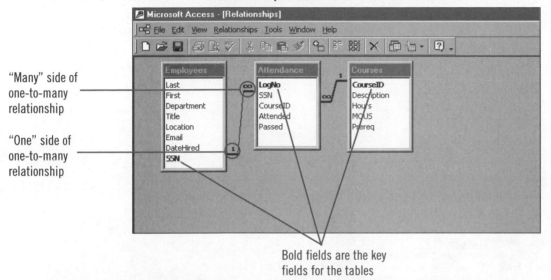

Bold fields are the key fields for the tables

FIGURE E-12: **A subdatasheet allows you to view related records**

Expand button

Collapse button

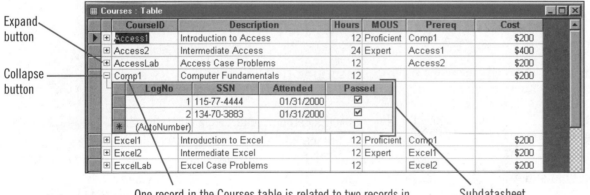

One record in the Courses table is related to two records in the Attendance table through the common CourseID field

Subdatasheet

Enforcing referential integrity

Referential integrity ensures that no orphaned records are entered or created in the database. An **orphan record** happens when information in the linking field of the "many" table doesn't have a matching entry in the linking field of the "one" table. For MediaLoft, referential integrity ensures that SSN entries added to the Attendance table are first recorded in the Employees table. Also, referential integrity prevents the user from deleting a record from the Employees table if a matching SSN entry is present in the Attendance table.

Practice

► Concepts Review

Identify each element of the table Design view shown in Figure E-13.

FIGURE E-13

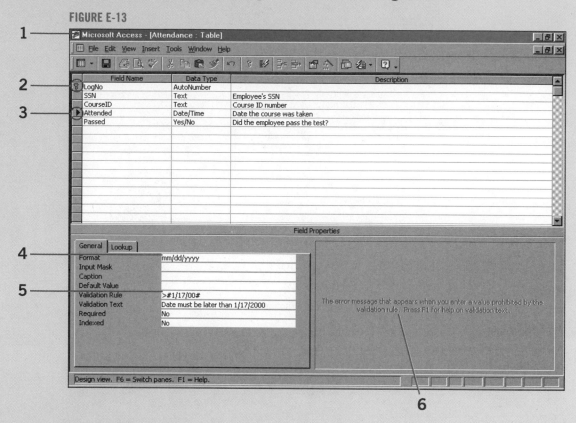

Match each term with the statement that describes its function.

7. **Primary Key**
8. **Field Properties**
9. **Design view**
10. **Validation Rule and Validation Text**
11. **Relational database**

a. Several tables linked together in one-to-many relationships
b. A field that holds unique information for each record in the table
c. Where all characteristics of a table, including field names, data types, field descriptions, field properties, and key fields, are defined
d. Characteristics that apply to each field of a table, such as field size, default values, or field formats
e. Helps you eliminate unreasonable entries by establishing criteria for the entry

Select the best answer from the list of choices.

12. **Which of the following steps would probably help eliminate fields of duplicate data in a table?**
    a. Redesign the database and add more tables.
    b. Redesign the database and add more fields.
    c. Change the formatting properties of the field in which the duplicate data existed.
    d. Change the validation properties of the field in which the duplicate data existed.

13. Which of the following is NOT defined in the table's Design view?
a. Key fields
b. Duplicate data
c. Field lengths
d. Data types

14. Which of the following is NOT a common data type?
a. Text
b. Alpha
c. Number
d. Date/Time

15. Which feature helps the database designer make sure that one-to-many relationships are preserved?
a. Validation Text property
b. Validation Rule property
c. Field formatting
d. Referential integrity

16. Which character is used to identify dates in a validation expression?
a. " (double quote)
b. ' (single quote)
c. # (pound sign)
d. & (ampersand)

17. Which Format Property Option displays all characters in the field as uppercase?
a. <
b. >
c. !
d. @

▶ Skills Review

1. Examine relational database requirements.
a. Examine your address book.
b. Write down the fields you will need.
c. Examine which fields contain duplicate entries.

2. Plan related tables.
a. Start Access.
b. Use the Blank Access Database option button to create a new database file.
c. Type "Membership-E" as the File name then create the database on your Project Disk.
d. Click Tables on the Objects bar, then click the New Table button.

3. Create related tables.
a. Use Design view to create the new table using the following field names with the given data types: First, Text; Last, Text; Street, Text; Zip, Text; Birthday, Date/Time; Dues, Currency; MemberNo, Text; CharterMember, Yes/No.
b. Identify MemberNo as the primary key field.

c. Save the table as "Names," then close it.

d. Use Design view to create a new table using the following fields with the given data types: Zip, Text; City, Text; State, Text.

e. Identify Zip as the primary key field.

f. Save the table as "Zips," then close it.

g. Use Design view to create a new table using the following fields with the given data types: MemberNo, Text Activity Date, Date/Time; Hours, Number.

j. Save the table without a primary key field, name it "Activities," then close it.

4. Define text field properties.

a. Open the Zips table in Design view.

b. Change the Field Size property of the State field to 2.

c. Change the Field Size property of the Zip field to 5.

d. Save the changes and close the Zips table.

e. Open the Names table in Design view.

f. Use the Input Mask Wizard to create the Input Mask property for the Zip field in both the Zips and Names tables. Choose the Zip Code input mask, and use the other default options provided by the Input Mask Wizard.

g. Change the Field Size property of the First, Last, and Street fields to 30.

h. Change the Field Size property of the MemberNo field to 5.

i. Save the changes and close the Names and Zips tables.

j. Open the Activities table in Design view.

k. Change the Field Size property of the MemberNo field to 5.

l. Save the change and close the Activities table.

5. Define number and currency field properties.

a. Open the Names table in Design view.

b. Change the Decimal Places property of the Dues field to 0.

c. Save the change and close the Names table.

d. Open the Activities table in Design view.

e. Change the Field Size property of the Hours field to Byte.

f. Save the change and close the Activities table.

6. Define the Date/Time and Yes/No field properties.

a. Open the Names table in Design view.

b. Change the Format property of the Birthday field to m/d/yyyy.

c. Check to ensure that the Display Control property of the CharterMember field is set to check box.

d. Save the changes and close the Names table.

e. Open the Activities table in Design view.

f. Change the Format property of the ActivityDate field to m/d/yyyy.

g. Save the change and close the Activities table.

7. Define field validation properties.

a. Open the Zips table in Design view.

b. Click the State field name, click the Validation Rule text box, then type ="IA" OR "KS" OR "MO"

c. Click the Validation Text text box, then type "State must be IA, KS, or MO"

d. Save the change and close the Zips table.

8. Create one-to-many relationships.

  a. Open the Relationships window.

  b. Add all three tables to the Relationships window in this order: Activities, Names, Zips.

  c. Close the Show Table dialog box.

  d. Drag the Zip field from the Zips table to the Zip field in the Names table, creating a one-to-many relationship from the Zips table to the Names table.

  e. Enforce Referential Integrity for the relationship.

  f. Drag the MemberNo field from the Names table to the MemberNo field in the Activities table, creating a one-to-many relationship from the Names table to the Activities table.

  g. Enforce Referential Integrity for the relationship.

  h. Save the changes to the Relationships layout.

  i. Print the Relationships window.

  j. Close the Relationships report, and save it with the given name.

  k. Close the Relationships window.

  l. Close the Memberships-E database.

▶ Independent Challenges

1. As the manager of a music store's instrument rental program, you have decided to create a database to track instrument rentals to school children. The fields you need to track can be organized with four tables: Instruments, Rentals, Customers, and Schools, as shown below.

To complete this independent challenge:

  a. Sketch how the fields could be organized into four tables: Instruments, Rentals, Customers, and Schools. The sketch should show the fields listed in a vertical field list similarly to how they appear in the Relationships window.

  b. Determine if there are key fields in the tables. Place a "K" beside those fields in your sketch.

  c. Determine how the tables should be linked using one-to-many relationships. This may involve adding a linking field to a table to establish the connection. Draw a linking line between these fields using the one-to-many symbols at the appropriate ends of the linking line.

  d. Create and save a database called "Music Store-E".

  e. Create the four tables in the Music Store-E database using the following information. Note that the Primary Key fields are bold in the table.

table	field name	data type	table	field name	data type
Customers	FirstName	Text	Instruments	Description	Text
	LastName	Text		**SerialNo**	Text
	Street	Text		MonthlyFee	Currency
	City	Text			
	State	Text			
	Zip	Text			
	CustNo	AutoNumber			
	SchoolNo	Number			
Schools	SchoolName	Text	Rentals	**RentalNo**	AutoNumber
	SchoolNo	AutoNumber		CustNo	Number
				SerialNo	Text
				Date	Date/Time

f. Change the Field Size property of the following fields:

table	fields	change the Field Size property to:
Customers	FirstName, LastName, Street, City	30
Customers	State	2
Customers	Zip	9
Instruments	SerialNo	10
Rentals	SerialNo	10

g. Add a Validation Rule property to the Date field of the Rentals table that only allows dates of 1/1/00 or later to be entered into the database. The property entry is >=#1/1/00#.

h. Add a Validation Text property to the Date field that states "Dates must be on or later than 1/1/2000".

i. Create one-to-many relationships to link the tables as follows. Be sure to enforce referential integrity as appropriate.

"one" table	"many" table	linking field
Customers	Rentals	CustNo
Instruments	Rentals	SerialNo
Schools	Customers	SchoolNo

j. Print the Relationships window of the database, making sure that all fields of each table are visible.

k. Compare the printout to your original sketch. How do the database designs differ?

2. You want to document the books you've read in a relational database. You will design the database on paper including the tables, field names, data types, and relationships.

To complete this independent challenge:

a. On paper, create three balanced columns by drawing two vertical lines from the top to the bottom of the paper. At the top of the first column write the label "Table." At the top of the second column write the label "Field Name," and at the top of the third column write the label "Data Type."

b. In the middle column, list all of the fields that need to be tracked to record information about the books you've read. You'll want to track such information as the book title, category (such as Biography, Mystery, or Science Fiction), rating (a numeric value from 1–10 that indicates how satisfied you were with the book), date you read the book, author's first name, and author's last name.

c. In the first column, identify the table where this field would be found. (*Hint:* You should identify two tables of information for this listing of fields.)

d. Identify the key fields found in the tables by circling the field name. If you do not find any fields that are good candidates for key fields, you may have to create additional fields. (*Hint:* Each book has an ISBN—International Standard Book Number—which is a unique number assigned to every book. To uniquely identify each author, you will have to create a new field called AuthorNo.)

e. In a third column, identify the appropriate data type for each field.

f. On a new piece of paper, sketch the fields as they would appear in the Relationships window of Access. Be sure to include these elements:
- Two tables with their respective field lists
- Circled key fields in each table

- A linking line drawn between the field common to each table. (*Hint:* To complete the linking line, you may have to add a field to one of the tables to create the common link. Remember that the "one" side of the relationship must be a key field.) Be sure that your linking line shows the "one" and "many" symbols at the appropriate ends of the linking line, just as it does in the Access Relationships window.

3. You have been asked by your employer to create a database that documents blood donations by employees over the year. You first design the database on paper and include the tables, field names, data types, and relationships, and then you create the database in Access.

To complete this independent challenge:

a. On paper, create three balanced columns by drawing two vertical lines from the top to the bottom of the paper. At the top of the first column write the label "Table." At the top of the second column write the label "Field Name," and at the top of the third column write the label "Data Type."

b. In the middle column, list all of the fields that need to be tracked to record information about the blood donations. You'll want to track information such as employee name, employee Social Security number, employee department, employee blood type, date of donation, and hospital the donation was given to. Also, you'll want to track basic hospital information, such as the hospital name and address.

c. In the first column, identify the table where this field would be found. (*Hint:* You should identify three tables of information for this listing of fields. Each employee can donate many times in one year, and each hospital can receive many donations.)

d. Identify the key fields found in the tables by circling the field name. If you do not find any fields that are good candidates for key fields, you may have to create additional fields. (*Hint:* Employees are uniquely identified by their SSN, and hospitals by a unique HospitalNo. An AutoNumber field called "DonationNo" uniquely identifies each donation.)

e. In a third column, identify the appropriate data type for each field.

f. On a new piece of paper, sketch the fields as they would appear in the Relationships window of Access. Be sure to include these elements:

- Three tables with their respective field lists.
- Circle the key fields in each table.
- Draw the linking line between the field common to each table. (*Hint:* To complete the linking line, you may have to add a field to one of the tables to create the common link. Remember that the "one" side of the relationship must be a key field.) Be sure that your linking line shows the "one" and "many" symbols at the appropriate ends of the linking line, just as it does in the Access Relationships window.

g. Start Access and open a new, blank database, then create the database you just designed.

h. Name the database "Donations", save and close Donations, then exit Access.

4. MediaLoft has developed a company intranet site that gives employees access to company-wide information. In this independent challenge, you'll check the intranet site to find new courses requested by MediaLoft employees.

a. Connect to the Internet and use your browser to go to the MediaLoft intranet site at http://www.course.com/illustrated/MediaLoft/.

b. Click the link for Training.

c. Click the link for New Courses, and print the Web page.

d. Start Access, then open the Training-E database.

e. Enter the three new courses found on the Web page into the Courses table.

f. Print the Courses table, then close the Courses table.

g. Close the Training-E database.

h. Exit Access.

▶ Visual Workshop

Open the Training-E database, create a new table called "Vendors" using the Table Design view shown in Figure E-14 to determine field names and data types. Additional property changes include changing the Field Size property of the VState field to 2, the VendorID and VPhone fields to 10, and all other text fields to 30. Be sure to specify that the VendorID field is the Primary Key field.

FIGURE E-14

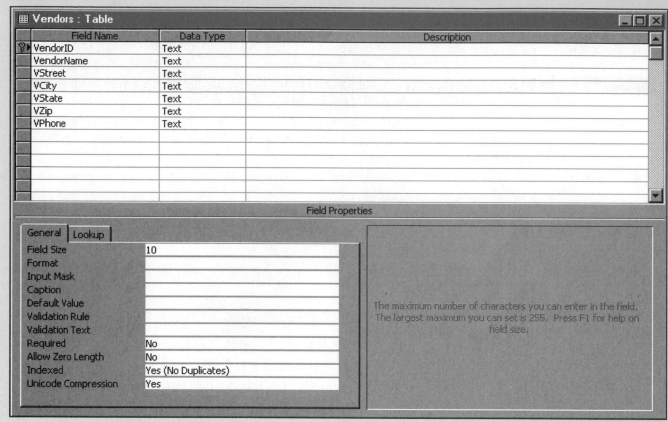

Unit
F

Creating
Multiple Table Queries

Objectives

- MOUS ► **Create select queries**
- MOUS ► **Sort a query on multiple fields**
- MOUS ► **Develop AND queries**
- MOUS ► **Develop OR queries**
- MOUS ► **Create calculated fields**
- MOUS ► **Build summary queries**
- ► **Create crosstab queries**
- ► **Modify crosstab queries**

In this unit, you will create **queries**, which are database objects that answer questions about the data by pulling fields and records that match specific criteria into a single datasheet. A **select query** retrieves data from one or more linked tables and displays the results in a datasheet. Queries can also be used to sort records, develop new calculated fields from existing fields, or develop summary calculations such as the sum or average of the values in a field. **Crosstab queries** present information in a cross-tabular report, similar to pivot tables in other database and spreadsheet products. ◄— David Dumont has spent several days entering information into the Attendance table to record which employees are taking which classes. Now, he can create select queries and crosstab queries to analyze the data in the database.

Access 2000

Creating Select Queries

You develop queries by using the Query Wizard or by directly specifying requested fields and query criteria in **Query Design view**. The resulting query datasheet is not a duplication of the data that resides in the original table's datasheet, but rather a logical view of the data. If you change or enter data in a query's datasheet, the data in the underlying table (and any other logical view) is updated automatically. Queries often are used to present and sort a subset of fields from multiple tables for data entry or update purposes. David creates a query to answer the question, "Who is taking what course?" He pulls fields from several tables into a single query object to display a single datasheet that answers this question.

1. Start Access and open the **Training-F** database on your Project Disk

2. Click the **Queries button** on the Objects bar in the Training-F Database window, then double-click **Create query in Design View**

   The Query1 Select Query Design view window opens and the Show Table dialog box opens listing all the tables in the database. You use the Show Table dialog box to add the tables that contain the fields you need to the Query Design view.

Trouble?

If you add a table to Query Design view twice by mistake, click the title bar of the extra field list, then press [Delete].

3. Click **Employees**, click **Add**, click **Attendance**, click **Add**, click **Courses**, click **Add**, then click **Close**

   The upper pane of Query Design view displays **field lists** for the three tables. Each table's name is in its field list title bar. You can drag the title bar of the field lists to move them or drag the edge of a field list to resize it. Key fields are bold, and serve as the "one" side of the one-to-many relationship between two tables. Relationships are displayed with **one-to-many join lines** between the linking fields, as shown in Figure F-1. The fields you want displayed in the datasheet must be added to the columns in the lower pane of the Query Design view.

QuickTip

Double-click a field name to place it in the next available column of the query grid.

4. Click the **First field** in the Employees table field list, then drag the **First field** to the Field cell in the first column of the query design grid

   The order in which the fields are placed in the query design grid is their order in the datasheet.

QuickTip

If you need to add a field to the query that isn't currently displayed, click the Show Table button to add the new table.

5. Drag the **Last field** from the Employees table to the Field cell in the second column, drag the **Attended field** from the Attendance table to the third column, drag the **Description field** from the Courses table to the fourth column, then drag the **Hours field** from the Courses table to the fifth column

   Your Query Design view should look like Figure F-2. You may delete a field from the lower pane by clicking the field selector above the field name and pressing [Delete]. Deleting a field from the query design grid removes it from the logical view of this query's datasheet, but does not delete the field from the database. A field is physically defined and the field's contents are physically stored in a table object only.

6. Click the **Hours field selector**, press **[Delete]** to remove the field from the query design grid, then click the **Datasheet View button** on the query Design toolbar

   The datasheet looks like Figure F-3. The resulting datasheet shows the four fields selected in Query Design view and displays 153 records. The records represent the 153 different times a MediaLoft employee has attended a MediaLoft class. Shayla Colletti appears in eleven records because she has attended eleven classes.

FIGURE F-1: Query Design view with multiple tables

Table names

Fields in the
Employees table

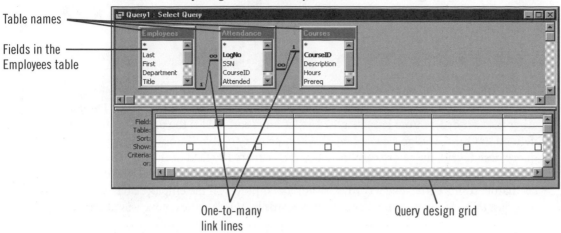

One-to-many
link lines

Query design grid

FIGURE F-2: Query Design view with five fields in the query grid

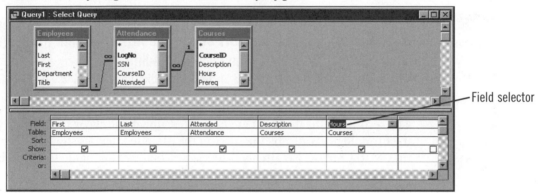

Field selector

FIGURE F-3: Query datasheet showing related information from three tables

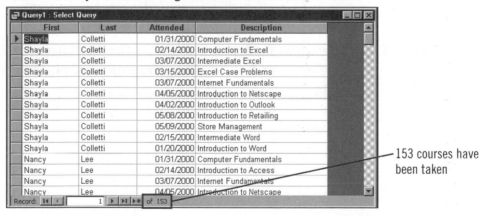

153 courses have
been taken

Resizing Query Design view

Drag the resize bar up or down to provide more room for the upper (field lists) or lower (query design grid) parts of Query Design view. By dragging the resize bar down, you may have enough room to enlarge each field list so that you can see all of the field names in each table, but still have enough room to show all of the information in the query design grid.

Sorting a Query on Multiple Fields

Sorting refers to reorganizing the records in either ascending or descending order based on the contents of a field. Queries allow you to specify more than one sort field in Query Design view, evaluating the sort orders from left to right. The leftmost sort field is the primary sort field. Sort orders defined in Query Design view are saved with the query object. If no sort orders are specified in the query design grid, the records are sorted by the primary key field of the first table that has a field in the query. ⬛ David wishes to put the records in alphabetical order based on the employee's last name. If more than one record exists for an employee (if the employee has attended more than one class), David wants to further sort the records by the date the course was attended.

1. **Click the Design View button** ⬛ **on the Query Datasheet toolbar**
   To sort the records according to David's plan, the Last field must be the primary sort, and the Attended field the secondary sort field.

QuickTip

You can resize the columns of a datasheet by pointing to the right column border that separates the field names, then dragging ✛ left or right to resize as needed. You can double-click ✛ to automatically adjust the column width to fit the widest entry.

2. **Click the Sort cell of the Last field in the query design grid, click the Sort list arrow, click Ascending, click the Sort cell of the Attended field in the query design grid, click the Sort list arrow, then click Ascending**
   The resulting query design grid should look like Figure F-4.

3. **Click the Datasheet View button** ⬛ **on the Query Design toolbar**
   The records of the datasheet are now listed alphabetically by the entry in the Last field, then in chronological order by the entry in the Attended field, as shown in Figure F-5. You notice that Maria Abbott has attended six classes, but that her name has been incorrectly entered in the database as "Marie." Fix this error in the query datasheet.

4. **Type Maria, then press [↓]**
   This update shows that you are using a properly designed relational database because changing any occurrence of an employee's name should cause all other occurrences of that name to be automatically updated. The employee name is physically stored only once in the Employees table, although it is displayed in this datasheet once for every time the employee has attended a course.

QuickTip

If you need to identify your printout, include your name or initials in the query name and it will print in the header of the datasheet.

5. **Click the Close Window button to close the Select Query, click Yes when prompted to save the changes, type Employee Progress Query in the Query Name text box, then click OK**
   The query is now saved and listed as an object in the Queries window in the Training-F database window.

FIGURE F-4: Specifying multiple sort orders in Query Design view

Records will be sorted by Last, then by Attended

Show check box

Resize columns by dragging right edge

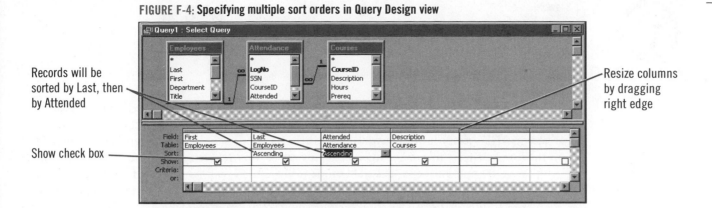

FIGURE F-5: Records sorted by Last, then Attended

Primary sort field

Secondary sort field

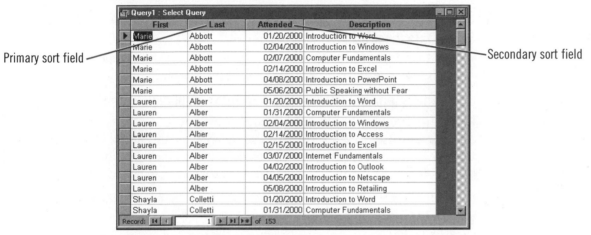

FIGURE F-6: Query grid for sorting out of order

Sort order is defined using fields that do not appear on the datasheet

Show check boxes are unchecked

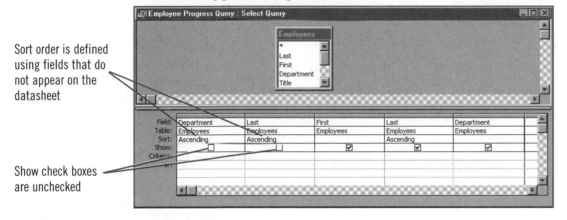

CLUES TO USE

Specifying a sort order different from the field order in the datasheet

You cannot modify the left-to-right sort order hierarchy in Query Design view. However, if you wish to have the fields in the datasheet appear in a different order than that by which they are sorted, there is a simple solution, as shown in Figure F-6. Suppose you want the fields First, Last, and Department to appear in a datasheet in that order, but want to sort the records by Department, then by Last. The Department and Last fields are the first two fields in the design grid with the appropriate sort order specified, but their Show Check Boxes are unchecked, so these columns do not display in the datasheet. The resulting datasheet would sort the records by Department, then Last, and display the First, Last, and Department fields.

Developing AND Queries

Using Access you can query for specific records that match two or more criteria. **Criteria** are tests, or limiting conditions, for which the record must be true to be selected for a datasheet. To create an **AND query** in which two or more criteria are present, enter the criteria for the fields on the same Criteria row of the query design grid. If two AND criteria are entered for the same field, the AND operator separates the criteria in the Criteria cell for that field. ◆◆◆ David is looking for a person to assist the Access teacher in the classroom. In order to compile a list of potential candidates, he creates an AND query to find all employees who have taken MediaLoft's Access courses and passed the exams.

1. Click the **Employee Progress query**, then click the **Design View button** 🔲 on the Query Datasheet toolbar
   Instead of creating a query from scratch, you can modify the Employee Progress query. The only additional field you have to add to the query is the Passed field.

2. Scroll the **Attendance table field list**, then double-click the **Passed field** to move it to the fifth column in the query design grid
   MediaLoft offers several Access courses, so the criteria must specify all the records that contain the word "Access" anywhere in the Description field. You'll use the asterisk (*), a **wildcard character** that represents any combination of characters, to create this criteria.

3. Click the **Description field Criteria cell**, type ***access***, then click the **Datasheet View button** 🔲 on the Query Design toolbar
   The resulting datasheet as shown in Figure F-7, shows thirteen records that match the criteria. The resulting records all contain the word "access" in some part of the Description field, but because of the placement of the asterisks, it didn't matter *where* (beginning, middle, or end) the word was found in the Description field entry. Additional criteria are needed to display a datasheet with only those records where the student passed the final exam.

4. Click the **Design View button** 🔲 on the Query Datasheet toolbar, click the **Passed field Criteria cell**, then type **yes**
   The resulting query design grid is shown in Figure F-8. Notice that Access entered double quotation marks around the text criterion in the Description field and added the **Like operator**. See Table F-1 for more information on Access operators.

5. Click **Datasheet View button** 🔲 on the Query Design toolbar to view the resulting records
   Multiple criteria added to the same line of the query design grid (AND criteria) must *each* be true for the record to appear in the resulting datasheet, thereby causing the resulting datasheet to display *fewer* records. Only nine records contain "access" in the Description field and "yes" in the Passed field.

6. Click **File** on the menu bar, click **Save As** to save this query with a new name, type **Potential Access Assistants** in the Save Query 'Employee Progress Query' To: text box, then click **OK**
   The query is saved with the new name, Potential Access Assistants, as a new object in the MediaLoft-F database.

7. Close the Potential Access Assistants datasheet

FIGURE F-7: Datasheet for Access records

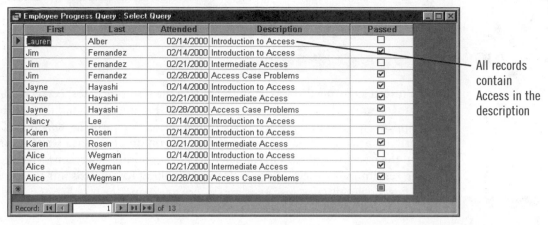

All records contain Access in the description

FIGURE F-8: AND criteria

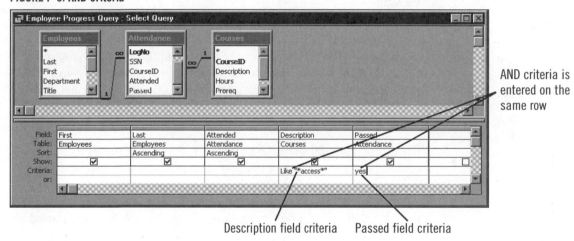

AND criteria is entered on the same row

Description field criteria   Passed field criteria

TABLE F-1: Comparison operators

operator	description	example	result
>	greater than	>50	Value exceeds 50
>=	greater than or equal to	>=50	Value is 50 or greater
<	less than	<50	Value is less than 50
<=	less than or equal to	<=50	Value is 50 or less
<>	not equal to	<>50	Value is any number other than 50
Between...And	finds values between two numbers or dates	Between #2/2/95# And #2/2/98#	Dates between 2/2/95 and 2/2/98, inclusive
In	finds a value that is one of a list	In("IA","KS","NE")	Value equals IA or KS or NE
Null	finds records that are blank	Null	No value has been entered
Is Not Null	finds records that are not blank	Is Not Null	Any value has been entered
Like	finds records that match the criteria	Like "A"	Value equals A
Not	finds records that do not match the criteria	Not 2	Numbers other than 2

Developing OR Queries

AND queries *narrow* the number of records in the resulting datasheet by requiring that a record be true for multiple criteria in one criteria row. **OR queries** *expand* the number of records that will appear in the datasheet because a record needs to be true *for only one* of the criteria rows. OR criteria are entered in the query design grid on different lines (criteria rows). Each criteria row of the query design grid is evaluated separately, adding the records that are true for that row to the resulting datasheet. ◄▬▬ David is looking for an assistant for the Excel courses. He modifies the Potential Access Assistants query to expand the number of records to include those who have passed Excel courses.

Steps

1. Click the **Potential Access Assistants** query, then click the **Design button** 🔲 in the Training-F database window
   To add OR criteria, you have to enter criteria in the "or" row of the query design grid.

2. Click the **or Description criteria cell** below Like "*access*", then type ***excel***
   As soon as you click elsewhere in the query grid, Access will assist you with criteria **syntax** (rules by which criteria need to be entered) by automatically entering the Like operator when necessary. It also automatically adds double quotes to surround text criteria in Text fields, and pound signs (#) to surround date criteria in Date/Time fields. The criteria in Number, Currency, and Yes/No fields are not surrounded by any characters.

3. Click the **or Passed criteria cell** below Yes, then type **yes**
   If a record matches *either* row of the criteria grid, it is included in the query's datasheet. Each row is evaluated separately, which is why it was necessary to put the Yes criteria for the Passed field in both rows of the grid. Otherwise, the second row would pull all records where "excel" is in the description regardless of whether the test was passed or not. Figure F-9 shows the OR criteria in the query design grid.

4. Click the **Datasheet View button** 🔲 on the Query Design toolbar
   The resulting datasheet displays 28 records, as shown in Figure F-10. All of the records contain course Descriptions that contain the word Access or Excel as well as "Yes" in the Passed field. Also, notice that the sort order (Last, then Attended) is still in effect.

5. Click **File** on the menu bar, click **Save As**, click between **"Access"** and **"Assistants"**, type **or Excel**, press **[Spacebar]**, then click **OK**
   This query is saved as a separate database object.

6. Close the Potential Access or Excel Assistants query
   The Training-F database displays the three queries you created.

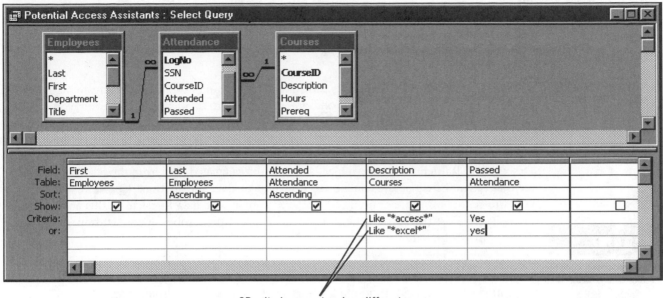

OR criteria are entered on different rows

FIGURE F-10: OR criteria adds more records to the datasheet

First	Last	Attended	Description	Passed
Maria	Abbott	02/14/2000	Introduction to Excel	☑
Lauren	Alber	02/15/2000	Introduction to Excel	☑
Shayla	Colletti	02/14/2000	Introduction to Excel	☑
Shayla	Colletti	03/07/2000	Intermediate Excel	☑
David	Dumont	02/14/2000	Introduction to Excel	☑
Jim	Fernandez	02/14/2000	Introduction to Access	☑
Jim	Fernandez	02/15/2000	Introduction to Excel	☑
Jim	Fernandez	02/28/2000	Access Case Problems	☑
Jayne	Hayashi	02/14/2000	Introduction to Access	☑
Jayne	Hayashi	02/21/2000	Intermediate Access	☑
Jayne	Hayashi	02/28/2000	Access Case Problems	☑
Cynthia	Hayman	02/14/2000	Introduction to Excel	☑
Cynthia	Hayman	03/07/2000	Intermediate Excel	☑
John	Kim	02/14/2000	Introduction to Excel	☑
John	Kim	03/07/2000	Intermediate Excel	☑
John	Kim	03/15/2000	Excel Case Problems	☑
Nancy	Lee	02/14/2000	Introduction to Access	☑

Record: ◄◄ ◄ 1 ► ►► ►* of 28

28 records found

Excel or Access records were found

Passed field is always "Yes"

Using wildcard characters in query criteria

To search for a pattern, use a ? (question mark) to search for any single character and an * (asterisk) to search for any number of characters. Wildcard characters are often used with the Like operator. For example, the criterion Like "10/*/97" would find all dates in October of 1997, and the criterion Like "F*" would find all entries that start with the letter F.

Access 2000

Creating Calculated Fields

Arithmetic operators and functions shown in Table F-2 and F-3, are used to create mathematical calculations within Access. **Functions** are special shortcut formulas that help you calculate common answers such as counts and subtotals on groups of records, a loan payment if working with financial data, or the current date. If you can calculate a new field of information based on existing fields in a database, never define the new piece of data as a separate field in the table's Design view. Rather, use a query object to create the calculated field from the raw data to guarantee that the new field always contains accurate, up-to-date information.   David has been asked to report on the "per hour" cost of each course. The data to calculate this answer already exists in the Cost (the cost of the course) and Hours (the number of contact hours per course) fields of the Courses table.

Steps

QuickTip

You can double-click an object in the Show Table dialog box to add it to Query Design view.

1. Click **Queries** on the Objects bar, double-click **Create query in Design view**, click **Courses**, click **Add**, then click **Close** in the Show Table dialog box
   The Courses field list is in the upper pane of the query window.

2. Double-click the **Description field**, double-click the **Hours field**, then double-click the **Cost field**
   A **calculated field** is created by entering a new descriptive field name followed by a colon in the Field cell of the query design grid followed by an expression. An **expression** is a combination of operators such as + (plus), – (minus), * (multiply), or / (divide); raw values (such as numbers or dates), functions; and fields that produce a result. Field names used in an expression are surrounded by square brackets.

QuickTip

If an expression becomes too long to fit completely in a cell of the query design grid, right-click the cell, then click Zoom to use the Zoom dialog box for long entries.

3. Click the blank **Field cell** of the fourth column, type **Hourly Rate:[Cost]/[Hours]**, then drag the ✛ on the right edge of the fourth column selector to the right to display the entire entry
   The query design grid should now look like Figure F-11.

4. Click the **Datasheet View button** 🔳 on the Query Design toolbar
   It is not necessary to show the fields used in the calculated expression in the datasheet (in this case, Hours and Cost), but viewing these fields beside the new calculated field helps confirm that your new calculated field is working properly. The Hourly Rate field appears to be accurate, but the data is not formatted well.

5. Click the **Design View button** 🔳 on the Query Datasheet toolbar, right-click the calculated **Hourly Rate field** in the query design grid, then click **Properties**
   The Field Properties dialog box opens. This new field represents dollars per hour.

6. Click the **Format text box**, click **Format property list arrow**, click **Currency**, close the property sheet, then click the **Datasheet View button** to display the records
   The data shown in the Hourly Rate field is now rounded to the nearest cent.

7. Press **[Tab]** twice, type **300** in the Introduction to Access Cost field, then press **[Enter]**
   The resulting datasheet is shown in Figure F-12. The Hourly Rate field was updated to the correct value as soon as the Cost field was updated.

Trouble?

If you have already moved to a new record, you must click the Undo button 🔄 to undo your last entry.

8. Press **[Esc]** to reverse the Introduction to Access Cost field change, click the **Save button** 🔳, type **Hourly Rate** in the Save As dialog box, click **OK**, then close the datasheet

FIGURE F-11: Entering a calculated field in Query Design view

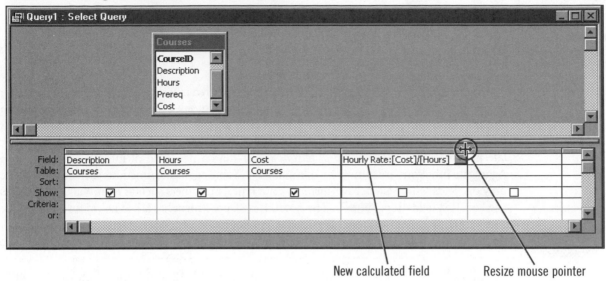

New calculated field   Resize mouse pointer

FIGURE F-12: Formatting and testing the calculated field

Description	Hours	Cost	Hourly Rate
▶ Introduction to Access	12	$300	$25.00
Intermediate Access	24	$400	$16.67
Access Case Problems	12	$200	$16.67
Computer Fundamentals	12	$200	$16.67
Introduction to Excel	12	$200	$16.67
Intermediate Excel	12	$200	$16.67
Excel Case Problems	12	$200	$16.67
Introduction to Internet Explorer	12	$200	$16.67
Intermediate Internet Explorer	12	$200	$16.67
Internet Fundamentals	12	$200	$16.67
Introduction to Netscape	12	$200	$16.67
Intermediate Netscape	12	$200	$16.67
Introduction to Networking	12	$200	

Record: 1 of 27

Calculated field with Currency format

Updated Cost field

TABLE F-2: Arithmetic operators

operator	description
+	Addition
–	Subtraction
*	Multiplication
/	Division
^	Exponentiation

TABLE F-3: Common functions

function	sample expression and description
DATE	DATE()-[BirthDate] Calculates the number of days between today and the date in the BirthDate field
PMT	PMT([Rate],[Term],[Loan]) Calculates the monthly payment on a loan where the Rate field contains the monthly interest rate, the Term field contains the number of monthly payments, and the Loan field contains the total amount financed
LEFT	LEFT([Lastname],2) Returns the first two characters of the entry in the Lastname field
RIGHT	RIGHT([Partno],3) Returns the last three characters of the entry in the Partno field
LEN	LEN([Description]) Returns the number of characters in the Description field

Building Summary Queries

As your database grows, you will probably be less interested in individual records and more interested in information about groups of records. A **summary query** can be used to calculate information about a group of records by adding appropriate **aggregate functions** to the Total row of the query design grid. Aggregate functions also create calculations, but are special functions in that they calculate information about a *group of records* rather than a new field of information for *each record*. Aggregate functions are summarized in Table F-4. Some aggregate functions such as Sum can be used only on fields with Number or Currency data types, but others such as Min, Max, or Count can be used on Text fields, too. ◄ The Accounting Department has asked David for a "cost by department" report that shows how many classes employees of each department have attended as well as the summarized costs for these courses. He builds a summary query to provide this information.

1. Click **Queries** on the Objects bar (if necessary), then double-click **Create query in Design view**
   You need all three tables to develop this query.

2. Click **Courses**, click **Add**, click **Attendance**, click **Add**, click **Employees**, click **Add**, then click **Close** in the Show Table dialog box

3. Double-click the **Department field** in the Employees table, double-click the **Cost field** in the Courses table, then double-click the **Cost field** in the Courses table again
   Even though you don't explicitly use fields from the Attendance table, you need this table in your query to tie the fields from the Courses and Employees tables together. You added the Cost field to the query grid twice because you wish to compute two different summary statistics on the information in this field (a subtotal and a count).

4. Click the **Totals button** 🔢 on the Query Design toolbar
   The Total row is added to the query grid below the Table row. This is the row that you use to specify how you want the resulting datasheet summarized. You want to group the resulting datasheet by the Department field, but summarize the data in the Cost fields.

5. Click the **Cost field Total cell** in the second column, click the **Group By list arrow**, click **Sum**, click the **Cost field Total cell** in the third column, click the **Group By list arrow**, then click **Count**
   Your Query Design view should look like Figure F-13.

QuickTip
You cannot enter or edit data in a summary query because each record represents the summarization of several records. The resulting datasheet is not updateable.

6. Click the **Datasheet View button** 📊 on the Query Design toolbar
   As you can see from the resulting datasheet, the Accounting Department had $3,500 of internal charges for the 16 classes its employees attended. By counting the Cost field in addition to summing it, you know how many records were combined to reach the total $3,500 figure. You can sort summary queries, too.

7. Click any entry in the **SumOfCost** field, then click the **Sort Descending button** 🔽 on the Query Datasheet toolbar
   The resulting datasheet is shown in Figure F-14, listing the in-house training costs in a highest to lowest order for all of the 11 departments at MediaLoft. If you wanted to permanently store this sort order, you would specify it in Query Design view, where it would be stored as part of the query object.

QuickTip
If you need to identify your printout, include your name or initials in the query name.

8. Click the **Save button** 💾, type **Internal Costs**, click **OK**, click the **Print button** 🖨 on the Query Datasheet toolbar, then close the datasheet

FIGURE F-13: Summary Query Design view

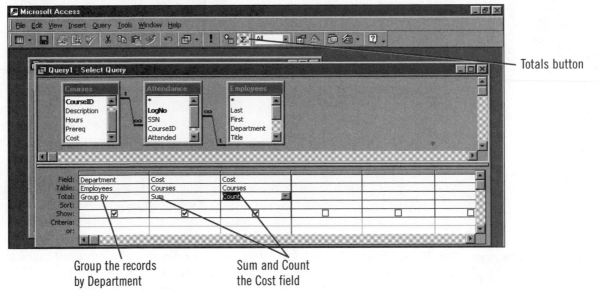

Totals button

Group the records by Department

Sum and Count the Cost field

FIGURE F-14: Summarized records sorted in descending order by SumOfCost

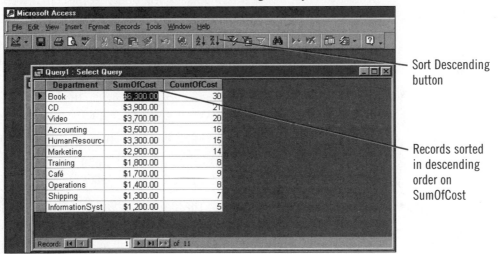

Sort Descending button

Records sorted in descending order on SumOfCost

TABLE F-4: Aggregate Functions

aggregate function	used to find the
Sum	Total of values in a field
Avg	Average of values in a field
Min	Minimum value in the field
Max	Maximum value in the field
Count	Number of values in a field (not counting null values)
StDev	Standard deviation of values in a field
Var	Variance of values in a field
First	Field value from the first record in a table or query
Last	Field value from the last record in a table or query

Access 2000

Creating Crosstab Queries

Crosstab queries provide another method of summarizing data by creating a datasheet in which one or more fields are chosen for the row headings, another field is chosen for the column headings, and a third field, usually a numeric field, is summarized within the datasheet itself. If you wish to base the crosstab query on fields from multiple tables, the first step to creating a crosstab query is to assemble the fields in a single select query. Then you create the final crosstab query based upon the intermediary query object by using the **Crosstab Query Wizard** to identify which fields will be the row and column headings, and which field will be summarized within the grid of the crosstab datasheet itself. ✎ David wishes to expand the information in the Internal Costs query to summarize the total cost for each course within each department. This is a good candidate for a crosstab query because he is summarizing information by two fields, one that will serve as the row heading (Description) and one that will serve as the column heading (Department) for the final crosstab datasheet.

Steps

1. Click **Queries** on the objects bar (if necessary), click **Internal Costs**, then click the **Design View button** 🖾 in the Training-F database window
   Instead of creating the intermediate select query from scratch, a couple of modifications to the Internal Costs query will quickly provide the fields you need.

2. Click the **Totals button** Σ on the Query Design toolbar, click the **Cost Field cell** for the third column, click the **Cost list arrow**, then click **Description**
   The intermediary select query should look like Figure F-15. You removed the summary functions (the Total row on the query design grid), then changed the second Cost field to the Description field. It is important to save the query with an appropriate name.

3. Click **File** on the menu bar, click **Save As**, type **Crosstab Fields** in the **Save Query 'Internal Costs' To:** text box, click **OK**, then close the query
   You can build the Crosstab query using the Crosstab Query Wizard.

Trouble?

The Create query by using wizard option from the database window is used only to create a select query, so you must click the New button to use the other query wizards.

4. Click the **New button** 🖾 in the database window, click **Crosstab Query Wizard** in the New Query dialog box, then click **OK**
   The Crosstab Query Wizard dialog box opens. The first question asks you which object contains the fields for the crosstab query.

5. Click the **Queries option button** in the View section, click **Crosstab Fields** in the list of available queries, then click **Next**
   The next questions from the Crosstab Query Wizard will organize how the fields are displayed in the datasheet.

QuickTip

You can click the Back button within any wizard to review previous choices.

6. Click **Description** for the row heading, click the **Select Single Field button** ⟩, click **Next**, click **Department** to specify the column heading, then click **Next**
   The next wizard dialog box asks you to identify the field that is summarized within the body of the crosstab report. Since the Cost field is the only field left, it is automatically chosen, but you still need to specify a function that will determine the way the Cost field is calculated.

7. Click **Sum** in the Functions list
   Your Query Wizard dialog box should look like Figure F-16.

8. Click **Next**, type **Crosstab Query** in the query name text box, then click **Finish**
   The final crosstab query is shown in Figure F-17.

9. Print the resulting datasheet

FIGURE F-15: Select query upon which the crosstab query will be based

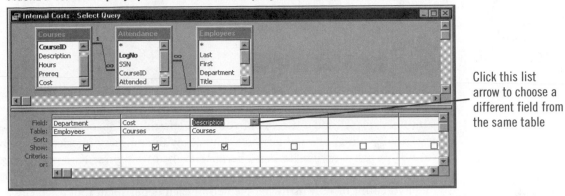

Click this list arrow to choose a different field from the same table

FIGURE F-16: Crosstab Query Wizard

Department field is the column heading

Description field is the row heading

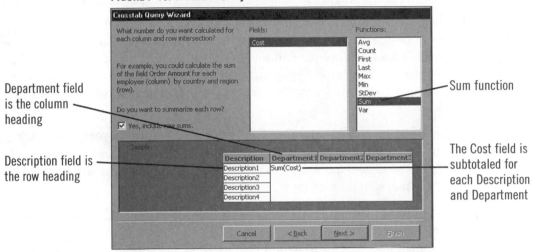

Sum function

The Cost field is subtotaled for each Description and Department

FIGURE F-17: Crosstab Query datasheet

Descriptions are row headings

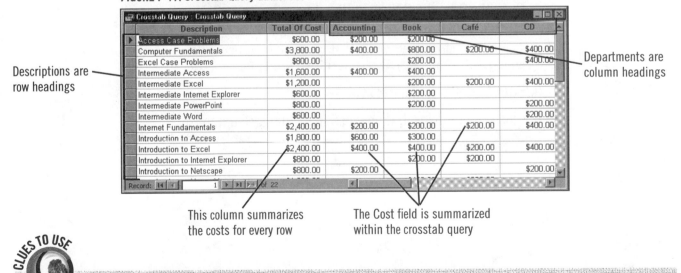

Departments are column headings

This column summarizes the costs for every row

The Cost field is summarized within the crosstab query

Defining types of Query Wizards

The **Simple Query Wizard** is an alternative way to create a select query, rather than going directly into Query Design view. The **Find Duplicates Query Wizard** is used to determine whether a table contains duplicate values in one or more fields. The **Find Unmatched Query Wizard** is used to find records in one table that don't have related records in another table. To invoke the Find Duplicates, Find Unmatched, or Crosstab Query Wizards, you must click the New button when viewing the query objects within the opening database window.

Modifying Crosstab Queries

Once a crosstab query is created, it can be modified in Query Design view, just like a select query can. Crosstab queries use two additional rows in the query grid: the "Totals" row (similar to a summary query) and a "Crosstab" row that determines the location of the field (column heading, row heading, or summarized value). As with summary queries, crosstab query datasheets cannot be used to update data, because every row represents a summarization of multiple records of data. ✐ David will use Query Design view to modify the crosstab query so that he has a count of how many people within each department took each class.

Steps

1. **Click the Design View button ▣ on the Query Datasheet toolbar**
   Query Design view for the Crosstab Query opens, as shown in Figure F-18. The Totals and Crosstab rows are displayed in the query grid. If you had not used the Query Wizard to create this query, you could still display these rows and, therefore, make any existing select query into a crosstab query by selecting the Query Type button and choosing the Crosstab Query from the list.

2. **Click Sum in the Total row for Cost field, click the list arrow, then click Count**
   This field determines the calculation performed on the field within the body of the crosstab report. Now it will count the number of people within each department that took each class rather than sum the Cost data.

3. **Click Sum in the Total row for the Total of Cost: Cost field, click the list arrow, then click Count**
   This field determines the second **row heading** and will now count how many courses of each description were taken for all departments.

4. **Click the Datasheet View button ▣ on the Query Design toolbar, then click the Save button ▣ on the Query Datasheet toolbar**
   The modified crosstab query that counts the number of times each course was taken for employees within each department is shown in Figure F-19.

5. **Print the resulting datasheet**

6. **Close the datasheet, then close the Training-F database**

7. **Exit Access**

FIGURE F-18: Query Design view of a crosstab query

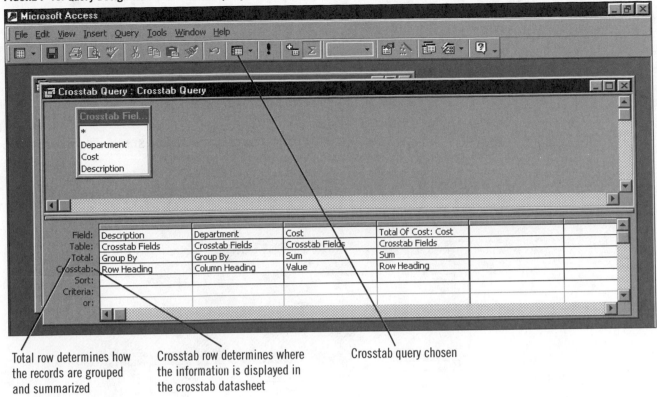

Total row determines how the records are grouped and summarized

Crosstab row determines where the information is displayed in the crosstab datasheet

Crosstab query chosen

FIGURE F-19: Modified crosstab query that counts courses taken

Description	Total Of Cost	Accounting	Book	Café	CD
Access Case Problems	3	1	1		
Computer Fundamentals	19	2	4	1	
Excel Case Problems	4		1		
Intermediate Access	4	1	1		
Intermediate Excel	6		1	1	
Intermediate Internet Explorer	3		1		
Intermediate PowerPoint	4		1		
Intermediate Word	3				
Internet Fundamentals	12	1	1	1	
Introduction to Access	6	2	1		
Introduction to Excel	12	2	2	1	
Introduction to Internet Explorer	4		1	1	
Introduction to Netscape	4	1			

Record: |◄| ◄ | 1 | ► | ►| | ►* | of 22

A total of 19 Computer Fundamentals courses were taken

Accounting Department employees took 2 Introduction to Excel courses

Practice

► Concepts Review

Identify each element of the Design view window and Select query window shown in Figure F-20.

FIGURE F-20

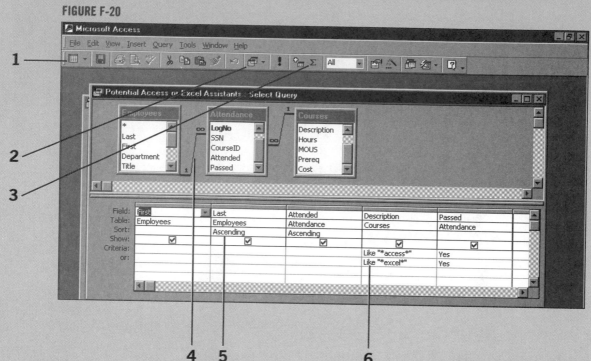

Match each term with the statement that describes its function.

7. Query
8. Arithmetic operators
9. And
10. Sorting
11. Criteria

a. Placing the records of a datasheet in a certain order
b. Used to create mathematical calculations in a query
c. A database object that answers questions about the data
d. Conditions that select only certain records
e. Operator used to combine two expressions

Select the best answer from the list of choices.

12. The query datasheet can best be described as a
   a. Duplication of the data in the underlying table's datasheet.
   b. Logical view of the selected data from an underlying table's datasheet.
   c. Separate file of data.
   d. Second copy of the data in the underlying tables.

13. **Queries are often used to:**
   a. Create copies of database files.
   b. Eliminate the need to build multiple tables.
   c. Create option boxes and list boxes from which to choose field values.
   d. Present a subset of fields from multiple tables.

14. **When you update data in a table that is displayed in a query:**
   a. You must also update the query.
   b. You must relink the query to the table.
   c. The data is automatically updated in the query.
   d. You have the choice whether or not you want to update the data in the query.

15. **To assemble several fields from different tables, use a(n):**
   a. Select Query.
   b. Update Query.
   c. Delete Query.
   d. Append Query.

16. **The order in which records are sorted is determined by:**
   a. The order in which the fields are defined in the underlying table.
   b. The alphabetic order of the field names.
   c. The left-to-right position of the fields in the query design grid.
   d. The ascending fields are sorted first in the query design grid, then the descending fields are sorted second.

17. **Crosstab queries are used to:**
   a. Summarize information based on fields in the column and row headings of the report.
   b. Update several records at the same time.
   c. Select fields for a datasheet from multiple tables.
   d. Calculate price increases on numeric fields.

► Skills Review

1. **Create select queries.**
   a. Start Access and open the database Membership-F.
   b. Create a new select query in Design View using both the Names and Zips tables.
   c. Add the following fields to the query design grid in this order:
      First, Last, and Street from the Names table
      City, State, and Zip from the Zips table
   d. Enter your own last name in the Last field of the first record.
   e. Save the query as "Basic Address List", view the datasheet, print the datasheet, then close the query.

2. **Sort a query on multiple fields.**
   a. Open the Design view for the Basic Address List query. You wish to modify the query so that it is sorted in ascending order by Last, then by First, but you do not want to change the order of the fields in the resulting datasheet.
   b. Drag another First field to the right of the Last field in the query design grid to make the first three fields in the query design grid First, Last, and First.

    c. Add the ascending sort criteria to the second column and third column fields, and uncheck the Show check box in the third column.

    d. Use Save As to save the query as "Sorted Address List", view the datasheet, print the datasheet, then close the query.

3. Develop AND queries.

    a. Return to the Design view for the Basic Address List. You wish to modify the "Basic Address List" query so that only those people from Kansas with a last name that starts with "M" are chosen.

    b. Enter M* (the asterisk is a wildcard) in the criteria row for the Last field to choose all people whose last name starts with M. Access assists you with the syntax for this type of criterion and enters "Like M*" in the cell when you click elsewhere in the grid.

    c. Enter "KS" as the criterion for the State field. Be sure to enter the criteria on the same line in the query design grid to make the query an AND query. You should have six records in this datasheet.

    d. Enter your own hometown in the City field of the first record.

    e. Save the query as "Kansas M Names", view, print, then close the datasheet.

4. Develop OR queries.

    a. Modify the "Kansas M Names" query so that only those people from KS with a last name that starts with either "M" or "C" are chosen. Do this by entering the OR criterion C* on the or row for the Last field in the query design grid.

    b. Be sure to also type the KS criterion on the or row for the State field in the query design grid to make sure that your query doesn't display all names that start with C, but only those who also live in Kansas.

    c. Save the query as "Kansas C or M Names", view the datasheet (there should be nine records), print the datasheet, then close the query.

5. Create calculated fields.

    a. Create a new select query using Design view using only the Names table. You want to determine the number of days old each person is based on the information in the Birthday field.

    b. Add the following fields from the Names table to the query design grid in this order: First, Last, Birthday.

    c. Create a calculated field called "Days Old" in the fourth column of the query design grid by entering the expression: Days Old:Date()-[Birthday].

    d. Sort the query in descending order on the calculated Days Old field.

    e. Select the calculated Days Old field, open the Property sheet, format the Days Old field with a Standard format, and enter "0" in the Decimal Places property text box. (*Hint:* You may need to view the datasheet then return to Design View to see the Decimal Places property.)

    f. Save the query as "Days Old", view the datasheet, print the datasheet, then close the query.

6. Build summary queries.

    a. Create a new select query using Design view, then add the Names and Activities tables.

    b. Add the following fields: First and Last from the Names table, Hours from the Activities table.

    c. Add the Total row to the query design grid and change the function for the Hours field from Group By to Sum.

    d. Sort in descending order by Hours.

    e. Save the query as "Total Hours", view the datasheet, print the datasheet, then close the query.

7. Create crosstab queries.

   a. First create a select query with the fields City and State from the Zips table, and Dues from the Names table. Save it as "Crosstab Fields".

   b. Click the New button when viewing query objects, then start the Crosstab Query Wizard, and base the crosstab query on the Crosstab Fields query you just created.

   c. Select City as the row heading and State as the column heading, and sum the Dues field within the crosstab datasheet.

   d. Save and name the query "Crosstab of Dues by City and State".

   e. View, print, then close the datasheet.

8. Modify crosstab queries.

   a. Open the Crosstab of Dues by City and State query in Design view.

   b. Change the Sum function to Count for both the Dues and the Total of Dues: Dues fields.

   c. View, print, then close the datasheet without saving it.

   d. Close the database, then exit Access.

▶ Independent Challenges

1. As the manager of a music store's instrument rental program, you have created a database to track instrument rentals to schoolchildren. Now that several rentals have been made, you wish to query the database for several different datasheet printouts to analyze school information.

To complete this independent challenge:

   a. Start Access and open the database Music Store-F.

   b. Create a query that pulls the following fields in the following order into a datasheet, then print the datasheet: SchoolName from Schools table, Date from Rentals table, Description from Instruments table. (*Hint:* You will need to add the Customers table to this query to make the connection between the Schools table and the Rentals table even though you don't need any Customers fields in this query's datasheet.)

   c. Sort ascending by SchoolName, then ascending by Date.

   d. Save the query as "School Rentals", enter your high school name in the first record, then print the datasheet.

   e. Modify the School Rentals query by deleting the Description field. Then, use the Totals button to group the records by SchoolName and to count the Date field. Print the datasheet and save the query as "School Count". (*Note:* Include your name or initials as part of the query name if you need to identify your prinout.)

   f. Use the Crosstab Query Wizard to create a crosstab query based on the School Rentals query. Use Description as the row heading and SchoolName as the column heading. Count the Date field.

   g. Save the query as "School Crosstab", then view, print, and close it.

   h. Modify the "School Rentals" query so that only those schools with the word "Elementary" in the SchoolName field are displayed. (*Hint:* You will have to use wildcard characters in the criteria.) Twelve elementary schools should be displayed.

   i. Save the query as "Elementary Rentals", then view, print, and close the datasheet.

   j. Close the Music Store-F database and exit Access.

Access 2000

2. As the manager of a music store's instrument rental program, you have created a database to track instrument rentals to schoolchildren. Now that several rentals have been made, you wish to query the database to analyze customer and rental information.

To complete this independent challenge:

a. Start Access and open the database Music Store-F.

b. Create a query that pulls the following fields in the following order into a datasheet, and print the datasheet:
FirstName and LastName from the Customers Table
Description and MonthlyFee from the Instruments Table
(*Hint:* You will need to add the Rentals table to this query to make the connection between the Customers table and the Instruments table even though you don't need any Rentals fields in this query's datasheet.)

c. Sort ascending by LastName.

d. Save the query as "Customer Rentals", enter your own last name in the first record's LastName field, and print the datasheet.

e. Modify the Customer Rentals query by deleting the FirstName and LastName fields. Then, use the Totals button to group the records by Description and to sum the MonthlyFee field.

f. Add another MonthlyFee field as a third column to the query grid, and use the Count function to find the total number of rentals within that group.

g. Sort ascending by the Description field.

h. Save the query as "Monthly Instrument Income".

i. View, print, and close the datasheet.

j. Close the Music Store-F database and exit Access.

3. As the manager of a music store's instrument rental program, you have created a database to track instrument rentals to schoolchildren. The database has already been used to answer several basic questions, and now that you've shown how easy it is to get the answers using queries, more and more questions are being asked. You will use queries to analyze customer and rental information.

To complete this independent challenge:

a. Start Access and open the database Music Store-F.

b. Create a query that pulls the following fields in the following order into a datasheet:
Description and MonthlyFee from the Instruments Table
Zip and City from the Customers Table
(*Hint:* You will need to add the Rentals table to this query to make the connection between the Customers table and the Instruments table even though you don't need any Rentals fields in this query's datasheet.)

c. Sort ascending by Zip, and within Zip by Description. (*Hint:* You will have to add the Zip field to the query grid twice to accomplish this task. Uncheck the Show check box on the Zip field column that you do not wish to display in the datasheet.)

d. Save the query as "Zip Analysis". (*Note:* Include your name or initials as part of the query name if you need to identify your printout.)

e. View, print, and close the datasheet.

f. Modify the Zip Analysis query by adding criteria to find the records where the Description is "viola".

g. Save this query as "Violas". The datasheet should have three records. Print the datasheet.

h. Modify the Violas query with AND criteria that further specifies that the City must be "Des Moines".

i. Save this query as "Violas in Des Moines". The datasheet should have only one record. Print the datasheet.

j. Modify the "Violas" query with OR criteria that finds all violas OR violins, regardless of where they are located.

k. Save this query as "Violas and Violins". The datasheet should have five records. Print and close the datasheet.

l. Using the Crosstab Query Wizard, create a crosstab query based on the School Analysis query that uses the Description field for the row headings and the SchoolName field for the column headings, and that counts the RentalNo field.

m. Save the crosstab query as "Crosstab School and Instrument", preview the datasheet, then print the datasheet in landscape orientation so that it fits on one page.

n. Close the Music Store-F database and exit Access.

4. Check the MediaLoft Intranet site to find cost information about public training courses that the Accounting Department has gathered. Then create a query to determine if your in-house courses are similar in length and cost.

To complete this independent challenge:

a. Connect to the Internet and use your browser to go to the MediaLoft Intranet site at http://www.course.com/illustrated/MediaLoft/

b. Click the link for Training.

c. Click the link for Public Courses, and print the Web page.

d. Start Access and open the Training-F database.

e. Create a query that lists the following fields from the Courses table in the following order: Description, Hours, Cost.

f. Sort the records in ascending order by Description.

g. Save the query as "Competitor Analysis". (*Note:* If you need to identify your printout, include your name or initials in the query name.)

h. View and print the resulting datasheet.

i. Compare the Competitor Analysis query to the results you found on the Web site. Who offers less expensive training, MediaLoft or the competition?

j. Print the datasheet, exit Access.

Access 2000

► Visual Workshop

Open the Training-F database and create a new query to display the datasheet as shown in Figure F-21. Notice that the records are sorted alphabetically by the date the course was attended, then by last name. Save the query as "History of Attendance". (*Note:* If you need to identify your work on the printout, add your initials as part of the query name). Print the query.

FIGURE F-21

History of Attendance : Select Query

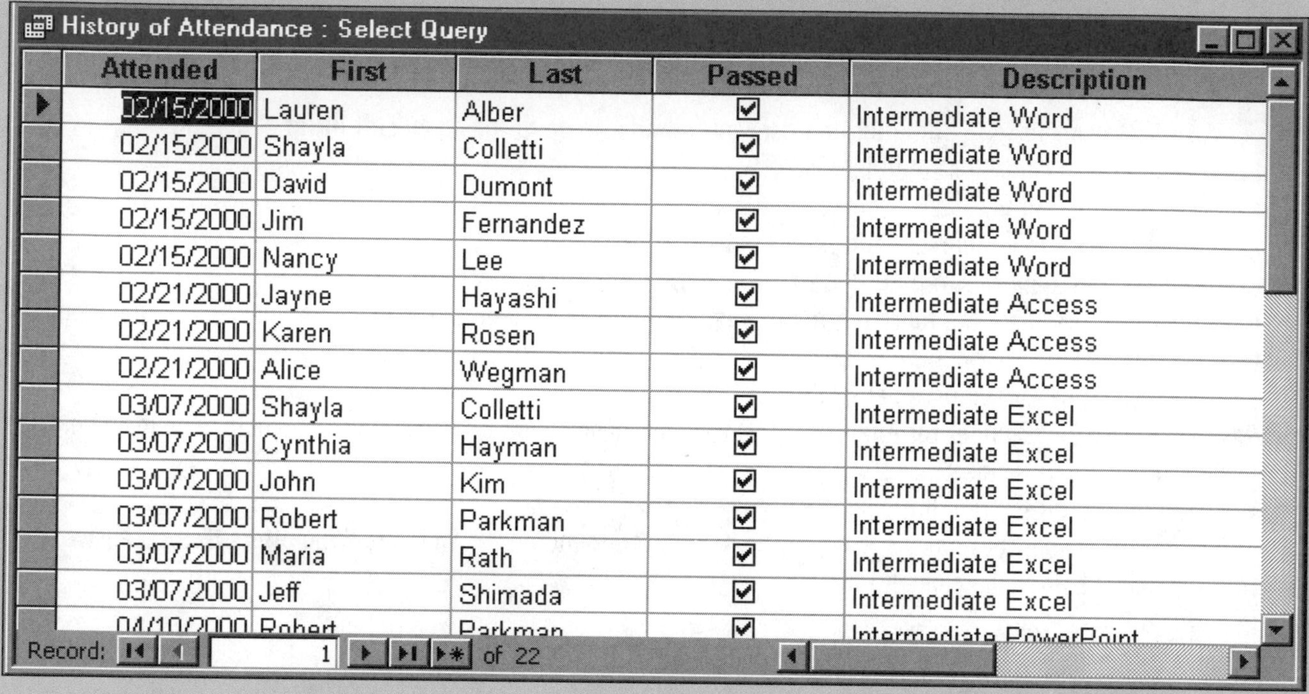

Attended	First	Last	Passed	Description
02/15/2000	Lauren	Alber	☑	Intermediate Word
02/15/2000	Shayla	Colletti	☑	Intermediate Word
02/15/2000	David	Dumont	☑	Intermediate Word
02/15/2000	Jim	Fernandez	☑	Intermediate Word
02/15/2000	Nancy	Lee	☑	Intermediate Word
02/21/2000	Jayne	Hayashi	☑	Intermediate Access
02/21/2000	Karen	Rosen	☑	Intermediate Access
02/21/2000	Alice	Wegman	☑	Intermediate Access
03/07/2000	Shayla	Colletti	☑	Intermediate Excel
03/07/2000	Cynthia	Hayman	☑	Intermediate Excel
03/07/2000	John	Kim	☑	Intermediate Excel
03/07/2000	Robert	Parkman	☑	Intermediate Excel
03/07/2000	Maria	Rath	☑	Intermediate Excel
03/07/2000	Jeff	Shimada	☑	Intermediate Excel
04/10/2000	Robert	Parkman	☑	Intermediate PowerPoint

Record: 1 of 22

Developing
Forms and Subforms

Objectives

- ▶ **Understand the form/subform relationship**
- ▶ **Create subforms using the Form Wizard**
- [MOUS] ▶ **Create subforms using queries**
- [MOUS] ▶ **Modify subforms**
- [MOUS] ▶ **Add combo boxes**
- [MOUS] ▶ **Add option groups**
- [MOUS] ▶ **Add command buttons**
- [MOUS] ▶ **Add records with a form/subform**

Viewing, finding, entering, and editing data in a database must be easy and straightforward for all database users. A **form** can be designed to present data in any logical screen arrangement and serve as the primary interface for most database users. Forms contain **controls** such as labels, text boxes, combo boxes, and command buttons to help identify and enter data. Forms with **subform** controls allow you to show a record and its related records from another object (table or query) at the same time. For example, on one screen you may wish to see customer information as well as all of the orders placed by the customer. Well-designed form/subforms will encourage fast, accurate data entry, and will shield the data entry person from the complexity of underlying tables, queries, and datasheets. ◄━━ David develops a single form that shows employee information at the top of the form and all of the classes that an employee has attended at the bottom. This requires a subform control. He also upgrades the usability of the forms by adding various controls such as combo boxes, option groups, and command buttons.

Understanding the Form/Subform Relationship

A **subform** control is actually a form within a form. The primary form is called the **main form**, and it contains the subform control. The subform shows related records that are linked to the single record currently displayed in the main form. The relationship between the main form and subform is often called a **parent/child relationship**, because the "parent" record in the main form is linked to many "children" records displayed in the subform. The link between the main form and subform is established through a linking field common to both, the same field that is used to establish the one-to-many relationship between underlying tables in the database.  Creating forms with subforms requires careful planning, so David studies form/subform planning guidelines before he attempts to create the forms in Access.

 Sketch the layout of the form/subform on paper, identifying which fields belong in the main form and which belong in the subform

David has sketched two forms with subforms that he wants to create. Figure G-1 displays employee information in the main form and attendance information in the subform. Figure G-2 displays course information in the main form and employee information in the subform.

 Determine whether you are going to create separate queries upon which to base the main form and subform, or if you are going to use the Form Wizard to collect fields from multiple tables upon which to create the form and subform objects

This decision may have important consequences later because it determines the form's recordset. The **recordset** is the fields and records that will appear on the form. To modify the recordset of forms created solely through the Form Wizard, you have to modify the form's **Record Source property**, where the recordset is defined. When the form is based on an intermediate query, changing the query object automatically updates the Record Source property for the form, because the query object name *is* the Record Source property entry for that form.

If you use the Form Wizard to create a form with fields from multiple tables without an intermediary query object, the Record Source property of the form often displays an **SQL (Structured Query Language) statement**. This SQL statement can be modified to change the recordset, but obviously requires some knowledge of SQL.

 Create the form and subform objects based on the appropriate intermediary queries. If intermediary queries were not created, use the Form Wizard to gather the fields for both the form and subform

David uses the Form Wizard technique as well as the intermediary query technique so that he can compare the two.

FIGURE G-1: Employees Main Form with Attendance Subform

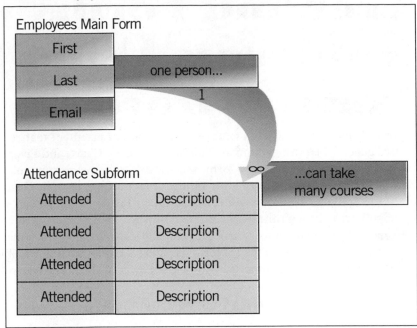

FIGURE G-2: Courses Main Form with Employee Subform

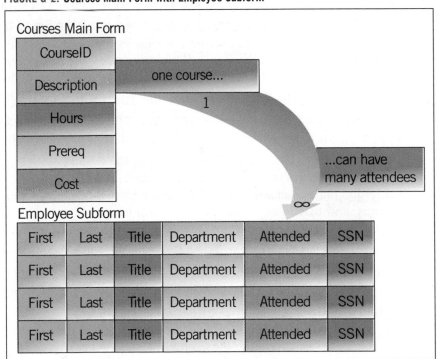

Creating Forms with Subforms Using the Form Wizard

A form displays the fields of a table or query in an arrangement that you design, based on one of five general **layouts**: Columnar, Tabular, Datasheet, Chart, and PivotTable. **Columnar** is the most popular layout for a main form, and **Datasheet** is the most popular layout for a subform. See Table G-1 for more information on the different form layouts. Once the main form is created, the subform control is added in the main form's Form Design view. If you create the form/subform through the Form Wizard, however, both objects are created in one process. ⤴ David creates a form and subform showing employee information in the main form and course information in the subform. He creates the form/subform objects without first creating intermediary query objects by using the power of the Form Wizard.

Steps

1. Start Access and open the **Training-G** database

2. Click **Forms** on the Objects bar, then double-click **Create form by using wizard** in the Training-G Database window
   The **Form Wizard** appears and prompts you to select the fields of the form. You need five fields that are stored in three different tables for the final form/subform.

3. Click the **Attended field**, click the **Select Single Field button** ▸, click the **Tables/Queries list arrow**, click **Table: Courses**, click the **Description field**, click ▸, click the **Tables/Queries list arrow**, click **Table: Employees**, click the **First field**, click ▸, click the **Last field**, click ▸, click the **Email field**, then click ▸
   The Form Wizard dialog box should look like Figure G-3. Next, you must decide how to view the data. Arranging the form by Employees places the fields from the Employees table in the main form, and the Attended and Description fields in a subform.

4. Click **Next**, click **by Employees**, click the **Form with subform(s) option button** (if necessary), click **Next**, click the **Datasheet option button** (if necessary) as the layout for the subform, click **Next**, click **Standard** (if necessary) as the style for the main form, click **Next**, then click **Finish** to accept the default form and subform names
   The final Employees main form and Attendance Subform is shown in Figure G-4. Two sets of navigation buttons appear, one for the main form and one for the subform. The navigation buttons show that 19 employees are in the recordset and that the first employee has attended 11 courses. You can resize the form and subform control to display more information.

5. Click the **Design View button** 🖳 on the Form View toolbar, click the **Employees Form Maximize button**, click the **subform control** so that sizing handles appear, then drag the subform control bottom middle sizing handle to the horizontal scroll bar at the bottom of the screen using ↕, as shown in Figure G-5
   The controls on the Attendance Subform appear within the subform control, and can be modified, just like controls in the main form.

6. Click the **Form View button** 🖽 on the Form Design toolbar to view the resized subform, click the **Save button** 🖫, then close the **Employees** form
   The Employees form and the Attendance Subform appear with other form objects in the Training-G database window.

FIGURE G-3: Form Wizard

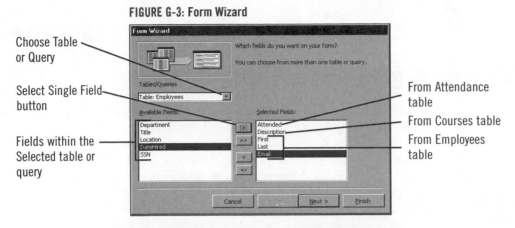

Choose Table or Query

Select Single Field button

Fields within the Selected table or query

From Attendance table

From Courses table

From Employees table

FIGURE G-4: Employees Main Form/Attendance Subform

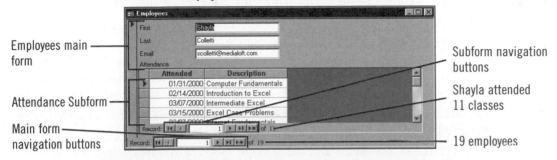

Employees main form

Attendance Subform

Main form navigation buttons

Subform navigation buttons

Shayla attended 11 classes

19 employees

FIGURE G-5: Resizing the Attendance Subform

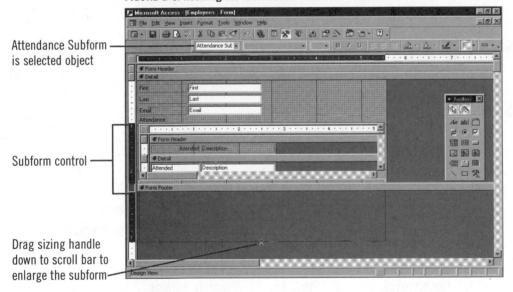

Attendance Subform is selected object

Subform control

Drag sizing handle down to scroll bar to enlarge the subform

TABLE G-1: Form layouts

layout	description
Columnar	Each field appears on a separate line with a label to its left, one record for each screen
Tabular	Each field appears as a column heading and each record as a row. Multiple records appear just like they do in a datasheet, but you have more design control and flexibility. For example, you can change elements such as colors, fonts, headers, or footers
Datasheet	Each field appears as a column heading and each record as a row. The datasheet layout shows multiple records, but formatting options, except for resizing columns, are limited
Chart	Numeric fields appear in a chart (graph) format
PivotTable	Fields are chosen for column and row headings, and a field is summarized in the intersection of the appropriate column and row in a cross-tabular format

Creating Subforms Using Queries

Another way to create a form with a subform is to create both forms separately, basing them on either table or query objects, then linking the two forms together in a form/subform relationship. Although creating the forms by building them on separate query objects takes more work than building the form/subform using the Form Wizard, the benefit is your ability to quickly change the form's recordset by modifying the underlying query. ✎ David creates a form and subform showing course information in the main form and employee information in the subform using query objects that he has already created.

Steps

Trouble?

If the property sheet doesn't show the word "Form" in the title bar, click the Form Selector button.

1. Double-click **Create form in Design View**, click the **Properties button** 🔲 on the Form Design toolbar to display the form's property sheet, click the **Data tab**, click the **Record Source list arrow**, then click **Employee Info**
   The Employee Info query's field list (which supplies the recordset for the form) opens. Another initial property to consider is the **Default View** property, which determines the form's appearance. Datasheet layout is a popular style for subforms because it arranges the fields horizontally.

2. Click the **Format tab**, click the **Default View text box**, click the **Default View list arrow**, click **Datasheet**, then click 🔲 to toggle the property sheet off
   With the Record Source and Default View specified, you are ready to add the fields to the form.

QuickTip

Point to the Field list title bar to display the object name as a ScreenTip.

3. Double-click the **Employee Info field list title bar**, drag the **selected fields** using 🗇 to the top of the Detail section at the **1" mark** on the horizontal ruler, as shown in Figure G-6, then click the **Field list button** 🔲 to toggle the field list off

4. Click the **Save button** 🔲 on the Form Design toolbar, the Save As dialog box opens, type **Employee Info Sub** in the Form Name text box, click **OK**, then close the form
   The subform will display the Employees who took each course.

5. Double-click **Create form in Design View**, click 🔲 to display the form's property sheet, click the **Data tab**, click the **Record Source property list arrow**, then click **Courses Info**
   The main form requires all of the fields from the Courses Info query.

Trouble?

If you drag and position the fields incorrectly on the form, click Undo 🔄 and try again.

6. Click 🔲 to close the property sheet, double-click the **Courses Info Field list title bar**, drag the **selected fields** using 🗇 to the top of the Detail section at the **1" mark** on the horizontal ruler, click 🔲 to close the Field list, then maximize the form
   The main form is created. Now add the subform to it.

Trouble?

If you get a message box to install the Subform Wizard, insert your Office 2000 CD, then follow the instructions to install the feature.

7. Click the **Toolbox button** 🔨 on the Form Design toolbar to display the Toolbox toolbar (if necessary), be sure the **Control Wizards button** 🔲 is selected, click the **Subform/Subreport button** 🔲 on the Toolbox toolbar, then use ⁺🔲 to drag a 6" wide and 2" high rectangle to place the subform just below the Cost controls as shown in Figure G-7
   If you drag a control beyond the edges of an existing form, the form will automatically enlarge to accept the control. The SubForm Wizard appears.

8. Click **Employee Info Sub** as the existing data for the subform, click **Next**, verify that **Show Employee Info for each record in Courses Info using CourseID** is selected, click **Next**, verify the name **Employee Info Sub**, click **Finish**, then click the **Form View button** 🔲
   The final form/subform is shown in Figure G-8. The first of 27 courses, Access1, is displayed in the main form. The six employees who completed that course are displayed in the subform.

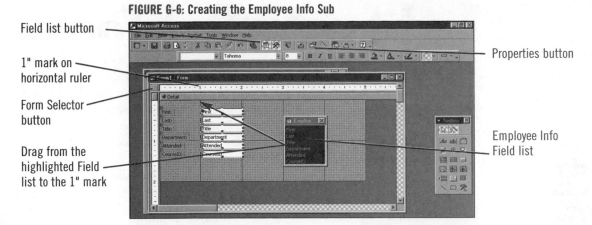

FIGURE G-6: Creating the Employee Info Sub

Field list button

1" mark on horizontal ruler

Form Selector button

Drag from the highlighted Field list to the 1" mark

Properties button

Employee Info Field list

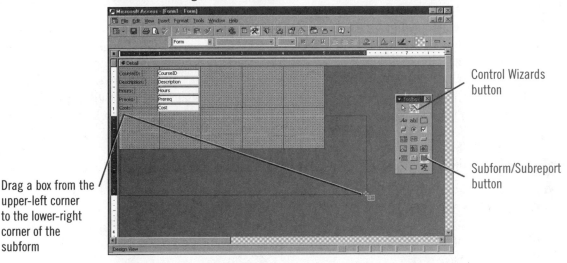

FIGURE G-7: Adding a subform control

Drag a box from the upper-left corner to the lower-right corner of the subform

Control Wizards button

Subform/Subreport button

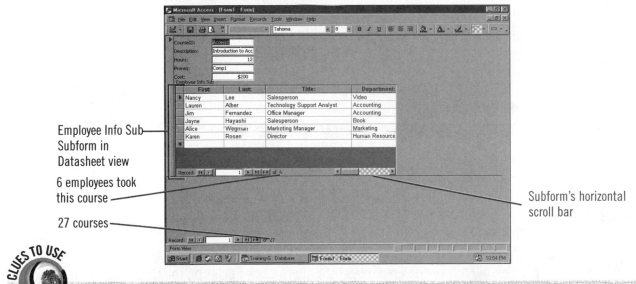

FIGURE G-8: Courses Main Form / Employee Info Subform

Employee Info Sub Subform in Datasheet view

6 employees took this course

27 courses

Subform's horizontal scroll bar

CLUES TO USE

Linking the form and subform

If the form and subform do not appear to be correctly linked, examine the subform's property sheet, paying special attention to the **Link Child Fields** and **Link Master Fields** properties on the Data tab. These properties tell you which field serves as the link between the main form and subform. The field specified for this property should be present in the queries that underlie the main and subforms, and is the same field that creates the one-to-many relationship.

Unit G
Access 2000

Modifying Subforms

Because the form/subform arrangement packs so much information on one screen, it is important to modify and format the form/subform to present the data clearly. If the subform is displayed in Datasheet view, you can use resize, hide, or move the columns. You can also change the subform's font, grid color, or background color directly in Form view. When viewing the subform control in Design view, you can directly modify the subform's controls just as you can directly modify the main form's controls. ▰▰▰ David likes the form/subform arrangement that displays each course in the main form and each employee who has taken that course in the subform, but he will improve upon the subform's design to display the employee subform information a little more clearly.

Steps

Trouble?
If sizing handles do not appear around the entire subform control or if the subform name is not in the object box on the Formatting Form/Report toolbar, click outside the control, then click the subform control again to select it.

1. **Click the Design View button** 🖾 **on the Form View toolbar, click the subform control, drag the middle right sizing handle to the 7" mark on the horizontal ruler, as shown in Figure G-9, then release the mouse button**
   Widening the subform control will allow you to display more fields at the same time. Even though the fields of the subform appear to be in a vertical arrangement in the subform control, the "Datasheet" Default View property forces them to display horizontally, like a datasheet. Other options for a form's Default View property are shown in Table G-2.

2. **Click the Form View button** 🖳 **on the Form Design toolbar to view the widened subform**
   The appearance of a horizontal scroll bar on the subform tells you that not all of the fields are visible on the subform's datasheet, but you can resize the columns of the datasheet directly in Form view.

Trouble?
You will not see ╋ when pointing within the datasheet itself. You must point to the edge of the field selector (between field names).

3. **Point to the First and Last field name column separator, double-click with ╋ to automatically adjust the column to accommodate the widest entry, then double-click each field name column separator in the subform**
   Your screen should look like Figure G-10. Notice that the horizontal scroll bar disappears when all fields within the subform are visible. Formatting the datasheet makes it more appealing to the user.

4. **Click any field in the subform, click the Line/Border color button list arrow** 🖉▾**, click the Dark Blue box (first row, second from right), click the Fill/Back color list arrow** 🖼▾**, then click the Light Blue box (last row, fourth from the right)**
   You can format the datasheet to best represent the data using line colors, special effects, and fill colors as well as changing the fonts and character formatting.

5. **Click the Save button** 🖫**, type Courses Main Form in the Form Name text box, click OK, then close the form**
   You can always sort, filter, and find records directly on a form or subform, but filters are not saved with the form object. By basing form objects on associated queries, however, you can easily modify the form's recordset by modifying the underlying query. MediaLoft's Accounting Department wants to use this form to display only those employees who attended class in January 2000.

Trouble?
Depending on your computer's date settings, you may have to enter the criteria as 1/*/2000.

6. **Click Queries on the Objects bar, click Employee Info, click the Design button** 🖾 **in the database window, click the Attended field Criteria cell, then type 1/*/00, as shown in Figure G-11**

7. **Click** 🖫**, close the Employee Info query, click Forms on the Objects bar, then double-click Courses Main Form to open it**
   The Employee InfoSub Subform is based on the Employee Info query and does not display any records for the first course, Access1, because no employees attended this course in January of 2000.

8. **Press [Page Down] three times to move to CourseID Comp1, which is record 4**
   The Comp1 course displays 10 records in the subform, indicating that 10 employees took this course in January 2000.

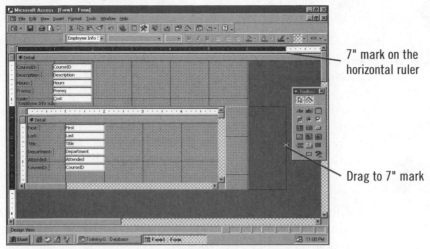

FIGURE G-9: Widening a subform

7" mark on the horizontal ruler

Drag to 7" mark

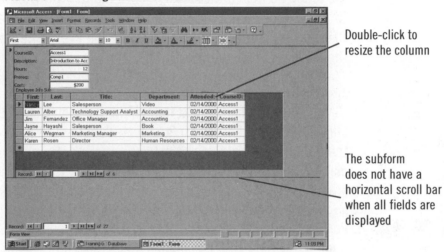

FIGURE G-10: Resizing columns of a subform

Double-click to resize the column

The subform does not have a horizontal scroll bar when all fields are displayed

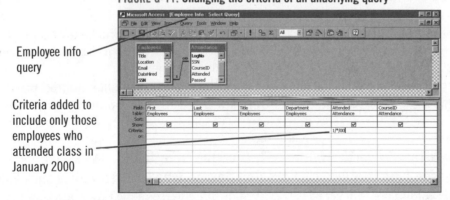

FIGURE G-11: Changing the criteria of an underlying query

Employee Info query

Criteria added to include only those employees who attended class in January 2000

TABLE G-2: Default View property options for forms

default view property	description
Single Form	Displays one record at a time. Gives the user full ability to format the controls placed on the form in Design view and is the most common Default View property entry.
Continuous Form	Displays multiple records at a time, and is often used as the Default View property for subforms. Gives the user the ability to format the controls in Design view.
Datasheet	Displays multiple records at the same time in a datasheet arrangement regardless of how they are formatted in Design view. This is the most common Default View property choice for subforms.

Adding Combo Boxes

By default, fields are added to a form as text boxes, but sometimes other controls such as list boxes, combo boxes, or options buttons would handle the data entry process more easily or quickly for a particular field. Both the **list box** and **combo box** controls provide a list of values from which the user can choose an entry. A combo box also allows the user to make an entry from the keyboard; therefore, it is a "combination" of the list box and text box controls. You can create a combo box by using the Combo Box Wizard to guide your actions, or you can change an existing text box into a combo box control. ![arrow] David changes the Prereq text box (which specifies if a prerequisite course is required in the main form) from a text box into a combo box to allow users to choose from the existing courses offered at MediaLoft.

Steps 1 2 3 4

1. Click the **Design View button** ![icon] click the **Prereq text box**, then press [**Delete**]
   You can add the Prereq field back to the form as a combo box.

2. Click the **Field List button** ![icon] to toggle it on (if necessary), click the **Toolbox button** ![icon] to toggle it on (if necessary), click the **Control Wizards button** ![icon] to toggle it on (if necessary), click the **Combo Box button** ![icon] on the Toolbox toolbar, click the **Prereq field** in the field list, then drag the **Prereq field** with ![icon] to the space where the Prereq text box was positioned
   The Combo Box Wizard appears. You want the Prereq combo box to display the CourseID and Description information from the Courses table.

3. Click **I want the combo box to look up the values in a table or query** (if necessary), click **Next**, click **Courses**, click **Next**, double-click the **CourseID field**, double-click the **Description field**, click **Next**, double-click **↔** on the right edge of the Description column selector to widen it, click **Next**, click **Next** to accept that the value will be stored in the Prereq field, then click **Finish** to accept the Prereq label
   Your screen will look similar to Figure G-12.

QuickTip
Press and hold [**Ctrl**], then press the →, ←, ↑, or ↓ keys to move the control precisely.

4. Position the **Prereq combo box** between the Hours and Cost fields, click the **Prereq combo box right resizing handle**, drag **↔** to the **3" mark** on the horizontal ruler, click the **Description text box**, then drag the **Description text box right sizing handle** with **↔** to the **3" mark** on the horizontal ruler
   Your screen will look similar to Figure G-13. Your final step will be to change the Cost text box into a combo box as well. MediaLoft has only three internal charges for its classes, $100, $200, and $400, which you want to display in the combo box.

5. Right-click the **Cost text box**, point to **Change To**, then click **Combo Box**
   This action changed the control from a text box to a combo box without the aid of the Combo Box Wizard. Therefore, you need to specify where the combo box will get its values directly in the control's property sheet.

6. Click the **Properties button** ![icon], click the **Data tab** (if necessary), click the **Row Source Type text box**, click the **Row Source Type list arrow**, then click **Value List**
   The combo box will get its values from the list entered in the Row Source property.

Trouble?
Be sure to enter semicolons between the values in the Row Source property.

7. Click the **Row Source property text box**, type **$100; $200; $400**, click the **Limit to List property list arrow**, click **Yes**, then click ![icon] to close the property sheet
   The entries in the Row Source property list become the values for the combo box's list. By changing the Limit to List property to "Yes," the user cannot enter a new entry from the keyboard.

8. Click the **Save button** ![icon], click the **Form View button** ![icon], click the **Cost combo box list arrow**, then click **$400**
   The updated form with two combo boxes should look like Figure G-14.

FIGURE G-12: Adding the Prereq combo box

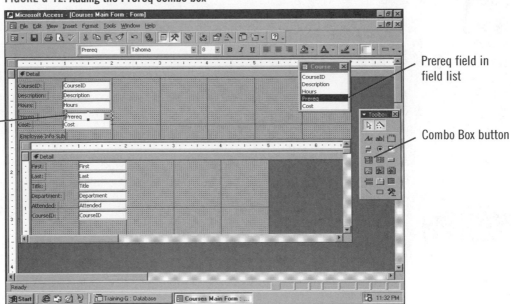

Prereq field added as a combo box

Prereq field in field list

Combo Box button

FIGURE G-13: Moving and resizing controls

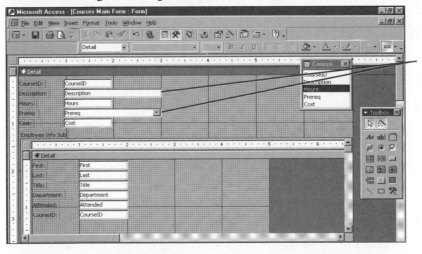

Controls are resized to 3" mark on the horizontal ruler

FIGURE G-14: Adding the Cost combo box

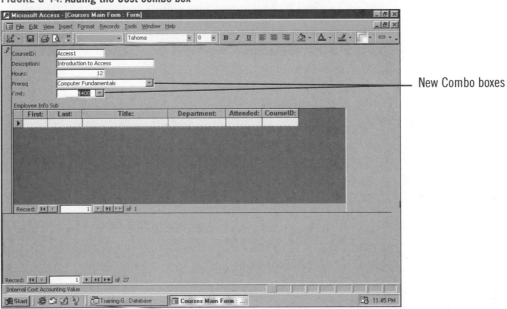

New Combo boxes

Adding Option Groups

An **option group** is a special type of bound control that is often used when a limited number of values are available for a field. The option group control uses **option button** controls (sometimes called radio buttons) to determine the value that is placed in the field. One option button exists for each possible entry. When the user clicks an option button, the numeric value associated with that option button is entered into the field bound to the option group. Option buttons within an option group are mutually exclusive, which means that only one can be chosen at a time. MediaLoft's classes are offered in 6-, 8-, 12-, and 16-hour formats. Because this represents a limited number of options, David uses an option group control for the Hours field to further simplify the Courses Main Form.

Steps

1. Click the **Design View button**, click the **Hours text box**, then press **[Delete]**
   You can add the Hours field back to the form as an option group.

2. Click the **Option Group button** on the Toolbox, click the **Hours field** in the field list, then drag the **Hours field** to the upper-right corner of the form at about the 5" mark on the horizontal ruler
   The Option Group Wizard appears to help guide the process of developing an option group. The first question asks about label names for the option buttons.

3. Type **6 hrs**, press **[Tab]**, type **8 hrs**, press **[Tab]**, type **12 hrs**, press **[Tab]**, type **16 hrs**, click **Next**, choose **No, I don't want a default**, then click **Next**
   The next question prompts you for the actual values associated with each option button.

4. Type **6**, press **[Tab]**, type **8**, press **[Tab]**, type **12**, press **[Tab]**, type **16**, click **Next**, click **Next** to accept **Hours** as the field that the value is stored in, click **Next** to accept **Option button controls** in an **Etched style**, type **Classroom Hours** as the caption, then click **Finish**
   An option group can contain option buttons, check boxes, or toggle button controls. The most common choice, however, are option buttons in an etched style. The **Control Source property** of the option group identifies the field it will update. The **Option Value property** of each option button identifies what value will be placed in the field when that option button is clicked. The new option group and option button controls are shown in Figure G-15.

5. Click the **Form View button** to view the form with the new control, then click the **16 hrs option button**
   Your screen should look like Figure G-16. You changed the Access1 course from 12 to 16 hrs. You just found out that MediaLoft is offering 24-hour classes, so you have to add another button to the group.

6. Click, click the **Option Button button** on the Toolbox toolbar, then click below the **16 hrs option button** in the new option group
   Your screen should look like Figure G-17. This option button in the group will represent 24-hour classes. Change the new option button's label and option value.

7. Click the **Option18 label** once to select it, double-click the **Option18 text**, then type **24 hrs**

8. Double-click the new **option button** to open the property sheet, click the **Data tab** (if necessary), double-click **5** in the **Option Value property text box** to select it, type **24**, click the **Properties button** to close the property sheet, move the **24 hrs option button control** as necessary to align it with the other option buttons, click the **Save button**, then click to observe the new option button

FIGURE G-15: Adding an Option Group with option buttons

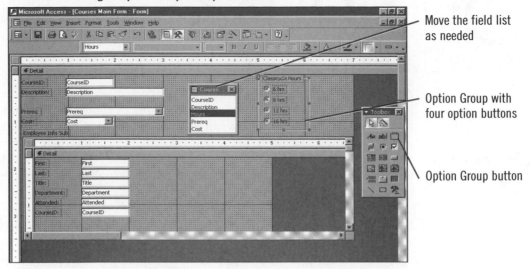

Move the field list as needed

Option Group with four option buttons

Option Group button

FIGURE G-16: Using an Option Group

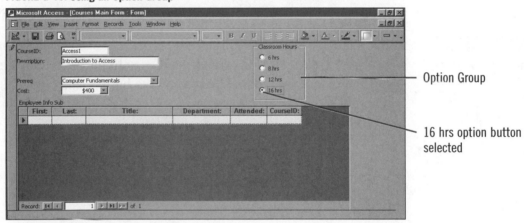

Option Group

16 hrs option button selected

FIGURE G-17: Adding another option button

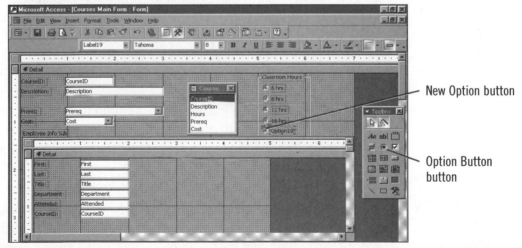

New Option button

Option Button button

CLUES TO USE

Protecting data

You may not want all the data that appears on a form to be able to be changed by all users who view that form. You can design forms to limit access to certain fields by changing the enabled and locked properties of a control. The Enabled property specifies whether a control can have the focus in Form view. The Locked property specifies whether you can edit data in a control in Form view.

Adding Command Buttons

A **command button** is a powerful unbound control used to initiate a common action such as printing the current record, opening another form, or closing the current form. In Form view, the user clicks a command button to run the specified action. Command buttons are often added to the **form header** or **form footer** sections. **Sections** determine where controls appear and print. See Table G-3 for more information on form sections. ✎ David adds a command button to the Courses Main Form form header section to help the users print the current record.

Steps 1 2 3 4

1. Click the **Design View button** ☒, click **View** on the menu bar, wait a second or two for the menu to expand (if necessary), then click **Form Header/Footer**
   The form header opens.

2. Click the **Command Button button** ▭ on the Toolbox toolbar, then click in the **Form Header at the 5" mark** on the horizontal ruler
   The Command Button Wizard opens, listing over 30 of the most popular actions for the command button, organized within six categories.

QuickTip

Resize the Form Header section to make more room for the button, if necessary.

3. Click **Record Operations** in the Categories list, click **Print Record** in the Actions list, click **Next**, click **Next** to accept the choice to display a **Picture of a Printer** on the button, type **Print Current Record** as the button name, then click **Finish**
   Your screen should look like Figure G-18. By default, the Print button 🖨 on the Standard toolbar prints the entire recordset displayed by the form creating a very long printout. Therefore, adding a command button to print only the current record is very useful.

QuickTip

To help identify your printouts, you can add your name as a label to the Detail section of the Courses Main Form.

4. Click the **Form View button** ▦ to view the new command button, press **[Page Down]** three times to navigate to the fourth record, click the new **Print Record command button**, then save and close the form
   The fourth record for the Computer Fundamentals class contains ten records in the subform that still displays only the January attendees as defined by the Employee Info query. You can adjust the left and right margins so that the printout fits neatly on one page.

5. Click **File** on the menu bar, click **Page Setup**, click the **Margins tab** (if necessary), press **[Tab]** three times to select **1** in the Left text box, type **0.5**, press **[Tab]** once to select **1** in the Right text box, type **0.5**, then click **OK**
   The **Display When** property of the Form Header controls when the controls in that section display and print.

6. Click ☒, double-click the **Form Header section** to open its property sheet, click the **Format tab** (if necessary), click the **Display When property text box**, click the **Display When list arrow**, click **Screen Only**, then click the **Properties button** 🖺 to close the property sheet
   You don't want the command button on the printouts.

Trouble?

If your printout is still too wide for one sheet of paper, pull the right edge of the form to the left in Form Design view to narrow it.

7. Click the **Save button** 🖫, click ▦, click the **Next Record button** ▶ several times on the Courses Main Form to navigate to the fourth record (Comp1), then click the **Print Record command button** to print the Comp1 record using the new command button
   Your final Courses Main Form should look like Figure G-19, and your printout should fit on one page, without displaying the form header.

8. Close the **Courses Main Form**

FIGURE G-18: Adding a command button

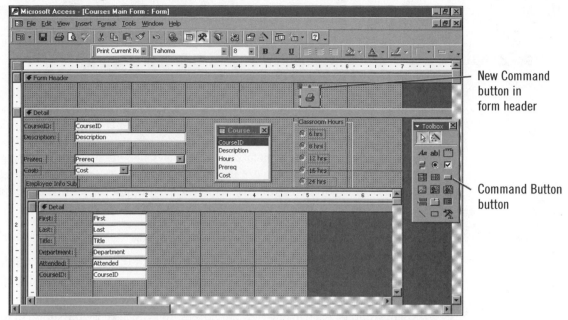

New Command button in form header

Command Button button

FIGURE G-19: The final Courses Main Form

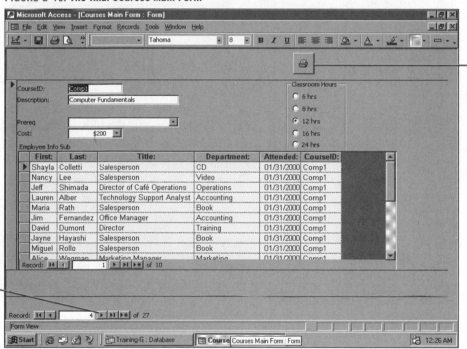

Print Record command button in form header

Next Record navigation button for Courses Main Form

TABLE G-3: Form Sections

section	description
Detail	Appears once for every individual record
Form Header	Appears at the top of the form and often contains command buttons or a label with the form's title
Form Footer	Appears at the bottom of the form and often contains command buttons or a label with instructions on how to use the form
Page Header	Appears at the top of a printed form with information such as page numbers or dates. The Page Header and Page Footer sections can be added to the form by clicking View on the menu bar, then clicking Page Header/Footer
Page Footer	Appears at the bottom of a printed form with information such as page numbers or dates

Adding Records with a Form/Subform

If you want to use the form/subform objects for data entry in addition to finding and viewing data, you must carefully plan the forms to make sure that all of the necessary fields are present that are required to add a record. For example, you cannot add a new employee to a main form unless the SSN field is present in the main form because the SSN is the key field. ✐ David built a form/subform for data entry purposes that displays all fields for each employee in the main form. The subform displays fields that reflect which classes that employee has attended. He uses this form/subform to add new employees as well as record new classes that employees have attended.

Steps 1 2 3 4

1. **Double-click the Employee Details Main Form in the database window, maximize the form, then press [Page Down] once to view the second record for Nancy Lee**
   Your screen should look like Figure G-20. Since the SSN field is listed in the main form, this form could be used to add new employees. You can also use the subform to add another class to the list that Nancy has attended.

2. **Click the New Record button ▶✱ on the subform navigation buttons, press [Tab] twice to move through the LogNo and SSN fields, then type Project1 in the CourseID field**
   The LogNo field is an AutoNumber data type, so it will automatically increase to the next available number as determined by the records in the Attendance table. The SSN field is automatically filled in with Nancy Lee's SSN because it serves as the linking field between the main and subforms.

3. **Press [Enter] to move the focus to the Description field, press [Enter], type 6/1/00 in the Attended field, press [Enter], press [Spacebar] to enter a check in the Passed field, then press [Enter] to complete the record**
   The CourseID entry (when added to the CourseID field of the Attendance table) automatically pulls the associated Description field entry from the Courses table, as shown in Figure G-21. Now enter a new employee into the main form.

QuickTip

A pencil icon in the margin of the form indicates the record is being edited.

4. **Click ▶✱ on the main form navigation buttons, click in the First Name text box, type Kelsey, press [Tab], type Wambold, press [Tab], type Video, press [Tab], type Salesperson, press [Tab], type San Francisco, press [Tab], type the address kwambold@medialoft.com, press [Tab], type 9/1/00, press [Tab], type 999881111, then press [Tab]**
   Kelsey has been added as a new employee in the database. When she starts taking courses, this form will be useful to track her attendance.

5. **Close the Employee Details Main Form, close the Training-G database, then exit Access**

FIGURE G-20: The Employee Details Main Form and Attendance Update Subform

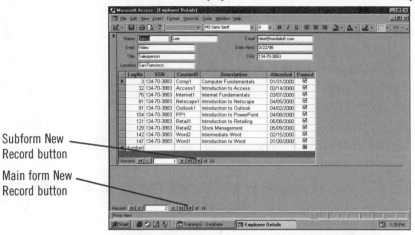

Subform New Record button

Main form New Record button

FIGURE G-21: Adding a record to the subform

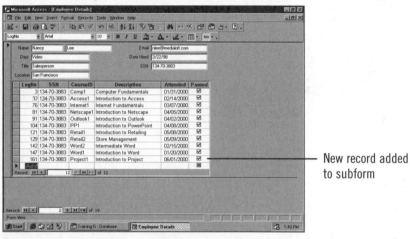

New record added to subform

FIGURE G-22: The Employee Details Main Form as a Web page

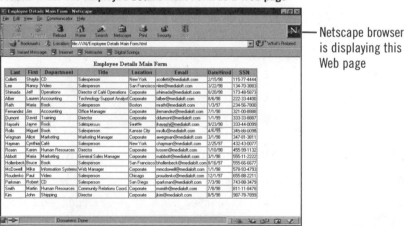

Netscape browser is displaying this Web page

 Access 2000

Saving a form as a Web page

You can save any form as a Web page in an **HTML** (Hypertext Markup Language, the language used to develop World Wide Web pages) file format. However, unless you create a **Data Access Page**, a database object used to create Web pages that interact with a live Access database, you will not be able to use the Web page to enter or edit data. Use the Export option on the File menu to save a form as an HTML document. You have the option of applying an HTML template that contains formatting instructions. Figure G-22 shows how the fields from the Employee main form would appear when they are exported from Access into an HTML file and are opened in browser software such as Microsoft Internet Explorer or Netscape Navigator.

Practice

► Concepts Review

Identify each element of the form's Design View shown in Figure G-23.

FIGURE G-23

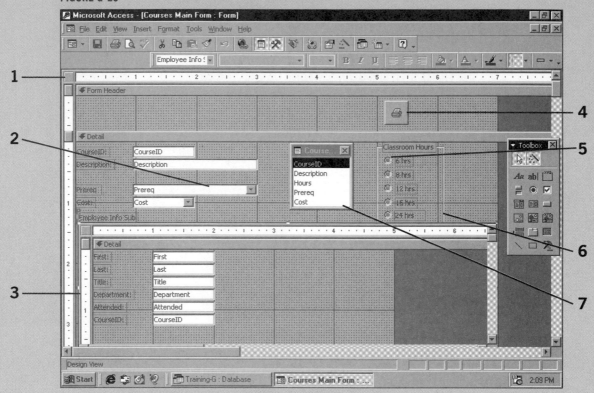

Match each term with the statement that describes its function.

8. **Option group**
9. **Controls**
10. **Command button**
11. **Subform**
12. **Combo box**

a. Elements you add to a form such as labels, text boxes, and list boxes
b. A control that shows records that are related to one record shown in the main form
c. An unbound control that, when clicked, executes an action
d. A bound control that is really both a list box and a text box
e. A bound control that displays a few mutually exclusive entries for a field

Select the best answer from the list of choices.

13. Which control would work best to display two choices for a field?
   a. Text box
   b. Label
   c. Option group
   d. Command button

14. Which control would you use to print a form?
   a. Option group
   b. List box
   c. Text box
   d. Command button

15. Which control would you use to display a drop-down list of 50 states?
   a. Check box
   b. Field label
   c. List box
   d. Combo box

16. To view linked records within a form use a:
   a. Subform.
   b. List box.
   c. Design template.
   d. Link control.

▶ Skills Review

1. Understand the form/subform relationship.
   a. Start Access and open the Membership-G database.
   b. Click the Relationships button on the Database toolbar.
   c. Click File on the menu bar, wait a second or two for the expanded menu to appear, then click Print Relationships.
   d. The Relationships for Membership-G will appear as a previewed report. Click the Print button on the Print Preview toolbar to print the report, close the preview window without saving the report, and then close the Relationships window. If you need to include your name on the printout, go to Design view and add your name as a label on the report.
   e. Based on the one-to-many relationships defined in the Membership-G database, sketch two form/subform combinations that you might want to create.

2. Create subforms using the Wizard.
   a. Click Forms on the Objects bar in the Membership-G database window.
   b. Double-click Create form by using wizard.
   c. Select all of the fields from both the Activities and the Names tables.
   d. View the data by Names.
   e. Accept a datasheet layout for the subform.
   f. Accept a standard style.
   g. Accept the default titles for the forms.
   h. Find the record for Lois Goode (record number 3) and enter your own first and last names in the appropriate text boxes.

   i. Resize the columns of the datasheet in the subform so that all of the data is clearly visible.

   j. Click File on the menu bar, then click Print. Click the Selected records option button in the Print dialog box to print only the data for your name.

   k. Close the Names form.

3. Create subforms using queries.

   a. Open the "Zips in IA or MO" query in Design view, and add the criteria to find only those records from IA or MO in the State field. View the datasheet, then save and close the query.

   b. Using either the Form Wizard or Form Design view, build a form based on the "Zips in IA or MO" query using all three fields in the query.

   c. Open the Zips in IA or MO form in Design view, and add a subform control about 5" wide by about 3" tall below the three text boxes.

   d. Use the Subform Wizard to specify that the subform will use an existing query, then select all of the fields in the Dues query to be part of the subform.

   e. Allow the wizard to link the form and subform so that they "Show Dues for each record in Zips in IA or MO using Zip".

   f. Accept Dues subform as the subform's name.

   g. Maximize the form, expand the size of the subform, move the subform as necessary, and resize the datasheet column widths so that all of the information in the subform is clearly visible. You will know you are done when the horizontal scroll bar does not display in Form view and text from the subform doesn't overlap the main form.

   h. Format the datasheet so the First field entry always appears as red text and the Zip field entry always appears as blue text.

   i. Find the record for Zip 64105 (the sixth record), enter your last name in the Last field of the first record, and print only that record.

   j. Save and close the Zips in IA or MO form.

4. Modify subforms.

   a. Click the Queries tab and open the Zips in IA or MO query in Design view.

   b. Delete the criteria that specifies that only the records with State values of IA or MO appear in the recordset.

   c. Save the modified query as "All Zips".

   d. Close the all Zips query.

   e. Click the Forms tab and open the Zips in IA or MO form in Design view.

   f. Open the property sheet for the form, and change the Record Source property from "Zips in IA or MO" to "All Zips".

   g. Save the form and navigate to record number 13, which displays Zip 64145 for Shawnee, Kansas.

   h. Change the city to the name of your hometown, then print this record.

   i. Close the form, then right-click it and choose Rename.

   j. Save the updated form with the name "Zips".

5. Add combo boxes.

   a. Open the Names form in Design view and delete the Zip text box.

   b. Add the Zip field back to the same location as a combo box, using the Combo Box Wizard.

   c. The Combo Box Wizard should look up values from a table or query.

   d. Choose the Zips table and the Zip field within the Combo Box Wizard.

   e. Store the value in the Zip field, label the Combo Box Zip.

   f. Reposition the new Zip label and combo box as necessary, save the form, and display it in Form view.

   g. Navigate to the second record, change the address to your own, and change the Zip to 50266 using the new combo box. Print the second record.

6. Add option groups.

a. Open the Names form in Design view, then delete the Dues text box.

b. Add the Dues field back to the form below the CharterMember check box control using an Option Group control with the Option Group Wizard.

c. Enter "$25" and "$50" as the label names, and accept $25 as the default choice.

d. Change the values to "25" and "50" to correspond with the labels.

e. Store the value in the Dues field, choose option buttons with an etched style, and enter the caption "Annual Dues".

f. Save the form, display it in Form view, find the record for Jerry Martin (you can use the Find command from the Edit menu), change the first name to your own, and change the Annual Dues to "$50".

g. Print the updated Martin record.

7. Add command buttons.

a. Open the Names form in Design view.

b. Open the Form Header to display about 0.5" of space, then add a command button to the upper-right corner using the Command Button Wizard.

c. Choose the Print Record action from the Record Operations category.

d. Display the text "Print Current Record" on the button, then name the button "Print".

e. Save the form and display it in Form view.

f. Navigate to the record with your own name, change the birth date to your own, and print the record using the new Print Current Record command button.

8. Add records with a subform.

a. Navigate to the first record for Mark Daniels, then click in the subform.

b. Add two records with the following information:

ActivityDate:	Hours:
3/1/00	4
3/2/00	8

c. Print the updated record using the Print Current Record command button.

d. Why is it unnecessary to enter the MemberNo data in the subform? Write a brief answer on your printout.

e. Use the Export option from the File menu to save the Names form as an HTML document on your Project Disk. Do not specify an HTML template.

f. Open the HTML document you created from the Names form in either Netscape or Internet Explorer, whichever browser is available on your system, then print the document.

g. Close the browser window, return to the Access window, close the Names form, close the Membership-G database, and exit Access.

► Independent Challenges

1. As the manager of a music store's instrument rental program, you have created a database to track instrument rentals to schoolchildren. Now that several rentals have been made, you wish to create a form/subform to facilitate the user's ability to enter a new rental record.

To complete this independent challenge:

a. Start Access and open the database Music Store-G.

b. Using the Form Wizard, create a new form based on all of the fields in the Customers and Rentals tables.

c. View the data by Customers, choose both a Datasheet layout for the subform and a Standard style, and accept the default form titles of "Customers" and "Rentals Subform."

d. Add another record to the rental subform by pressing [Tab] through both the RentalNo and CustNo fields, which will be filled in automatically, and typing "888335" as the SerialNo entry and "5/1/00" as the Date entry.

e. Close the new Customers form.

f. Add the description of the instrument to the subform information. To do this, create a new query in Design view.

g. Add the Rentals and Instruments tables, then close the Show Table dialog box.

h. Add all of the fields from the Rentals table and the Description field from the Instruments table to the query, save the query with the name "Rental Description", and close it.

i. Open the Rentals Subform in Design view, then change the Record Source property of the form from "Rentals" to "Rental Description".

j. Open the form's field list and drag the Description field to the right of the Date text box in the Detail section. Don't worry if the field doesn't perfectly line up with the others or if the Description label seems to be "on top" of other controls. Because the Default view of this form is set to Datasheet, this form will appear as a datasheet regardless of the organization of the controls in Design view.

k. Close the property sheet and the Rentals Subform, saving it when prompted.

l. Open the Customers form and note the new field in the subform that describes the type of instrument rented. Enter your last name in the LastName text box that currently displays "Bacon" and print the first record.

m. Close the Music Store-G database, save the changes, and exit Access.

2. As the manager of a music store's instrument rental program, you have created a database to track instrument rentals to schoolchildren. You add command buttons to a form to make it easier to use.

To complete this independent challenge:

a. Start Access and open the database Music Store-G.

b. Using the Form Wizard, create a form/subform using all the fields of both the Customers and Schools tables.

c. View the data by Schools, use a Datasheet layout for the subform, and a Standard style.

d. Accept the default names of "Schools" and "Customers Subform" for the titles.

e. Maximize the form and resize the columns of the subform so that as many fields as possible can be displayed. Save the form.

f. In Design view, widen the subform to the 6.5" mark on the horizontal ruler.

g. In Design view, add two command buttons in the Form Header using the Command Button Wizard. The first button should print the current record and display the text "Print School Record." The second button should add a new record and display the text "Add New School." Name the buttons appropriately.

h. Modify the Form Header "Display When" property so that this section appears only on the screen and not when printed.

i. Display the form in Form view, resize the columns of the datasheet (if necessary) to display all fields, add your own name and address as a new record in the datasheet of the first record, then use the Print School Record button to print that record.

j. Click the Add New School button, then add the name of your elementary school to the SchoolName field, allow the SchoolNo to increment automatically, and add the name of an elementary school teacher as the first record within the subform.

k. Use the Print School Record button to print this new school record.

l. Close the Schools form, saving it if prompted, then close the Music Store-G database and exit Access.

3. As the manager of a music store's instrument rental program, you have created a database to track instrument rentals to schoolchildren. Now that the users are becoming accustomed to forms, you add a combo box and option group to make the forms easier to use.

To complete this independent challenge:

a. Start Access and open the database Music Store-G.

b. Using the Form Wizard, create a form/subform using all the fields of both the Instruments and Rentals tables.

c. View the data by Instruments, use a datasheet layout for the subform, and a Standard style.

d. Enter the names "Instruments Main Form" and "Rental Information" as the form and subform titles, respectively.

e. Maximize the form, open it in Design view, and delete the Condition text box and label.

f. Using the Field List and the Toolbox toolbar, add the Condition field to the same location using the Combo Box Wizard. Choose "I will type in the values that I want", then enter "Poor", "Fair", "Good", and "Excellent" as the values for the first and only column.

g. Store the value in the Condition field, and label the new combo box as "Condition".

h. Move and resize the new combo box as necessary.

i. Delete the MonthlyFee textbox and associated label.

j. Using the Field List and the Toolbox toolbar, add the MonthlyFee field to the upper-right corner of the form using the Option Group Wizard.

k. Enter the Label Names as "$35", "$40", "$45", and "$50"; there should be no default option, and the values entered should be "35", "40", "45", and "50", respectively.

l. Store the value in the Monthly Fee field, and use option buttons with an etched style.

m. Caption the option group "Monthly Fee", then save the form and view it in Form view.

n. Navigate to the record for the cello, Serial Number 1234568, change the Monthly Fee to "$45", choose "Excellent" for the Condition, and add a new rental record in the subform. The RentalNo is an AutoNumber field and will record "20" automatically, enter "10" for the CustNo, tab through the SerialNo field that is already linked to the main form, and enter the date of your next birthday as the Date entry.

o. Use the Selected Record option in the Print dialog box, invoked by clicking Print from the File menu, to print only that record.

p. Save and close the Instruments Main Form, exit Music Store-G, and exit Access.

4. MediaLoft developed an intranet site that provides internal information to their employees. The Accounting Department created an example of a form that they would like to develop and add as a Web page on the MediaLoft intranet for easy access by others. In this independent challenge, you will find the prototype form on the intranet site. Print it, then create the form in the Training-G database.

a. Connect to the Internet and use your browser to go to the MediaLoft intranet site at http://www.course.com/illustrated/MediaLoft/

b. Click the link for Training.

c. Click the link for User Requests, and print the Web page.

d. Disconnect from the Internet, start Access, then open the Training-G database.

e. Create a query with the following fields: Department from the Employees table, LogNo and Attended from the Attendance table, and Description, Hours, and Cost from the Courses table.

f. Sort the query by Department, and then by Attended. Add criteria so that only the records in the Accounting Department are shown. (You should have 16 records.) Save and name the query "Accounting Query".

g. Create a new form in Form Design view, and set the form's Record Source property to the Accounting Query and the Default View property to Datasheet. Add all fields from the field list to the form. Save the form as "Accounting Form".

h. View the Accounting Form in form view, change the date on the first record by entering "1/21/00" in the Attended field, then save and close the Accounting Form.

i. Use the Export option from the File menu to export the Accounting Form to your floppy disk (A:\) as an HTML document. (*Hint*: Change the Save as type: option in the Export Form 'Accounting Form' As dialog box to HTML Documents). When prompted, click OK without specifying a special HTML template.

j. Start your browser (Internet Explorer or Netscape), use the Open option from the File menu to open the Accounting Form HTML file from your Project Disk, print it, and compare it to the earlier printout from the intranet site. The printouts should look exactly the same, except for the updated date in the first record.

k. Close your browser window, close the Training-G database, and exit Access.

Visual Workshop

Start Access, then open the Training-G database. Create a new form, as shown in Figure G-24, using the Form Wizard. The First, Last, and Department fields are pulled from the Employees table, the Description field comes from the Courses table, and the Attended and Passed fields come from the Attendance table. Name the form "Employee Basics" and the subform "Test Results." The Department combo box contains the following entries: Accounting, Book, Café, CD, Human Resources, Marketing, Operations, Shipping, Training, and Video. The command buttons in the Form Header print the current record and close the form.

FIGURE G-24

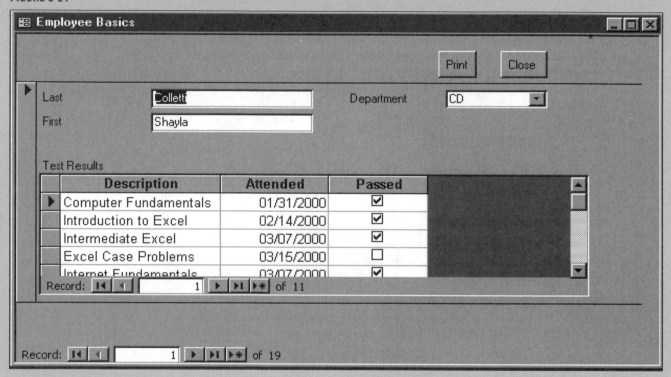

Building

Complex Reports

Objectives

- MOUS ▶ **Use the Database Wizard**
- MOUS ▶ **Import data**
- MOUS ▶ **Create a report from a parameter query**
- MOUS ▶ **Enhance reports**
- MOUS ▶ **Add lines and rectangles**
- MOUS ▶ **Use the Format Painter and AutoFormats**
- MOUS ▶ **Insert an image**
- MOUS ▶ **Secure the database**

Although you can print data in forms and datasheets, **reports** give you more control over how data is printed and greater flexibility in presenting summary information such as subtotals on groups of records. Because a report definition (the report object itself) can be saved, it can be created once and then used many times. Printed reports always reflect the most up-to-date data in a consistent format each time they are printed. As with form designs, report designs allow you to add bound controls such as text boxes and calculated controls, and unbound controls such as lines, graphics, or labels. ◢━━━ Other departments have noted the initial success of David's Training database, and now he is being asked to report the information in new ways. David uses the database to report information electronically, by using the Access import and export features. David also uses database management features such as database compacting to make the database easier to manage. Advanced reporting and formatting features such as parameter prompts, group footer calculations, conditional formatting, images, colors, and lines help David enhance his reports.

Access 2000

Using the Database Wizard

The **Database Wizard** is a powerful Access tool that creates a sample database file for a general purpose such as inventory control, event tracking, or expenses. It also creates objects that you can use or modify. ➤ The Accounting Department tracks a training budget to determine how various departments are using MediaLoft's in-house classes. Although David could create a quarterly paper report with this information, he decides to report this information electronically by creating a separate Access database for the Accounting Department into which he can send historical information on course attendance and costs from the Training database.

Steps

QuickTip

If Access is started, click the **New button** 🗋 on the Database toolbar to open the New dialog box.

1. Start Access, click the **Access database wizards, pages, and projects option button** in the Microsoft Access dialog box, click **OK**, then click the **Databases tab**
   The Databases tab of the New Dialog box is shown in Figure H-1.

2. Click **Expenses** in the New dialog box, then click **OK**
   When you create a new database, you must first name the database file regardless of whether it is created by a wizard or from scratch.

Trouble?

The files for this unit will not fit on one floppy disk. Be sure to save this file to Project Disk 1, which also contains the files DeptCodes.xls and Training.mdb.

3. Click the **Save In: list arrow**, click the **3½ Floppy (A:)** option to save the file on your Project Disk, double-click **expenses1** in the File name text box, type **Accounting**, click **Create**, then click **Next**
   The dialog box shown in Figure H-2 opens. The sample database will include four tables and their associated fields.

Trouble?

If the Office Assistant opens, right-click it, then click Hide.

4. Click **Expense report information** in the Tables list to view the fields in this table, then click **Next**

5. Click **Standard**, click **Next**, click **Corporate**, click **Next**, type **Accounting** as the database title, click **Next**, make sure the **Yes, start the database check box** is checked, then click **Finish**
   It takes several seconds for Access to build all of the objects for the Accounting database and then open the Main Switchboard form, as shown in Figure H-3. When you use the Database Wizard, Access creates a **switchboard**, a special Access form that displays command buttons that help make the database easier to use.

Trouble?

The Accounting database window is minimized in the Access Window.

6. Click the **Main Switchboard Close button**, maximize the **Accounting database window**, review the available forms, click **Reports** on the Objects bar, then click the **Tables** on the Objects bar
   These objects can be used, modified, or deleted like any user-created object.

7. Click the **Employees table**, click the **Design button** 🖾, click the **Insert Rows button** 📑 on the Table Design toolbar, type **Department**, press **[Tab]**, click the **Data Type list arrow**, then click **Lookup Wizard**
   The Lookup Wizard opens. Use the Lookup Wizard to provide department choices.

8. Click **I will type in the values that I want option button**, click **Next**, press **[Tab]**, then type **Accounting**, press **[Tab]**, type **Book**, press **[Tab]**, type **Cafe**, press **[Tab]**, type **CD**, press **[Tab]**, type **Human Resources**, press **[Tab]**, type **Information Systems**, press **[Tab]**, type **Marketing**, press **[Tab]**, type **Operations**, press **[Tab]**, type **Shipping**, press **[Tab]**, then type **Video**

9. Click **Next**, click **Finish** to accept the Department label, click the **Datasheet View button** 🖩, click **Yes** to save the table, then click the **Department field list arrow**
   The Lookup Wizard provides the values in the Department list, but you could also type a new value into the Department field if desired.

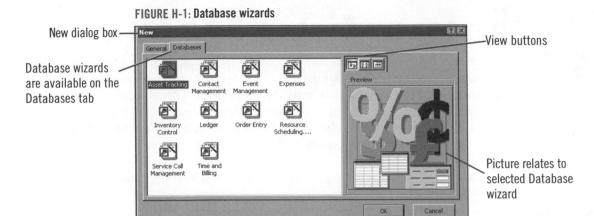

FIGURE H-1: Database wizards

New dialog box

Database wizards are available on the Databases tab

View buttons

Picture relates to selected Database wizard

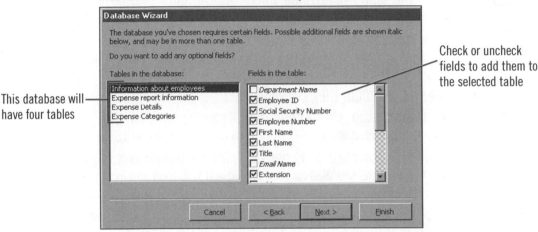

FIGURE H-2: Tables and fields within the Expenses Database Wizard

Check or uncheck fields to add them to the selected table

This database will have four tables

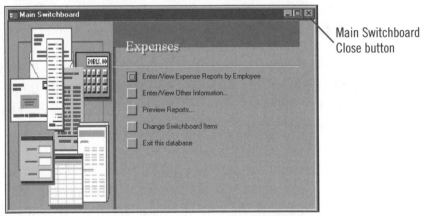

FIGURE H-3: Main Switchboard form for the Accounting database

Main Switchboard Close button

CLUES TO USE

Using the Lookup Wizard

The **Lookup Wizard** is a powerful Access feature that allows a field to "look up" values from a list you type (called a **value list**) or from another table or query. It is not a data type such as Text, Number, or Yes/No. However, the Lookup Wizard helps you determine the final data type for the field based on the values you enter in the list. A lookup field often improves data entry speed, accuracy, and comprehension. A field that has lookup properties will automatically appear as a combo box control when added to a form or viewed on a datasheet. Lookup properties for a specific field can be examined on the Lookup Tab of the field's properties in Table Design view.

Importing Data

Importing is a process to quickly convert data from an external source, such as Excel or another database program, into an Access database. The Access import process copies the data from the original source and pastes the data in the Access database. Therefore, if you update data in either the original source or in the imported copy in Access, the other copy is not updated. See Table H-1 for more information on the types of data that Access can import. ◀━━ Now that the Accounting database has been created, David imports the historical cost and attendance information into it. The integrity of the information will remain intact because the Accounting Department will not be updating or changing the data, but only creating reports.

Steps

Trouble?

You can't import from the Training database if it is opened in another Access window.

1. Click the **Employees table Close button**, click **File** on the menu bar, point to **Get External Data**, click **Import**, click the **Look in list arrow**, locate your **Project Disk**, click **Training**, then click **Import**
   The Import Objects dialog box opens, as shown in Figure H-4. Any object in the Training-H database can be imported into the Accounting database.

2. Click **1QTR-2000**, click **Courses**, click the **Queries tab**, click **Accounting Query**, click the **Reports tab**, click **Accounting Report**, then click **OK**
   The four selected objects are imported into the Accounting database.

3. Click **Tables** on the Objects bar, then click the **Details button** 🔲 in the database window
   The Created and Modified dates of both the 1QTR-2000 and the Courses tables should be today's date. If you update these tables in the future, the Modified date will change, but not the Created date.

QuickTip

By default, objects in the database window are sorted by name.

4. Click the **Modified column heading** to sort the Table objects in ascending order on the date they were modified, then click the **Name column heading**

5. Click **Queries** on the Objects bar to make sure that the Accounting Query has been imported, click **Reports** (Your screen should look like Figure H-5.), point to the **Name column heading divider** to display the ↔ pointer, then double-click ↔
   The column expands to accommodate the widest entry in the Name column. This database will also track department codes that are stored in an Excel spreadsheet.

6. Click **File** on the menu bar, point to **Get External Data**, click **Import**, click the **Look in: list arrow**, locate your **Project Disk**, click the **Files of type list arrow**, click **Microsoft Excel**, click **Deptcodes**, then click **Import**
   The Import Spreadsheet Wizard guides you through the rest of the import process.

7. Click **Next**, make sure the **First Row Contains Column Headings** check box is checked, click **Next**, make sure the **In a New Table option button** is selected, click **Next**, click **Next** to accept the default field information, click the **Choose my own primary key option button**, make sure **Code** is displayed in the primary key list box, click **Next**, type **Codes** in the Import to Table text box, click **Finish**, then click **OK**
   The Deptcodes spreadsheet is now a table in the Accounting database.

8. Double-click **Codes** to open it, then review the codes as a datasheet
   The Accounting Department has more work to do before they can use their new database. They must determine if they are going to use the other tables created by the Database Wizard; if they are going to add, modify, or delete any of the existing fields; and most importantly, how they are going to link the tables in one-to-many relationships.

9. Close the codes datasheet, then close the Accounting database

FIGURE H-4: Import Objects dialog box

Tables tab is chosen ──

Table objects in the ── Training-H database

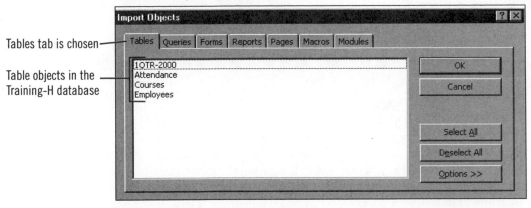

FIGURE H-5: Database window with Details

Resize column pointer ──

Column heading for Name of object ──

Details button ──

Column heading for Created date ──

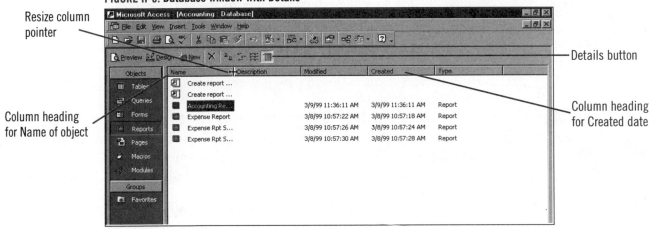

TABLE H-1: Data sources Microsoft Access can import

data source	version or format supported
Microsoft Access database	2.0, 7.0/95, 8.0/97, 9.0/2000 (Note: Access version 7.0 is also known as Access version 95. Access version 8.0 is also known as Access 97, and so forth.)
Microsoft Access project	9.0/2000
dBASE	III, III+, IV, and 5
Paradox, Paradox for Windows	3.x, 4.x, and 5.0
Microsoft Excel	3.0, 4.0, 5.0, 7.0/95, 8.0/97, and 9.0/2000
Lotus 1-2-3	.wks, .wk1, .wk3, .wk4
Microsoft Exchange	All versions
Delimited text files	All character sets
Fixed-width text files	All character sets
HTML	1.0 (if a list) 2.0, 3.x (if a table or list)
SQL tables, Microsoft Visual Foxpro, and other data sources that support ODBC protocol	ODBC (Open Database Connectivity) is a protocol for accessing data in SQL (Structured Query Language) database servers.

Creating a Report from a Parameter Query

If you create a report or form by basing it on a **parameter query**, it will display a dialog box prompting you for criteria to customize the **recordset** of the object each time you use it. For example, you might base a report on a parameter query that prompts for date, department, or state criteria so that only those records that are true for that are used for the report. ◀━━ David has been asked by many departments to provide a paper report of which employees have attended which classes. Rather than create a query and corresponding report object for each department, he builds one parameter query that prompts for the Department field criteria and one report object based on this parameter query.

Steps 1 2 3 4

Trouble?

If you are using floppy disks, the Training-H database is on the second Project Disk.

1. Open the **Training-H** database from your Project Disk, click **Queries** 🔲 on the Objects bar, click **Department Query**, then click the **Design button** 📐
Department Query opens in Design view. It uses fields from all three of the original tables: Courses, Attendance, and Employees.

Trouble?

The parameter criteria must be surrounded by [square brackets], not by (parentheses), <angle brackets>, or {curly brackets}.

2. Click the **Department field Criteria cell**, type **[Enter department name:]**, press **[Enter]**, place the pointer on the **right edge of the Department field column selector**, then drag the ↔ pointer to the right to display the entry
You can see the entire parameter criteria entry, as shown in Figure H-6. Query criteria, including parameter criteria, are not case sensitive.

3. Click the **Datasheet view button** 🔲, type **cd** in the Enter department name text box in the Enter Parameter Value dialog box, then click **OK**
The resulting datasheet shows that the CD department employees attended 21 classes. The parameter criteria entry works.

4. Click the **Save button** 🔲, then close the Department Query datasheet
Use the Report Wizard to quickly create a report based on the Department Query.

5. Click **Reports** 🔲 on the Objects bar, double-click **Create report by using wizard**, click the **Tables/Queries list arrow**, click **Query: Department Query**, click the **Select All Fields button** >> , click **Next**, then click **by Attendance**
View choices are actually ways to group the records with multiple fields in the group header.

6. Click **Next**, click **Department**, click the **Select Single Field button** > , click **Next**, click the **first sort order list arrow**, click **Last**, click the **second sort order list arrow**, click **First**, click the **third sort order list arrow**, then click **Attended**
Your Report Wizard sorting and summary dialog box should look like Figure H-7. The rest of the wizard options determine group calculations (summary options), layout, and style information. The Summary Options dialog box allows you to calculate the subtotal, average, or minimum or maximum value for several fields.

QuickTip

If you want to customize your printouts, place a label control in the Report Header section that contains your name.

7. Click the **Summary Options button**, click the **Hours Sum check box**, click **OK**, click **Next**, click the **Stepped option button**, click the **Portrait option button**, click **Next**, click **Corporate** for the style, click **Next**, type **Department Report** in the title text box, then click **Finish**
Because the report is based on the Department Query (a parameter query), the entry in the dialog box will determine which department's records will appear on the report.

8. Type **video**, then click **OK**
The final report should look similar to Figure H-8.

9. Click the **Print button** 🖨 on the Print Preview toolbar

FIGURE H-6: Creating a parameter query

Resize column pointer

Parameter criteria entry

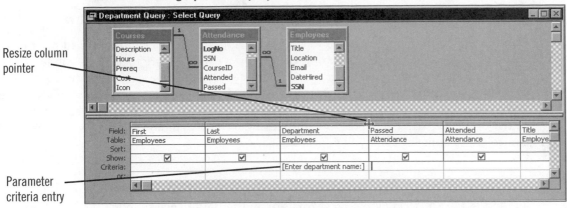

FIGURE H-7: Report Wizard sorting order and Summary Options dialog box

First sort order

Second sort order

Third sort order

Summary Options button

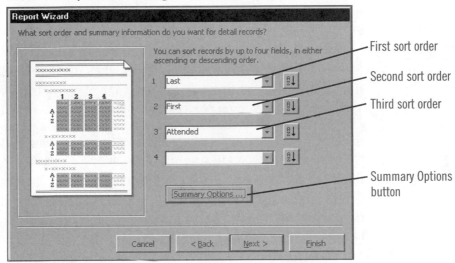

FIGURE H-8: Final Department Report

Records are grouped by Department

Only the Video department is displayed

Records are sorted by Last name

Because there are not two employees with the same last and first name, the records are further sorted by the date in the Attended field

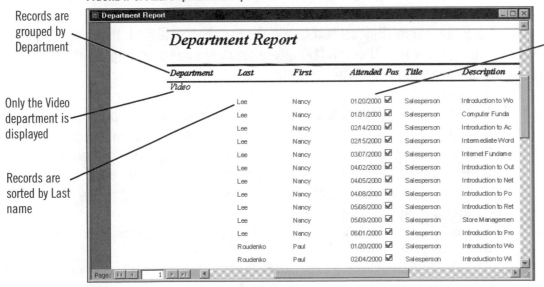

Enhancing Reports

Conditional formatting allows you to change the appearance of a control on a form or report based on criteria you specify. **Grouping controls** is a handy feature that allows you to identify several controls in a group in order to quickly and easily apply the same formatting properties to them. Other report embellishments such as hiding duplicate values and group footer calculations improve the clarity of the report. David wants to improve the appearance and clarity of the Department Report by using techniques such as hiding duplicate values, grouping controls, and applying conditional formatting.

Steps

QuickTip

Clicking a control within a *selected group* selects just that single control.

1. Click the **Design View button** , click the **Last text box** in the Detail section, press and hold **[Shift]**, click the **First text box** in the Detail section, click the **Title text box**, release **[Shift]**, click **Format** on the menu bar, then click **Group**

The three text boxes have been grouped and can now be formatted or modified simultaneously. Group selection handles surround the group, so when you click on *any* control in a group, you select *every* control in the group.

QuickTip

The title bar of the Property sheet indicates that multiple controls have been selected.

2. Click the **Properties button** on the Report Design toolbar, click the **Format tab** on the Multiple selection property sheet, click the **Hide Duplicates text box**, click the **Hide Duplicates list arrow**, click **Yes**, then click to close the property sheet

With the Hide Duplicates property set to Yes, the First, Last, and Title values will print only once per employee. Because only one department shows on this report, there is no need for the Department Footer because the Report Footer presents the same calculation. To subtotal the number of hours of class attendance for each person, you need a Last Footer section.

3. Click the **Sorting and Grouping button** , select the **Department field**, click the **Group Footer list arrow**, click **No**, click **Yes** to delete the group section, click the **Last field**, click the **Group Footer list arrow**, click **Yes** to display a footer every time the Last field changes, then click to close the Sorting and Grouping dialog box

The Department Footer section was removed and the Last Footer section was added.

Trouble?

The =Sum([Hours]) text box is not wide enough to display the entire expression, but you can still copy and paste it.

4. Click the **=Sum([Hours]) text box** in the Report Footer, click the **Copy button** on the Report Design toolbar, click the **Last Footer section**, then click the **Paste button**

Your screen should look like Figure H-9. This calculated control in the Last group footer summarizes the number of hours for each person.

5. Click the **=Sum([Hours]) text box** in the Last Footer section, then use the pointer to drag the **=Sum([Hours]) text box** to the right edge of the report, directly under the Hours text box in the Detail section

Both calculated controls will be selected for conditional formatting.

QuickTip

The Font/Fore Color button displays the last color selected.

6. Click the **=Sum([Hours]) text box** in the Last Footer section, press and hold **[Shift]**, click the **=Sum([Hours]) text box** in the Report Footer section, release **[Shift]**, click **Format** on the menu bar, click **Conditional Formatting**, click the **between list arrow** in the Conditional Formatting dialog box, click **greater than**, click the text box, type **100**, click the **Bold button** , click the **Font/Fore Color list arrow** , then click the **Red box** on the palette

Your screen should look like Figure H-10. The conditional formatting will display the subtotaled hours in bold and red if the calculation exceeds 100.

QuickTip

Maximize the report window and scroll to view the entire report.

7. Click **OK** in the Conditional Formatting dialog box, click the **Save button** , click the **Print Preview button** , type **book** in the Enter Parameter Value dialog box, then click **OK**

The Department Report for the Book department should look like Figure H-11.

8. Close the Print Preview window, save the report, then close it

FIGURE H-9: Department Report in Design view

Last Footer section

Pasted
=Sum([Hours]) text
box

Report Footer section

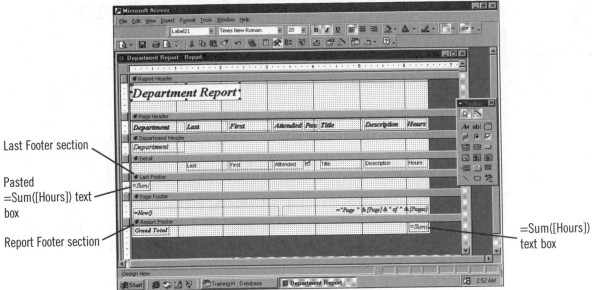

=Sum([Hours])
text box

FIGURE H-10: Conditional Formatting dialog box

Select "greater than"

100 is the criteria

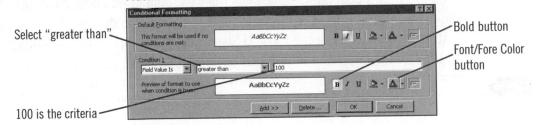

Bold button

Font/Fore Color
button

FIGURE H-11: Final Department Report for the Book department

Duplicate values
are hidden

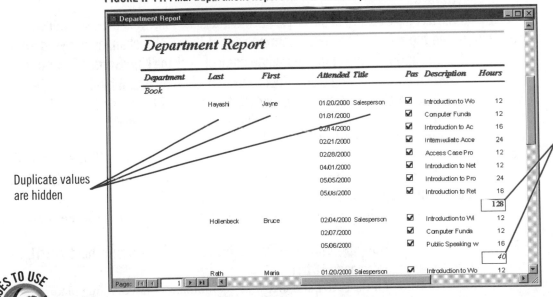

Hours are subtotaled
for each person, and
conditional formatting
is applied for values
greater than 100

Applying Conditional Formatting

Conditional Formatting is an excellent tool to high-light important data in a report. For example, you could change the color, background, or style of a text box control, such as a Sales field, if its value exceeds $1,000. Later, if the value of the Sales field becomes less than $1,000, Access would reapply the default for-matting for the control.

Adding Lines and Rectangles

Unbound controls such as labels, lines, and rectangles can enhance the clarity of the report. The Report Wizard often creates line controls at the bottom of the Report Header, Page Header, or Group Header sections that visually separate the parts of the report. Lines and boxes can be formatted in many ways. ✐ The Personnel Department has asked David to create a report that lists all of the courses and subtotals the courses by hours and costs. David uses line and rectangle controls to enhance the appearance of this report.

Steps

1. Double-click **Create report by using wizard**, click the **Tables/Queries list arrow**, click **Query: Course Summary Query**, click the **Select All Fields button** [>>], click **Next**, click **by Attendance**, click **Next**, double-click **Department** to add it as a grouping field, then click **Next**

   After determining the grouping field(s), the wizard prompts for the sort fields.

2. Click the **first sort field list arrow**, click **Attended** to sort the detail records by the date the classes were attended, then click the **Summary Options button**

3. Click the **Hours Sum check box**, click the **Cost Sum check box**, click **OK**, click **Next**, click the **Outline 2 Layout option button**, click the **Landscape Orientation option button**, click **Next**, click the **Formal** Style, click **Next**, type **Course Summary Report** as the report title, click **Finish**, then click the **Zoom Out pointer** 🔍 on the report

   Figure H-12 shows several line and rectangle controls. These controls are sometimes very difficult to locate in Design view because they are placed against the edge of the section or the border of other controls. The easiest place to click the line control in the Detail section is between the Passed check box and Description text box controls.

4. Click the **Design View button** 🖹, click the **line control** in the Detail section, then press **[Delete]**

   To find the rectangle control in the Department Header section, expand the size of that section.

5. Point to the **top edge of the Detail section** so that the pointer changes to ✚, drag down 0.5", click the **bottom edge of the rectangle control**, click the **Line/Border Color button list arrow** 🖌️▾ on the Formatting (Form/Report) toolbar, click the **bright blue box** in the second row, click the **Line/Border Width list arrow** ▾, then click **2** (a measurement of line width)

   Your screen should look like Figure H-13. Short double lines under the calculations in the Report Footer section indicate grand totals.

6. Click the **Line button** ╲ on the Toolbox toolbar, press and hold **[Shift]**, drag a line from the **left edge =Sum([Hours]) text box** to the **right edge of the =Sum([Cost]) text box** in the Report Footer section, then release **[Shift]**

   Copying and pasting lines create an exact duplicate of the line that can be moved to a new location.

7. Click the **Copy button** 📋, click the **Paste button** 📋, press and hold **[Ctrl]**, press **[↑]** five times, then release **[Ctrl]**

   Moving a control with the **[Ctrl]** and arrow key combination moves it one picture element (**pixel**) at a time.

8. Click the **line control** below the Course Summary Report label in the Report Header section, point to the **line** so the pointer changes to ✋, drag the **line** straight down until it rests just above the Page Footer section, click the **Print Preview button** 📄, then click the **Last Page Navigation button** [▶|]

   Your screen should look like Figure H-14.

FIGURE H-12: First page of Course Summary Report

Rectangle control

Line controls

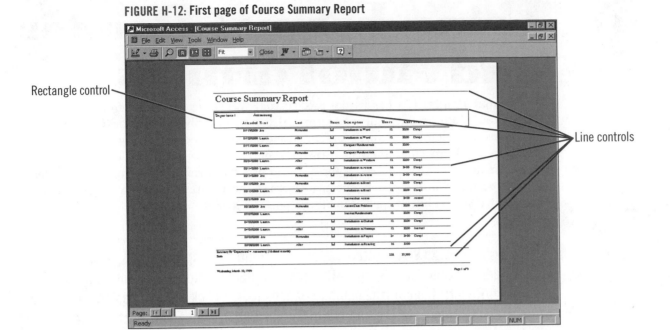

FIGURE H-13: Course Summary Report in Design view

Line/Border Width button

Line/Border Color button

Line control deleted

Drag top edge of Detail section down to expand the Department Header section

Rectangle control is selected

Line button

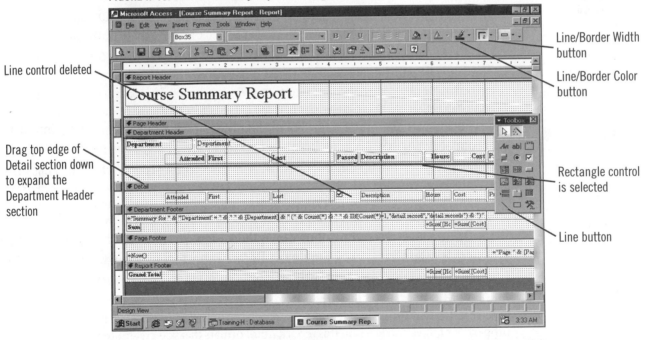

Line was moved from the bottom of the Report Header section to the bottom of the Department Footer section

Lines added to indicate a grand total

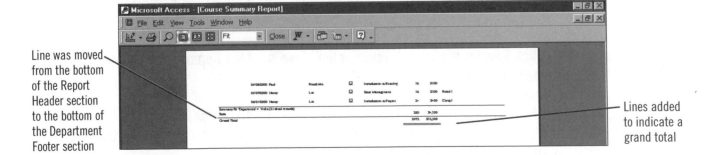

Using Format Painter and AutoFormats

The **Format Painter** is a handy tool used to copy formatting properties from one control to another. **AutoFormats** are predefined formats that you can apply to a form or report and include such items as background pictures, font, color, and alignment choices. Once you have developed a form or report format that you wish to save and apply to other objects, you can add it to the list of AutoFormats provided by Access. ➤ David uses the Format Painter to change the characteristics of other lines on the report, then saves the report's formatting scheme as a new AutoFormat so that he can apply it to other reports he creates.

Steps

QuickTip

Double-clicking the Format Painter button will allow you to "paint" more than one control.

1. Click the **Design View button** 🔲, click the **blue rectangle control** in the Department Header section, double-click the **Format Painter button** 🖌 on the Formatting (Form/Report) toolbar (the pointer changes to ⬙), click the **line control** in the Report Header section, click the **line control** in the Department Footer section, then click 🖌 to release the paintbrush

   Both lines are now bright blue and the same width as the rectangle control.

QuickTip

Press [Esc] to release the Format Painter.

2. Click the **Attended label** in the Department Header section, click the **Font list arrow** | Times New Roman ▼ | on the Formatting (Form/Report) toolbar, click **Arial**, click the **Font size list arrow** |10 ▼| click **11**, click the **Align Left button** ▤, double-click 🖌, click the **First, Last, Passed, Description, Hours, Cost,** and **Prereq labels** in the Department Header section, then click 🖌

   The Format Painter copied the font face, font size, and alignment properties from the Attended label in the Department Header section to the other labels, as shown in Figure H-15.

3. Click **Format** on the menu bar, click **AutoFormat**, click the **Customize button** in the AutoFormat dialog box, click the **Create a new AutoFormat based on the Report 'Course Summary Report' option button**, click **OK**, type **Blue Lines-(Your Name)**, then click **OK**

   The AutoFormat dialog box should look similar to Figure H-16 (many other AutoFormats may appear). Saving the formatting characteristics of the report as a new AutoFormat will allow you to apply them later to other reports in the Training-H database.

4. Click **OK** to close the AutoFormat dialog box, click **Window** on the menu bar, click **Training-H : Database**, click **Employee Detail Report**, click the 🔲, click **Format** on the menu bar, click the **AutoFormat**, click **Blue Lines-[Your Name]** in the Report AutoFormats list, then click **OK**

   Your screen should look like Figure H-17. The AutoFormat you applied changed the formatting properties of lines and labels in this report. AutoFormats that you create are available every time you use the Report Wizard (report AutoFormats) and Form Wizard (form AutoFormats).

5. Click the **Save button** 🔲, close the report, then click the **Course Summary Report button** on the taskbar

   The Design view of the Course Summary Report appears on your screen.

6. Click **File** on the menu system, click **Save As**, type **Department Summary Report**, then click **OK**

   Delete the **Blue Lines-[Your Name]** AutoFormat.

7. Click **Format** on the menu bar, click **AutoFormat**, click **Blue Lines-[Your Name]**, click **Customize**, click the **Delete 'Blue Lines-[Your Name]' option button**, click **OK**, then click **Close**

8. Save and close the Department Summary Report

FIGURE H-15: Using the Format Painter

Font list arrow

Format Painter button

Attended label

Align Left button

Font size list arrow

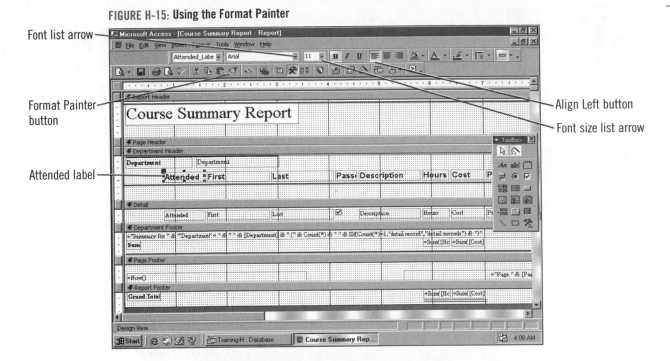

FIGURE H-16: The AutoFormat dialog box

New Report AutoFormat

Customize button

Sample shows the new AutoFormat characteristics

FIGURE H-17: Applying a saved AutoFormat to a different report

Label formatting changed

Line formatting changed

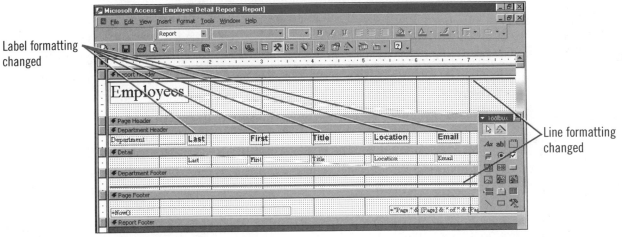

CLUES TO USE

Displaying only summary reports

Sometimes you may not want show all the details of a report, but only a portion of it, such as the group summary information that is calculated in the Group Footer section. You can accomplish this by deleting all controls in the Detail section. Calculated controls in a Group Footer section will still calculate properly even if the individual records used within the calculation are not displayed on the report.

Inserting an Image

Multimedia controls are those that display picture, sound, motion, or other nontextual information. A control that displays an unbound logo would most likely be placed in the Report Header section, and a control that is bound to a field that contains multimedia information for each record (for example a picture of each employee) would be placed in the Detail section. See Table H-2 for more information on multimedia controls. ✒ David added an Icon field to the Courses table that contains a descriptive picture that represents the course's content. He uses the Bound Object Frame control to display this picture for each course in a new report.

1. Double-click **Create report by using wizard**, click the **Tables/Queries list arrow**, click **Query: Microsoft Office Classes**, click the **Select All Fields button** [>>], click **Next**, click **by Attendance**, then click **Next**

2. Double-click **Description**, click **Next**, click the **first sort order list arrow**, click **Last**, click the **Summary Options button**, click the **Hours Sum check box**, click the **Cost Sum check box**, click **OK**, then click **Next**
   This report groups the records by Description, sorts them by Last (name) within Description (of the course), and summarizes both the Cost and Hours fields.

3. Click the **Outline 1 Layout option button**, click the **Landscape Orientation option button**, click **Next**, click the **Casual** style, click **Next**, type **Microsoft Office Classes** as the report title, click **Finish**, then click the 🔍 on the Print Preview screen
   The first page of the report appears in miniature, as shown in Figure H-18. The wizard created a large control for the picture for each course.

Trouble?
Close the Field list if necessary.

4. Click the **Design View button** [⊞], click the large **icon bound image control** in the Detail section, press and hold **[Shift]**, click the **Icon label** in the Description Header section, click the **Description label** in the Description Header section, release **[Shift]**, then press **[Delete]**
   The Icon field can be added to the Description Header section to help announce that the following group of records are all for the same course.

Trouble?
Be sure to delete the Description label control on the left and not the Description text box control on the right.

5. Point to the **top edge of the Description Footer section**, drag the ↕ pointer up to the bottom of the controls in the Detail section, click the **Bound Object Frame button** 🔲 on the Toolbox toolbar, click in the **upper-left corner of the Description Header section**, place the pointer on the **Bound Object Frame control lower-right corner sizing handle**, then drag ↖ up and to the left to the **0.5" mark** on both the horizontal and vertical rulers
   Your screen should look like Figure H-19. Every time you add a control from the Toolbox toolbar, you get an accompanying label. In this case, you do not need the label.

Trouble?
The label control is partially behind the new frame.

6. Click the new **label control**, press **[Delete]**, place the pointer on the **top edge of the Detail section**, then drag ↕ up to the bottom of the controls in the Description Header section
   You need to **bind** the frame to the Icon field, which means you change a bound control's **source property** to the associated field name of the field it will represent.

7. Double-click the **Bound Object Frame control** to open its property sheet, click the **Data tab**, click the **Control Source property list arrow**, click **Icon**, click the **Format tab**, click the **Border Style property list arrow**, click **Transparent**, click the **Properties button** 🗐 to close the property sheet, click the **Save button** 🔲, click the **Print Preview button** 🔍, click 🔍 on the screen, then maximize the report window
   Your screen should look like Figure H-20. The icons for both Access and Excel appear in their respective course Description Header sections.

8. Print the report, close the Print Preview window, then close the Microsoft Office Classes report

FIGURE H-18: Microsoft Office Classes report

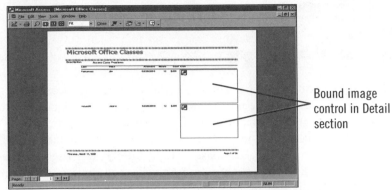

Bound image
control in Detail
section

FIGURE H-19: Microsoft Office Classes report in Design view

New label

Bound Object Frame

Resized Detail
section

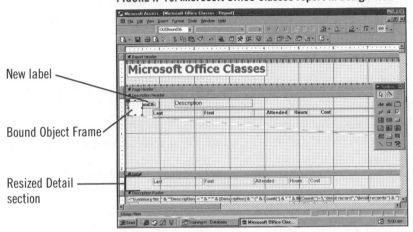

FIGURE H-20: Final Microsoft Office Classes report

Bound Object
Control displays
the Icon picture
in the Description
Header section

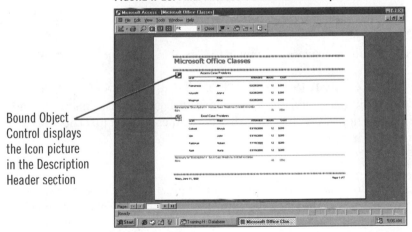

TABLE H-2 Multimedia controls

control name	toolbox icon	bound or unbound	used to display	form/report section where this control is most likely placed	
Image		Unbound	an unbound picture, piece of clip art, or logo	Form Header	Report Header or Page Header
Unbound Object Frame		Unbound	a sound or motion clip a document or spreadsheet	Form Header	Report Footer
Bound Object Frame		Bound	information contained in a field with an OLE data type	Detail	Detail or Group Header

Access 2000

Securing the Database

When you delete data and objects in an Access database, the database can become fragmented and use disk space inefficiently. **Compacting** the database rearranges the data and objects to improve performance by reusing the space formerly occupied by the deleted objects. The compact process also checks to see if the database is damaged and, if so, attempts to repair it. A good time to back up a database is right after it has been compacted. If hardware is stolen or destroyed, a recent backup (most database administrators recommend that databases be backed up each night) can minimize the impact of that loss to the business. Use Windows Explorer to copy individual database files and floppy disks, or use back-up software like Microsoft Backup to create back-up schedules to automate the process. ◤▬▬ David needs to secure the Training database. He starts by compacting the database, then backing it up by using Windows Explorer to make a copy.

Steps 1234

1. Click **Tools** on the menu bar, point to **Database Utilities**, click **Compact and Repair Database**
   Access 2000 allows you to compact and repair an open database, but it's a good practice to use the "Compact on Close" feature, which compacts the database every time it is closed.

> **QuickTip**
>
> When working with databases on storage disks of limited size such as floppies, always check the Compact on Close feature.

2. Click **Tools** on the menu bar, click **Options**, click the **General tab** of the Options dialog box, then click the **Compact on Close** check box (if it is not already checked)
   The Options dialog box is shown in Figure H-21. **Compact on Close** automatically compacts and repairs the database when you close it if the size can be reduced by at least 256 KB. It is not checked (turned on) by default.

> **Trouble?**
>
> Be sure that your Project Disk is in drive A: and that you have a blank disk ready to complete the step.

3. Click **OK**, close the **Training-H** database, exit **Access**, right-click the **Start button**, then click **Explore**
   You'll use Windows Explorer, as shown in Figure H-22, to make a copy of your Project Disk.

4. Right-click **3½ Floppy (A:)** in the Folders list, then click **Copy Disk**
   The Copy Disk dialog box opens, as shown in Figure H-23. This command allows you to copy an entire floppy disk from one disk to another without first copying the contents to the computer's C: hard drive.

5. Click **Start**
   Windows Explorer will start copying your original Project Disk, the **source disk**, and will prompt you to insert the blank disk, the **destination disk**, where the files will be pasted.

6. When you are prompted to insert the destination disk, do so and click **OK**
   Explorer was able to copy all of the files from the Project Disk to the blank disk with one process. Sometimes you are prompted to reinsert the source disk and then the destination disk because all of the files cannot be copied in one process.

7. Click **Close** in the Copy Disk dialog box, then close **Windows Explorer**

8. Label the disk and place it in a safe place

FIGURE H-21: Options dialog box

General tab —

Compact on Close —

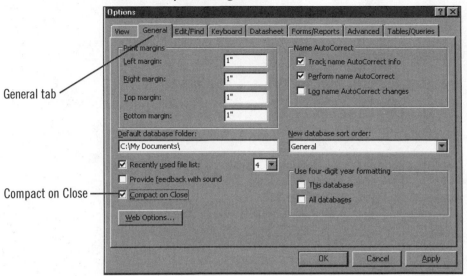

FIGURE H-22: Windows Explorer

3½ Floppy (A:) —

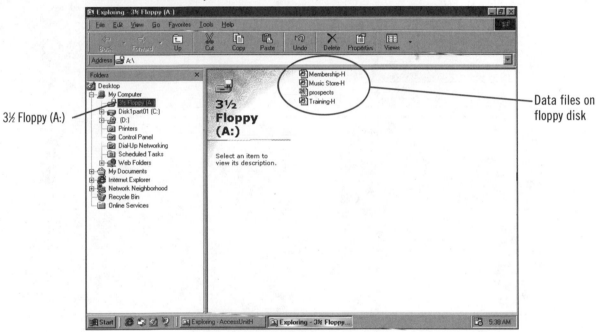

— Data files on floppy disk

FIGURE H-23: Copy Disk dialog box

Make sure 3½ Floppy (A:) is chosen in both the Copy from: and Copy to: locations

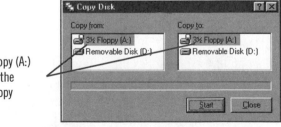

Compacting a database automatically

Microsoft Access can automatically compact a database file every time you close it. Choose the Options from the Tools menu, then click the General tab. Click the Compact on Close check box, then click OK.

Compacting does not occur when you close the database unless the file size would be reduced by more than 256 KB. It also does not occur if you close the database while another person is using it.

Practice

▶ Concepts Review

Identify each element of the form's Design view shown in Figure H-24.

FIGURE-H-24

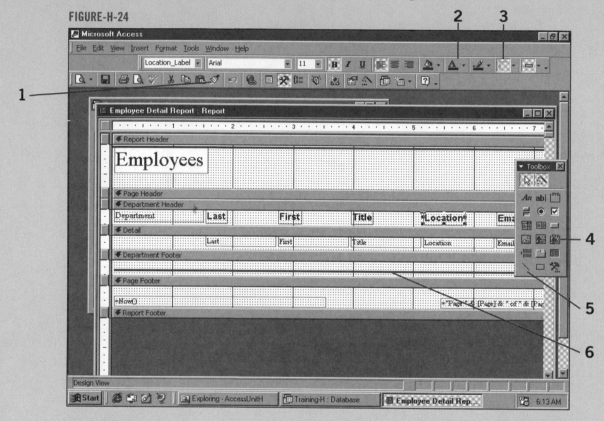

Match each term with the statement that describes its function.

7. Image control
8. Parameter Query
9. Bound Object Frame
10. Format Painter
11. Importing

a. A process to quickly convert data from an external source into an Access database

b. This displays a dialog box prompting you for criteria each time you open it

c. Used to display information contained in a field with an OLE data type

d. Used to copy formatting properties from one control to another

e. Used to display an unbound picture, clip art item, or logo

Select the best answer from the list of choices.

12. **Which control would work best to present sound clips of each employee's voice stored in a Voice field with an OLE data type?**
    a. Text box
    b. Label
    c. Bound Object Frame
    d. Unbound Object Frame

13. **Which control would you use to separate groups of records on a report?**
    a. Option group
    b. Image
    c. Bound Object Frame
    d. Line

14. **Which wizard would you use to create a database from scratch?**
    a. Database Wizard
    b. Table Wizard
    c. Records Wizard
    d. Lookup Wizard

15. **Which wizard would you use to provide a value list for a field?**
    a. Database Wizard
    b. Lookup Wizard
    c. Value List Wizard
    d. Field Wizard

16. **Which of the following programs or file types cannot serve as a source for data imported into Access?**
    a. Excel
    b. Lotus 1-2-3
    c. Lotus Notes
    d. HTML

▶ Skills Review

1. **Use the Database Wizard.**
   a. Start Access, click the Access database wizards, pages, and projects option button in the Microsoft Access dialog box, then click OK.
   b. Double-click the Contact Management Wizard, and create the new database with the name "Contacts" on a new, blank Project Disk.
   c. Follow the prompts of the Database Wizard and accept all of the default field suggestions. Use the Standard style for screen displays and the Soft Gray style for printed reports.
   d. Accept the name Contact Management as the title of the database.
   e. After all of the objects are created, close the Main Switchboard form, then close the Contacts database.

2. **Import Data.**
   a. Use Windows Explorer to copy the Excel file prospects from Project Disk 2 to the new Project Disk that contains the Contacts database.
   b. Open the Contacts database.
   c. Click File on the menu bar, point to Get External Data, then click Import.
   d. In the Import dialog box, click the Files of type list arrow, click Microsoft Excel, click prospects on your Project Disk, then click the Import button in the Import dialog box.

e. In the Import Spreadsheet Wizard, make sure that the Show Worksheets option button is selected, click Next, check the First Row Contains Column Headings check box, click Next, click the In an Existing Table list arrow, click Contacts, click Next, then click Finish.

f. Click OK when prompted that the import was successful, then open the Contacts table in Design view.

g. Modify the Region field using the Lookup Wizard Data Type by typing the following values. Press [Tab] as you type each value in the column: East, Midwest, North, South, West. Use "Region" for the label.

h. Save the table, then open it in Datasheet view.

i. Add your personal information as a new record using "East" as the entry for the Region, regardless of where you live.

j. Print the datasheet in landscape orientation, then close the datasheet.

3. Create a Report from a Parameter Query.

a. Start a new query in Design view, then add the Contacts table.

b. Add the following fields to the Query Design grid in this order: FirstName, LastName, City, StateOrProvince, Region.

c. Enter the following parameter criteria to the Region field: [Enter Region:].

d. Save the query, naming it "Customer Regions", then close the query.

e. Using the Report Wizard, create a new report basing it on the Customer Regions query.

f. Select all the fields, group the report by Region, sort ascending by LastName, and choose a Block layout, a Portrait orientation, and a bold style.

g. Accept the name Customer Regions for your report title.

h. When prompted for the region, enter "East".

i. Open the report in Design view and add a label to the Report Footer with the text "Created by [Your Name]".

j. Save, print, and close the report.

k. Close the Contacts database.

4. Enhance Reports.

a. Open the Membership-H database.

b. Using the Report Wizard, create a report on the Query: Member Activity Log using all of the fields in that query.

c. Group the fields by Last, sort ascending by ActivityDate, and Sum the Hours field.

d. Use the Outline 2 layout, Portrait orientation, Compact style, and accept the name Member Activity Log as the report title.

e. Open the report in Design view and select the =Sum([Hours]) calculated field in the Last Footer section.

f. Use the Conditional Formatting from the Format menu to change Font/Fore color to bold and bright blue if the value is greater than or equal to 10.

g. Add a label to the Report Footer section, with the text "Created by [Your Name]", then save the report and print the last page.

h. Open the property sheet for the First text box in the Detail section and set the Hide Duplicates property to Yes.

i. Group the controls in the Report Footer section, then format the group with a bright blue Font/Fore color.

j. Save and print the report.

5. Add Lines and Rectangles.

a. Open the Member Activity Log report in Design view, then delete the following controls:
Last, First, and Dues labels in the Last Header section
First and Dues text boxes in the Detail section
Line in the Detail section (*Hint*: It is between the ActivityDate and Hours text boxes.)
Line in the Last Header section (*Hint*: It is a short line just above the Last text box.)
Rectangle in the Last Header section (*Hint*: You will probably have to expand the section to find it.)

b. Move the ActivityDate label in the Last Header section and the ActivityDate text box in the Detail section to the right, so that they are right beside the Hours controls.

c. Move the line control at the top of the Last Footer section to the bottom of the Last Footer section.

d. Draw two short lines under the =Sum([Hours]) control in the Report Footer to indicate a grand total.

e. Use the Save As option from the File menu to save the report as the "Simplified Member Activity Log" and print the first page.

6. **Use the Format Painter and AutoFormats.**

a. Open the Simplified Member Activity Log in Design view.

b. Format the ActivityDate label in the Last Header section with a bold Tahoma font.

c. Use the Format Painter to copy that format to the Last text box and the Hours label in the Last Header section.

d. Change the color of the lines in the Report Header section to bright red.

e. Create a new AutoFormat named "Red Lines-[Your Name]" based on the Simplified Member Activity Log report.

f. Print the first page of the Simplified Member Activity Log report, then save and close it.

g. Open the Member Activity Log report in Design view, and use the AutoFormat option from the Format menu to apply the Corporate format.

h. Use the Customize button in the AutoFormat dialog box to delete the "Red Lines-[Your Name]" style.

i. Preview, then print the first page of the Member Activity Log report. Save and close the report.

7. **Insert an Image.**

a. Use the Report Wizard to create a report using all the fields from the Team Members query except for the Team field.

b. Do not group the records, but sort them in ascending order on the Last, then on the First fields.

c. Use a Columnar layout and a Portrait orientation.

d. Apply a Bold style, and accept the name Team Members as the title.

e. In Design view, use the Bound Object Frame control to add a frame to the right of the Last text box in the Detail section. Delete the frame's accompanying label. Be sure to move and resize the frame and right edge of the report so that they do not go beyond the 6.5" mark.

f. On the Data tab of the property sheet for the frame, change the Control Source property to Team.

g. On the Format tab of the property sheet for the frame, change the Size Mode property to Zoom and change the Border Style to Transparent.

h. Put a label control in the Report Header that displays your name, then save, preview, and print the report.

i. Close the Membership-H database and exit Access.

8. **Secure the Database.**

a. Start Access.

b. Use the Database Utilities option on the Tools menu to Compact and Repair the database.

c. Close the Membership-H database and exit Access.

d. Start Explorer, right-click on the 3½ Floppy (A:) option, then click Copy Disk.

e. Follow the prompts to make a back-up copy of your Project Disk to a new, blank disk.

f. Exit Windows Explorer.

▶ Independent Challenges

1. As the manager of a music store's instrument rental program, you have created a database to track instrument rentals to schoolchildren. Now that several instruments have been purchased, you often need to print a report listing the particular instruments in inventory. You will create a single instrument inventory report based on a parameter query that prompts the user for the type of instrument to be displayed on the report.

To complete this independent challenge:

a. Start Access and open the database Music Store-H.

b. Create a query with the following fields from the Instruments table:
Description, SerialNo, MonthlyFee, Condition

c. Add the following parameter criteria entry in the Description field:
[Enter the type of instrument:]

d. Save the query with the name "Instruments by Type".

e. Using the Report Wizard, create a report on the Instruments by Type query, and select all of the fields.

f. Group by the Description field, sort in ascending order by the SerialNo field, use a Stepped layout, use a Portrait orientation, apply a Corporate style, and title the report "Instruments in Inventory".

g. Enter "Cello" when prompted for the type of instrument.

h. Open the report in Design view and add a rectangle control to the left side of the Report Footer about 1" tall and 2" wide.

i. Add a label control to the Report Footer inside the rectangle control that displays your name.

j. Display the report with the Cello criteria, and print it.

k. Save and close the Instruments in Inventory report.

l. Close the Music Store-H database and exit Access.

2. As the manager of a music store's instrument rental program, you have created a database to track instrument rentals to schoolchildren. Now that several instruments have been rented, you need to create a conditionally formatted report that lists which school has the highest number of rentals from the store.

To complete this independent challenge:

a. Start Access and open the database Music Store-H.

b. Open the Schools table in Datasheet view and click the expand button to the left of Oak Hill Elementary to show the related records in the students table, then print the datasheet.

c. Click the collapse button, then close the datasheet.

d. Using the Report Wizard, create a report with the following fields from the following tables:
Schools: SchoolName
Instrument: Description, MonthlyFee
Rentals: Date

e. View and group the data by SchoolName, sort in ascending order by Date, and Sum the MonthlyFee field.

f. Use an Outline 1 layout, Portrait orientation, and Casual style.

g. Title the report "School Summary Report".

h. Open the report in Design view and click the =Sum([MonthlyFee]) control in the SchoolNo Footer section.

i. Use the Conditional Formatting option on the Format menu to specify that the field be Bold and have a bright yellow Fill/Back Color if it is greater than or equal to 200.

j. Add a label to the right side of the report that displays your name, and save the report.

k. Print the first page of the report.

l. Close the School Summary Report, then close the Music Store-H database and exit Access.

3. As the manager of a music store's instrument rental program, you have created a database to track instrument rentals to schoolchildren. Build a report that shows pictures of instruments.

To complete this independent challenge:

a. Start Access and open the database Music Store-H.

b. Double-click the Create a report in Design View option.

c. Click the Properties button, then choose "Instrument Sampler" as the Record Source property on the Data tab.

d. Open the Field list, then drag the three fields (Description, MonthlyFee, and Picture) to the left side of the Detail section, and arrange them in a vertical column.

e. Open the Properties sheet for the Picture Bound Object Frame. Make sure that the Size Mode property is set to Zoom (which resizes the picture to the size of the control and is especially necessary when the picture itself is larger than the actual control) and the Border Style property is set to Transparent.

f. Use the Page Header/Footer option on the View menu to close the Page Header and Page Footer sections.

g. Use the Report Header/Footer option on the View menu to open the Report Header and Report Footer sections.

h. Add a label to the Report Header section that displays your name.

i. Apply the Bold Autoformat.

j. Add a horizontal line to the bottom of the Detail section to separate the individual records.

k. Save the report with the name "Instrument Sampler Report".

l. Preview and print the first page of the report.

m. Close the Instrument Sampler Report, exit Music Store-H, and exit Access.

4. MediaLoft has developed a Web site that provides internal information to their employees. The Information Systems Department has created a sample report (just a mock up) that they would like to have developed, and have placed it as a Web page on the MediaLoft intranet for easy access by others. In this independent challenge, you'll find the prototype form on the Web site, print it, then create the real thing in the Training-H database.

a. Connect to the Internet and use your browser to go to the MediaLoft intranet at http://www.course.com/illustrated/MediaLoft/

b. Click the link for Training.

c. Click the link for User Report Requests, and print the Web page.

d. Close your browser window and disconnect from the Internet, start Access, then open the Training-H database.

e. Using the Report Wizard, create a report using the Description field from the Courses table, and Attended and Passed fields from the Attendance table.

f. View the data by Courses, group by Passed, and sort in ascending order by Attended.

g. Use a Stepped layout, a Portrait orientation, and a Formal style.

h. Title the report "Achievement Report".

i. In Design view, click the Sorting and Grouping button, change the CourseID Group Footer and the Passed Group Footer property to Yes, and close the Sorting and Grouping dialog box.

j. Add a text box control to the Passed Footer section just below the Attended text box with the expression =Count([Attended]), then delete the extra label that was created in the Passed Footer section.

k. Add a horizontal line to the CourseID Footer, then compare your report with the one you printed in step c. In Design view, make any changes to the report necessary to more closely match the request from the Information Systems Department.

l. Add a label to the Report Header section with your name, save the report, then print the first page.

m. Close the Achievement Report and the Training-H database.

n. Exit Access.

▶ Visual Workshop

Open the Training-H database and create a new report as shown in Figure H-25 using the Report Wizard. Gather the First, Last, and Department fields from the Employees table and the Description and Hours fields from the Courses table. Sum the Hours, sort in ascending order by the Description, and use the Outline 1, Portrait, and Corporate Wizard options. Enter your name as a label in the Report Header if you need to identify your printout.

FIGURE H-25

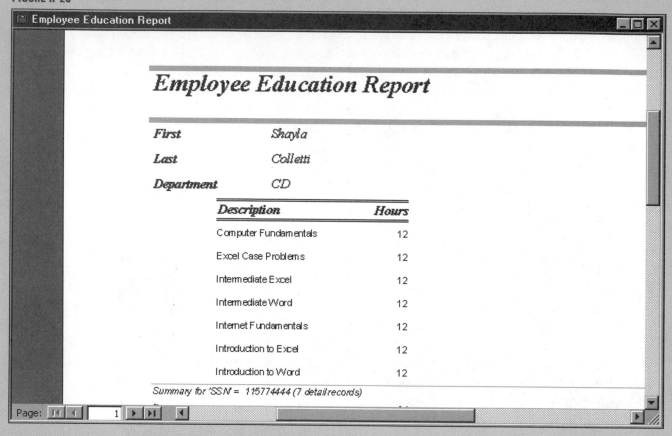

Access 2000 MOUS Certification Objectives

Below is a list of the Microsoft™ Office User Specialist program objectives for Core Access 2000 skills showing where each MOUS objective is covered in the Lessons and Practice. This table lists the Core certification skills covered in the units in this book (Units A-H). For more information on which Illustrated titles meet MOUS certification, please see the inside cover of this book.

MOUS standardized coding number	Activity	Lesson page where skill is covered	Location in lesson where skill is covered	Practice
AC2000.1	**Planning and designing databases**			
AC2000.1.1	Determine appropriate data inputs for your database	Access B-2 Access E-2	Details, Table B-1 Details	Skills Review, Independent Challenges 1–4, Visual Workshop
AC2000.1.2	Determine appropriate data outputs for your database	Access A-4 Access E-4	Table A-2 Details	Skills Review, Independent Challenges 1–4
AC2000.1.3	Create table structure	Access B-4 Access E-6	Steps 2–7 Steps 2–5	Skills Review, Independent Challenges 1–4
AC2000.1.4	Establish table relationships	Access E-16	Steps 1–5	Skills Review, Independent Challenges 1–4
AC2000.2	**Working with Access**			
AC2000.2.1	Use the Office Assistant	Access A-18	Steps 3–6	Skills Review
AC2000.2.2	Select an object using the Objects Bar	Access A-8 Access B-8	Steps 5–6 Steps 1–2	Skills Review, Independent Challenges 1–4

MOUS standardized coding number	Activity	Lesson page where skill is covered	Location in lesson where skill is covered	Practice
AC2000.2.3	Print database objects (tables, forms, reports, queries)	Access A-16 Access C-14 Access C-16	Steps 1–7 Step 7 Step 8	Skills Review, Independent Challenges 1–4
AC2000.2.4	Navigate through records in a table, query, or form	Access A-10 Access C-14	Steps 2–6 Steps 3–5	Skills Review, Independent Challenges 1–4
AC2000.2.5	Create a database (using a Wizard or in Design View)	Access H-2	Steps 1–6	Skills Review
AC2000.3	**Building and modifying tables**			
AC2000.3.1	Create tables by using the Table Wizard	Access B-4	Step 1	Skills Review, Independent Challenges 1–2
AC2000.3.2	Set primary keys	Access B-4 Access E-6	Steps 6–7 Step 6	Skills Review, Independent Challenges 1–4
AC2000.3.3	Modify field properties	Access B-6 Access E-6	Steps 5–6 Step 5	Skills Review, Independent Challenges 1–4
AC2000.3.4	Use multiple data types	Access B-6 Access E-6	Step 2 Steps 3–5	Skills Review, Independent Challenges 1–4
AC2000.3.5	Modify tables using Design View	Access B-6 Access E-6	Steps 1–8 Steps 3–6	Skills Review, Independent Challenges 1–4
AC2000.3.6	Use the Lookup Wizard	Access H-2	Steps 7–9	Skills Review
AC2000.3.7	Use the Input Mask wizard	Access E-8	Steps 4–8	Skills Review

MOUS standardized coding number	Activity	Lesson page where skill is covered	Location in lesson where skill is covered	Practice
AC2000.4	**Building and modifying forms**			
AC2000.4.1	Create a form with the Form Wizard	Access C-4	Steps 1–3	Skills Review, Independent Challenges 1–3
AC2000.4.2	Use the Control Toolbox to add controls	Access C-10 Access C-16	Steps 1–7 Steps 2–5	Skills Review, Independent Challenges 2–3
AC2000.4.3	Modify Format Properties (font, style, font size, color, caption, etc.) of controls	Access C-8 Access C-10	Steps 2–5 Steps 5–6	Skills Review, Independent Challenges 2–3
AC2000.4.4	Use form sections (headers, footers, detail)	Access C-6 Access C-12 Access C-16	Steps 1–6 Steps 2–5 Steps 2–5	Skills Review, Independent Challenges 2–3
AC2000.4.5	Use a Calculated Control on a form	Access C-10	Steps 2–7	Skills Review, Independent Challenges 2
AC2000.5	**Viewing and organizing information**			
AC2000.5.1	Use the Office Clipboard	Access D-10	Clues to Use	Skills Review, Independent Challenges 2–3
AC2000.5.2	Switch between object Views	Access B-6 Access B-18	Step 7 Step 6	Skills Review, Independent Challenges 1–4, Visual Workshop
AC2000.5.3	Enter records using a datasheet	Access A-12 Access E-12	Steps 2–4 Step 7	Skills Review Independent Challenges 3–4, Visual Workhop

MOUS standardized coding number	Activity	Lesson page where skill is covered	Location in lesson where skill is covered	Practice
AC2000.5.4	Enter records using a form	Access C-14 Access G-16	Step 2 Steps 2–4	Skills Review, Independent Challenge 1, Visual Workshop
AC2000.5.5	Delete records from a table	Access A-14	Step 9	Skills Review
AC2000.5.6	Find a record	Access B-10 Access B-12 Access B-14	Details Steps 4–7 Steps 4–8	Skills Review, Independent Challenge 1, Visual Workshop
AC2000.5.7	Sort records	Access B-10 Access B-12	Steps 1–3 Details	Skills Review, Independent Challenges 1–4
AC2000.5.8	Apply and remove filters (filter by form and filter by selection)	Access B-10 Access B-14	Details Steps 1–6	Skills Review
AC2000.5.9	Specify criteria in a query	Access B-16 Access B-18	Step 6 Step 4	Skills Review, Independent Challenges 1–4, Visual Workshop
AC2000.5.10	Display related records in a subdatasheet	Access E-16 Access H-22	Step 8	Independent Challenge 2
AC2000.5.11	Create a calculated field	Access C-10 Access F-10	Steps 1–6 Steps 2–3	Skills Review, Independent Challenge 3
AC2000.5.12	Create and modify a multi-table select query	Access F-2 Access F-6	Steps 2–6 Steps 2–4	Skills Review, Independent Challenges 1–4, Visual Workshop

MOUS standardized coding number	Activity	Lesson page where skill is covered	Location in lesson where skill is covered	Practice
AC2000.6	**Defining relationships**			
AC2000.6.1	Establish relationships	Access E-16	Steps 1–8	Skills Review, Independent Challenges 1–4, Visual Workshop
AC2000.6.2	Enforce referential integrity	Access E-16	Step 4	Skills Review, Independent Challenges 1–4
AC2000.7	**Producing reports**			
AC2000.7.1	Create a report with the Report Wizard	Access D-4 Access H-6 Access H-14	Steps 2–5 Steps 5–6 Step 1	Skills Review, Independent Challenges 1–4, Visual Workshop
AC2000.7.2	Preview and print a report	Access D-6 Access H-14	Step 7 Step 8	Skills Review, Independent Challenges 1–4, Visual Workshop
AC2000.7.3	Move and resize a control	Access D-12 Access H-14	Steps 2–5 Steps 4–6	Skills Review, Independent Challenges 1–4, Visual Workshop
AC2000.7.4	Modify format properties (font, style, font size, color, caption, etc.)	Access D-14 Access H-10	Steps 2–7 Steps 3–6	Skills Review, Independent Challenges 1–4, Visual Workshop
AC2000.7.5	Use the Control Toolbox to add controls	Access D-6 Access H-10 Access H-14	Steps 3–6 Step 6 Step 5	Skills Review, Independent Challenges 1–4, Visual Workshop
AC2000.7.6	Use report sections (headers, footers, detail)	Access D-3 Access D-6 Access H-14	Table Steps 1–7 Steps 3–6	Skills Review, Independent Challenges 1–4, Visual Workshop

MOUS standardized coding number	Activity	Lesson page where skill is covered	Location in lesson where skill is covered	Practice
AC2000.7.7	Use a Calculated Control in a report	Access D-12	Step 4	Skills Review, Independent Challenge 1
AC2000.8	**Integrating with other applications**			
AC2000.8.1	Import data to a new table	Access H-4	Steps 6–7	Skills Review
AC2000.8.2	Save a table, query, form as a Web page	Access G-17	Clues to Use	Skills Review, Independent Challenge 4
AC2000.8.3	Add Hyperlinks	Access C-17	Clues to Use	
AC2000.9	**Using Access Tools**			
AC2000.9.1	Print Database Relationships	Access E-16	Step 6	Skills Review, Independent Challenges 1
AC2000.9.2	Backup and Restore a database	Access H-16	Steps 4–6	Skills Review
AC2000.9.3	Compact and Repair a database	Access H-16	Steps 1–2	Skills Review

Project Files List

To complete many of the lessons and practice exercises in this book, students need to use a Project File that is supplied by Course Technology and stored on a Project Disk. Below is a list of the files that are supplied, and the unit or practice exercise to which the files correspond. For information on how to obtain Project Files, please see the inside cover of this book. The following list only includes Project Files that are supplied; it does not include the files students create from scratch or the files students create by revising the supplied files.

Unit	File supplied on Project Disk	Location file is used in unit
Access Unit A	MediaLoft-A.mdb	Lessons
	Recycle-A.mdb	Skills Review
	Recycle-A.mdb	Independent Challenge 2
	Recycle-A.mdb	Independent Challenge 3
	MediaLoft-A.mdb	Independent Challenge 4
	Recycle-A.mdb	Visual Workshop
Access Unit B	MediaLoft-B.mdb	Lessons
	Doctors-B.mdb	Skills Review
	Doctors-B.mdb	Independent Challenge 2
	MediaLoft-B.mdb	Independent Challenge 4
	MediaLoft-B.mdb	Visual Workshop
Access Unit C	MediaLoft-C.mdb Smallmedia.bmp	Lessons
	Membership-C.mdb Handin1.bmp	Skills Review
	Clinic-C.mdb	Independent Challenge 1
	Clinic-C.mdb	Independent Challenge 2
	Clinic-C.mdb Medical.bmp	Independent Challenge 3
	Clinic-C.mdb Medstaff.bmp	Visual Workshop
Access Unit D	MediaLoft-D.mdb	Lessons
	Club-D.mdb	Skills Review
	Therapy-D.mdb	Independent Challenge 1
	Therapy-D.mdb	Independent Challenge 2
	Club-D.mdb	Visual Workshop
Access Unit E	Training-E.mdb	Lessons
	Training-E.mdb	Independent Challenge 4
	Training-E.mdb	Visual Workshop
Access Unit F	Training-F.mdb	Lessons
	Training-F.mdb	Independent Challenge 4
	Training-F.mdb	Visual Workshop
	Music Store-F.mdb	Independent Challenges 1–3
	Membership-F.mdb	Skills Review

Unit	File supplied on Project Disk	Location file is used in unit
Access Unit G	Training-G.mdb	Lessons
	Training-G.mdb	Independent Challenge 4
	Training-G.mdb	Visual Workshop
	Membership-G.mdb	Skills Review
	Music Store-G.mdb	Independent Challenges 1–3
Access Unit H	Training.mdb (*Disk 1*) Training-H.mdb (*Disk 2*)	Lessons
	Prospects.xls (*Disk 3*) Membership-H.mdb (*Disk 3*)	Skills Review
	Music Store-H.mdb (*Disk 3*)	Independent Challenges 1–3
	Training-H.mdb (*Disk 2*)	Lessons
	Training-H.mdb (*Disk 2*)	Independent Challenge 4
	Training-H.mdb (*Disk 2*)	Visual Workshop
	Deptcodes.xls (*Disk 1*)	Lessons

Glossary

Aggregate functions Special functions used in a summary query that calculate information about a group of records rather than a new field of information about each record.

And criteria Criteria placed in the same row of the query design grid. All criteria on the same row must be true in order for a record to appear on the resulting datasheet.

AND query A query which contains AND criteria (two or more criteria present on the same row of the query design grid. Both criteria must be true for the record to appear on the resulting datasheet).

Arguments The pieces of information a function needs to create the final answer. In an expression, multiple arguments are separated by commas. All of the arguments are surrounded by a single set of parentheses.

Arithmetic operators Plus (+), minus (-), multiply (*), divide (/), and exponentiation (^) characters used in a mathematical calculation.

Ascending order A sequence in which information is placed in alphabetical order or from smallest to largest. For a text field, numbers sort first, then letters.

Text ascending order: 123, 3H, 455, 98, 98B, animal, Iowa, New Jersey
Date ascending order: 1/1/57, 1/1/61, 12/25/61, 5/5/98, 8/20/98, 8/20/99
Number ascending order: 1, 10, 15, 120, 140, 500, 1200, 1500

AutoFormats Predefined formats provided by Access that contain background pictures and font, color, and alignment choices that can quickly be applied to an existing form or report.

AutoNumber A data type in which Access enters a sequential integer for each record added into the datasheet. Numbers cannot be reused even if the record is deleted.

Bound control A control used in either a form or report to display data from the underlying record source; also used to edit and enter new data in a form.

Bound image control A bound control used to show OLE data such as a picture on a form or report.

Calculated control A control that uses information from existing controls to calculate new data such as subtotals, dates, or page numbers; used in either a form or report.

Calculated field A field created in Query Design view that results from an expression of existing fields, Access functions, and arithmetic operators. For example the entry Profit: [RetailPrice]-[WholesalePrice] in the field cell of the query design grid creates a calculated field called Profit that is the difference between the RetailPrice and WholesalePrice fields.

Caption property A field property used to override the technical field name with an easy-to-read caption entry when the field name appears on datasheets, forms, and reports.

Check box Bound control used to display "yes" or "no" answers for a field. If the box is "checked" it indicates "yes" information in a form or report.

Clipboard toolbar A toolbar that shows the contents of the Office Clipboard; contains buttons for copying and pasting items to and from the Office Clipboard.

Collapse button A "minus sign" to the left of a record displayed in a datasheet that when clicked, collapses the subdatasheet that is displayed.

Combo box A bound control used to display a list of possible entries for a field in which you can also type an entry from the keyboard. It is a "combination" of the list box and text box controls.

Command button An unbound control used to provide an easy way to initiate an action or run a macro.

Compacting Rearranging the data and objects on the storage medium so that space formerly occupied by deleted objects is eliminated. Compacting a database doesn't change the data, but it generally reduces the overall size of the database.

Conditional formatting Formatting that is based on specified criteria. For example, a text box may be conditionally formatted to display its value in red if the value is a negative number.

Control Source property The most important property of a bound control on a form or report because it etermines which field the bound control will display.

Controls Any element on a form or report such as a label, text box, line, or combo box. Controls can be bound, unbound, or calculated.

Criteria The entry that determines which records are displayed when finding or filtering records in a datasheet or form, or when building a query.

Crosstab query A query that presents data in a cross-tabular layout (fields are used for both column and row headings), similar to pivot tables in other database and spreadsheet products.

Crosstab Query Wizard A wizard used to create crosstab queries that helps identify which fields will be used for row and column headings, and which fields will be summarized within the datasheet.

Currency A data type used for monetary values.

Current record symbol A black triangle symbol that appears in the record select box to the left of the record that has the focus in either a datasheet or a form.

Data The unique entries of information that you enter into the fields of the records.

Data Access Page See *Page*.

Database A collection of data associated with a topic (for example, sales of products to customers).

Database software Software used to manage data that can be organized into lists of things such as customers, products, vendors, employees, projects, or sales.

Database window The window that includes common elements such as the Access title bar, menu bar, and toolbar. It also contains an Objects bar to quickly work with the seven different types of objects within the database by clicking the appropriate object button.

Database Wizard A powerful Access wizard that creates a sample database file for a general purpose such as inventory control, event tracking, or expenses. The objects created by the Database Wizard can be used and modified.

Datasheet A spreadsheet-like grid that shows fields as columns and records as rows.

Datasheet view A view that lists the records of the object in a datasheet. Table, query, and most form objects have a Datasheet view.

Data type A required property for each field that defines the type of data that can be entered in each field. Valid data types include AutoNumber, Text, Number, Currency, Date/Time, OLE Object, Memo, Yes/No, and Hyperlink.

Date/Time A data type used for date and time fields.

Descending order A sequence in which information is placed in reverse alphabetical order or from largest to smallest. For a text field, letters sort first, then numbers.

Text descending order: Zebra, Victory, Langguth, Bunin, 99A, 9854, 77, 740, 29, 270, 23500, 1
Date descending order: 1/1/99, 1/1/98, 12/25/97, 5/5/97, 8/20/61, 8/20/57
Number descending order: 1500, 1400, 1200, 140, 120, 15, 10, 1

Design view A view in which the structure of the object can be manipulated. Every Access object has a Design view.

Detail section The section of the form or report that contains the controls that are printed for each record in the underlying query or table.

Edit mode The mode in which Access assumes you are trying to edit that particular field, so keystrokes such as [Ctrl][End], [Ctrl][Home], [¨], and [Æ] move the insertion point within the field.

Edit record symbol A pencil-like symbol that appears in the record selector box to the left of the record that is currently being edited in either a datasheet or a form.

Expand button A "plus sign" to the left of a record displayed in datasheet view that when clicked, will show related records in a subdatasheet.

Expression A combination of values, functions, and operators that calculates to a single value. Access expressions start with an equal sign and are placed in a text box in either Form or Report Design view.

Field The smallest piece or category of information in a database such as the customer's name, city, state, or phone number.

Field list A list of the available fields in the table or query that it represents.

Field names The names given each field in Table Design or Table Datasheet view. Field names can be up to 64 characters long.

Field Property See *Properties*.

Filter A temporary view of a subset of records. A filter can be saved as a query object if you wish to apply the same filter later without recreating it.

Filter window A window that appears when you click the Filter by Form button when viewing data in a datasheet or in a form window. The Filter window allows you to define the filter criteria.

Find Duplicates Query Wizard A wizard used to create a query that determines whether a table contains duplicate values in one or more fields.

Find Unmatched Query Wizard A wizard used to create a query that finds records in one table that doesn't have related records in another table.

Focus The property that refers to which field would be edited if you started typing.

Footer Information that prints at the bottom of every printed page (or section when using forms and reports).

Form An Access object that provides an easy-to-use data entry screen that generally shows only one record at a time.

Form Design toolbar The toolbar that appears when working in Form Design View with buttons that help you modify a form's controls.

Form footer A section that appears at the bottom of screen in Form View for each record, but prints only once at the end of all records when the form is printed.

Form header A section that appears at the top of the screen in Form View for each record, but prints only once at the top of all records when the form is printed.

Form View toolbar The toolbar that appears when working in Form View with buttons that help you print, edit, find, filter, and edit records.

Format Painter A tool used within Form and Report Design view to copy formatting characteristic from one control, and paint them on another.

Formatting Enhancing the appearance of the information in a form, report or datasheet.

Function A special, predefined formula that provides a shortcut for a commonly used calculation, for example, AVERAGE.

Functions A special, predefined formula that provides a shortcut for a commonly used calculation, for example, SUM

Graphic See *Image*.

Group Footer section The section of the report that contains controls that print once at the end of each group of records.

Group Header section The section of the report that contains controls that print once at the beginning of each group of records.

Grouping controls Specifying that several controls in the Design view of a form or report are in a "group" so that you can more productively format, move, and change them.

Grouping records In a report, grouping records means to sort them based on the contents of a field, plus provide a group header section that precedes the group of records as well as a group footer section that follows the group of records.

Handles See *Sizing handles*.

Header Information that prints at the top of every printed page (or section when using forms and reports).

Help system Pages of documentation and examples that are available through the Help menu option, the Microsoft Access Help button on the Database toolbar, or the Office Assistant.

HTML (Hypertext Markup Language) The programming language used to develop World Wide Web pages.

Hyperlink A data type that stores World Wide Web addresses.

Image A nontextual piece of information such as a picture, piece of clip art, drawn object, or graph. Because images are graphical (not numbers or letters), they are sometimes referred to as *graphical images*.

Imported table A table created in another database product or application such as Excel, that is copied and pasted within the Access database through the import process.

Importing A process to quickly convert data from an external source, such as Excel or another database application, into an Access database

Input mask A field property that controls both the values that the users can enter into a text box, as well as provides a visual guide for users as they enter data.

Input mask wizard A wizard that helps you determine the three parts of the input mask property.

Key field A field that contains unique information for each record. Also known as *Primary key field*. A key field cannot contain a null entry.

Key field combination Two or more fields that as a group, contain unique information for each record.

Key field symbol In a table's Design view, the symbol that appears as a miniature key in the field indicator box to the left of the field name. It identifies the field that contains unique information for each record.

Label An unbound control that displays static text on forms and reports.

Layout The general arrangement in which a form will display the fields in the underlying recordset. Layout types include Columnar, Tabular, Datasheet, Chart, and PivotTable. Columnar is most popular for a form, and Datasheet is most popular for a subform.

Line control An unbound control used to draw lines on a form or report that divide it into logical groupings.

Link Childs field A subform property that determines which field will serve as the "many" link between the subform and main form.

Link Masters fields A subform property that determines which field will serve as the "one" link between the main form and the subform.

Linked table A table created in another database product or application such as Excel, that is stored outside of the open database, but which can still be used within Access to modify and use its data.

List box A bound control that displays a list of possible choices from which the user can choose. Used mainly on forms.

Lookup Wizard A wizard used in Table Design view that allows one field to "lookup" values from another table or query. For example, you might use the Lookup Wizard to specify that the CustomerNumber field in the Sales table display the CustomerName field entry from the Customers table.

Macro An Access object that stores a collection of keystrokes or commands such as printing several reports in a row or providing a toolbar when a form opens.

Main form A form that contains a subform control.

Memo A data type used for lengthy text such as comments or notes. It can hold up to 64,000 characters of information.

Module An Access object that stores Visual Basic programming code that extends the functions and automated processes of Access.

Multimedia controls Non-textual controls such as those that display picture, sound, or motion information.

Navigation buttons Buttons in the lower-left corner of a datasheet or form that allow you to quickly navigate between the records in the underlying object as well as add a new record.

Navigation mode A mode in which Access assumes that you are trying to move between the fields and records of the datasheet (rather than edit a specific field's contents), so keystrokes such as [Ctrl][Home] and [Ctrl][End] move you to the first and last field of the datasheet, respectively.

New Record button A button that, when clicked, presents a new record for data entry. It is found on both the Form View and Datasheet toolbars as well as part of the Navigation buttons.

Null The term that refers to a state of "nothingness" in a field. Any entry such as 0 in a numeric field or an invisible space in a text field is *not* null. It is common to search for empty fields by using the criteria "Is Null" in a filter or query. "Is Not Null" criteria finds all records where there is an entry of any kind.

Number A data type used for numeric information used in calculations, such as quantities.

Object A table, query, form, report, page, macro, or module.

Objects bar In the opening database window, the toolbar that presents the seven Access objects. When you click an object button on the Objects bar, options and wizards to create an object of that type as well as existing objects of that type appear in the main portion of the database window.

Office Assistant An animated character that appears to offer tips, answer questions, and provide access to the program's Help system.

Office Clipboard A temporary storage area shared by all Office programs that can be used to cut, copy and paste multiple items within and between Office programs. The Office Clipboard can hold up to 12 items collected from any Office program. See also *Clipboard toolbar.*

OLE Object A data type that stores pointers that tie files created in other programs to a record such as pictures, sound clips, word-processing documents, or spreadsheets.

One-to-many line The line that appears in the Relationships window that shows which field is duplicated between two tables to serve as the linking field. The one-to-many line displays a "1" next to the field that serves as the "one" side of the relationship and an infinity symbol next to the field that serves as the "many" side of the relationship when referential integrity is specified for the relationship. Also called one-to-many join line.

One-to-many relationship The relationship between two tables in an Access database in which a common field links the tables together. The field is a key field in the "one" table of the relationship, but can be listed "many" times in the "many" table of the relationship.

Option Button A bound control used to display a limited list of mutually exclusive choices for a field such as "female" or "male" for a gender field in a form or report. Also called a radio button.

Option Group A bound control placed on a form that is used to group together several option buttons that provide a limited number of values for a field.

Or criteria Criteria placed on different rows of the query design grid. A record will appear in the resulting datasheet if it is true for any single row.

OR query A query that contains OR criteria (two or more criteria present on different rows in the query design grid. A record will appear on the resulting datasheet if it is true for either criteria.)

Orphan record A record in a "many" table that doesn't have a linking field entry in the "one" table. Orphan records can be avoided by using referential integrity.

Page An Access object that creates Web pages from Access objects as well as provides Web page connectivity features to an Access database. Also called Data Access Page.

Page Footer section The section of the form or report that contains controls that print once at the bottom of each page.

Page Header section The section of the form or report that contains controls that print once at the top of each page. On the first page of the report, the Page Header section prints below the Report Header section.

Parameter query A query that displays a dialog box prompting you for criteria each time you run it.

Parent/Child relationship The relationship between the main form and subform. The main form acts as the parent, displaying the information about the "one" side of a one-to-many relationship between the forms. The subform acts as the "child" displaying as many records as exist in the "many" side of the one-to-many relationship.

Primary key field See *Key field.*

Primary sort field In a query grid, the left-most field that includes sort criteria. It determines the order in which the records will appear and can be specified "ascending" or "descending."

Print Preview A window that displays how the physical printout will appear if the current object is printed.

Properties Characteristics that further define the field (if field properties), control (if control properties), section (if section properties), or object (if object properties).

Property sheet A window that displays an exhaustive list of properties for the chosen control, section, or object within the form or report Design view.

Query An Access object which provides a spreadsheet-like view of the data similar to tables. It may provide the user with a subset of fields and/or records from one or more tables. Queries are created when the user has a "question" about the data in the database.

Query design grid The bottom pane of the Query Design view window in which you specify the fields, sort order, and limiting criteria for the query.

Query Design view The window in which you develop queries by specifying the fields, sort order, and limiting criteria that determine which fields and records are displayed in the resulting datasheet.

Raw data The individual pieces of information stored in the database in individual fields.

Record A group of related fields, such as all demographic information for one customer.

Record selector box The small square to left of a record in a datasheet that marks the current record or edit record symbol when the record has focus or is being edited. Clicking the record selector box selects the entire record. In Form view, the record selector box expands to the entire height of the form because only one record is viewed at a time.

Record source In a form or report, either a table or query object that contains the fields and records that the form will display. It is the most important property of the form or report object. A bound control on a form or report also has a record source property. In this case, the record source property identifies the field to which the control is bound.

Record source property The most important property of a form or report because it determines the recordset that the form or report will display.

Recordset The fields and records that are displayed by the object.

Rectangle control An unbound control used to draw rectangles on the form that divide the other form controls into logical groupings.

Referential integrity Ensures that no orphaned records are entered or created in the database by making sure that the "one" side of a linking relationship (CustomerNumber in a Customer table) is entered before that same value can be entered in the "many" side of the relationship (CustomerNumber in a Sales table).

Relational database A database in which more than one table, such as the customer, sales, and inventory tables, can share information. The term "relational database" comes from the fact that the tables are linked or "related" with a common field of information. An Access database is relational.

Report An Access object that creates a professional printout of data that may contain such enhancements as headers, footers, and calculations on groups of records

Report Footer section On a report, a section that contains controls that print once at the end of the last page of the report.

Report Header section On a report, a section that contains controls that print once at the top of the first page of the report.

Row selector The small square to the left of a field in Table Design view.

ScreenTip A pop-up label that appears when you point to a button. It provides descriptive information about the button.

Secondary sort field In a query grid, the second field from the left that includes sort criteria. It determines the order in which the records will appear if there is a "tie" on the primary sort field. (For example, the primary sort field might be the State field. If two records both contained the data "IA" in that field, the secondary sort field, which might be the City field, would determine the order of the IA records in the resulting datasheet.)

Section A location of a form or report that contains controls. The section in which a control is placed determines where and how often the control prints.

Select query The most common type of query that retrieves data from one or more linked tables and displays the results in a datasheet.

Show Check Box A check box in Query Design View that determines whether the chosen field will be displayed on the datasheet or not.

Simple Query Wizard A wizard used to create a select query.

Sizing handles Small squares at each corner of a selected control. Dragging a handle resizes the control. Also known as *handles*.

Sort To place records in an order (ascending or descending) based on the values of a particular field.

Source document The original paper document that records raw data such as an employment application. In some databases, there is no source document because raw data is entered directly into the computer.

Specific record box Part of the Navigation buttons that indicates the current record number. You can also click in the specific record box and type a record number to quickly move to that record.

SQL (structured query language) statement, A standard programming language for selecting and manipulating data stored in a relational database.

Status bar The bar at the bottom of the Access window that provides informational messages and other status information (such as whether the Num Lock is active or not).

Subdatasheet A datasheet that shows related records. It appears when the user clicks a record's expand button.

Subform A form placed within a form that shows related records from another table or query. A subform generally displays many records at a time in a datasheet arrangement.

Summary query A query used to calculate and display information about records grouped together.

Tab control An unbound control used to create a three-dimensional aspect to a form so that other controls can be organized and shown in Form view by clicking the "tabs."

Tab order The sequence in which the controls on the form receive the focus when pressing [Tab] or [Enter] in Form view.

Table An Access object which is a collection of records for a single subject, such as all of the customer records. Tables can be linked with a common field to share information and therefore minimize data redundancy.

Table Datasheet toolbar The toolbar that appears when you are viewing a table's datasheet.

Text A data type that allows text information or combinations of text and numbers such as a street address. By default, it is 50 characters but can be changed to 50 characters. The maximum length of a text field is 255 characters.

Text box A common control used on forms and reports to display data bound to an underlying field. A text box can also show calculated controls such as subtotals and dates.

Toggle button A bound control used to indicate "yes" or "no" answers for a field. If the button is "pressed" it displays "yes" information.

Toolbox toolbar The toolbar that has common controls that you can add to a report or form when working in the report or form's Design view.

Unbound controls Controls that do not change from record to record and exist only to clarify or enhance the appearance of the form, such as labels, lines, and clip art.

Unbound image control An unbound control used to display clip art that doesn't change as you navigate from record to record on a form or report.

Validation rule A field property that establishes criteria for an entry to be accepted into the database.

Validation text A field property that determines what message will appear if a user attempts to make a field entry that does not pass the validation rule for that field.

Wildcard characters Special characters used in criteria to find, filter, and query data. The asterisk (*) stands for any group of characters. For example, the criteria I* in a State field criteria cell would find all records where the state entry was IA, ID, IL, IN, or Iowa. The question mark (?) wildcard stands for only one character. The pound sign (#) can only be used as a wildcard in a numeric field and stands for a single number.

Wizard An interactive set of dialog boxes that guides you through an Access process such as creating a query, form, or report.

Yes/No A data type that stores only one of two values (Yes/No, On/Off, True/False).

Index

Index

Index